ESSENTIAL BUSINESS BOOKS

ESSENTIAL BUSINESS BOOKS

BLOOMSBURY

A BLOOMSBURY REFERENCE BOOK
Created from the Bloomsbury Business Database
www.ultimatebusinessresource.com

First published in 2003 by
Bloomsbury Publishing Plc
38 Soho Square
London W1D 3HB

British Library Cataloguing in Publication Data
A CIP record for this book is available from the British Library.

ISBN 0-7475-6238-5

Design by Fiona Pike, Pike Design, Winchester
Typeset by RefineCatch Limited, Bungay, Suffolk
Printed in Great Britain by Clays Ltd, St Ives plc

Contents

Contents

User's Guide

Essential Business Books contains accessible and time-saving digests of the most influential business books ever written.

A vast amount of literature on business and the world of work exists already, and a host of new publications emerges each year. *Essential Business Books* aims to distil the main lessons from the best and most influential titles ever published in an easy-to-read format.

Taking in the perspectives of authors, practitioners, and theorists around the world and across the centuries, the contents range from timeless texts on strategy such as *The Art of War* and *The Prince*, to classics such as *The Practice of Management*, to comment on modern life at work in *Dilbert*.

Each digest contains the following features:

- a capsule introduction to why each book is a must-read
- **Getting Started**—an introduction to the main themes that each book sets out to address
- **Contribution**—more detailed information on the key points raised in each book
- **Context**—an overview of each book's impact, and the reaction of others to it and its message
- **The Best Sources of Help**—essential bibliographic information on each title

---

For more information about BUSINESS: The Ultimate Resource™ and other related titles, please visit:

www.ultimatebusinessresource.com

To register for free electronic upgrades, please go to
www.ultimatebusinessresource.com/register, type in your e-mail address, and key in your password: **Belbin**

ESSENTIAL
BUSINESS
BOOKS

Action Learning
by Reg Revans

What is the difference between a puzzle and a problem? According to Revans, there is an existing solution to a puzzle and it simply needs to be found. There is no existing solution to a problem. The solution has to be worked out by a process of inquiry that begins at the point where one does not know what to do next and expertise is no help. *Action Learning* explains that process and offers an alternative method of learning to the traditional one, which is based on programmed knowledge instead of encouraging students to ask questions and roam widely around a subject.

GETTING STARTED

As a young man, Reg Revans competed in the 1928 Olympics and worked in the famous Cavendish laboratories at Cambridge, alongside such fathers of nuclear physics as Ernest Rutherford and J.J. Thompson. Action learning is his systematisation of the methods used by the Cambridge team to deal with problems. He developed them further when working for the National Coal Board after the second world war. He also later went on to become Britain's first professor of industrial administration at the University of Manchester.

Action Learning is all about an alternative to traditional education and training.

Action Learning is all about an alternative to traditional education and training. The method it sets out is a form of 'learning by doing', but its proponents are careful to distinguish it from simply 'learning on the job' or 'learning by experience'. It involves a collaborative effort, humility, a 'trading of one's confusion with that of others', and deep reflection on one's experience and on the nature of the problem. Its outcome is personal growth, as much as a way out of a current difficulty.

CONTRIBUTION

Action learning. The concept of 'action learning' is based on a simple equation: $L = P + Q$. Learning (L) occurs through a combination of programmed knowledge (P) and the ability to ask insightful questions (Q).

It does not deny all usefulness to existing knowledge, but its focus is on asking questions. Learning must be opened up. Programmed knowledge is one-dimensional and rigid; the ability to ask questions opens up other dimensions and is free-flowing.

The first step towards asking constructive questions is to acknowledge one's own ignorance. Too many people are concealing their ignorance under a veneer of knowledge. Instead of hiding our ignorance, according to Revans, we should be bartering it.

The essence of action learning is to become better acquainted with the self through observing what one actually tries to do, endeavouring to ascertain the reasons for attempting it, and tracing the consequences that result from it. Revans said he sought 'to focus [his] own doubt by keeping away from experts with prefabricated answers'.

The importance of small-team learning. The structure linking the two elements in the equation is the small team or set. The central idea of this approach is collaboration within the set; its members strive to learn with and from each other as they confess failures and expand on victories.

A better way to develop managers. Action learning is also the antithesis of the traditional approach to developing managers. We keep solving the same problems because we do not learn from them. We bring in consultants to provide solutions or send managers on courses where they are taught a lot but learn little. Action learning is about teaching little and learning a lot.

Collaboration counts. In industry, managers and workers need to acknowledge the problems they face and then attempt to solve them. When doctors listen to nurses, patients recover more quickly. If mining engineers pay more attention to their workers than to their machinery, the pits are more efficient. It is neither books nor seminars from which managers learn much, but from here-and-now exchanges about the operational job in hand.

According to Revans, 'The ultimate power of a successful general staff lies not in the brilliance of its individual members, but in the cross-fertilisation of its collective abilities'.

CONTEXT

For a long time Revans's ideas were comparatively little known and comparatively under-valued—at least in the English-speaking world. His ideas were received much better in mainland Europe (and in Belgium in particular), however, and he himself spent the final period of his working life abroad. Many management ideas that are currently fashionable, however, such as teamworking, re-engineering, and the learning organisation, contain elements of 'action learning'.

One of the critical points about action learning is its relation to action. In a way it appears misnamed. The name at first sight suggests learning in practical situations or performing tasks, rather than studying theory. It tends to conceal the centrality of reflection, question-ing—especially questioning one's own actions in a deliberate and precise way—ignorance-bartering, and collaborative effort to the process. The solutions that are eventually arrived at must be tested in action, but that is very much the final stage.

Interest in Revans's ideas nevertheless continues to grow. The Pentagon is said to be enthusiastic; the ANC has taken up action learning; General Electric uses action teams to tackle particular problems. There is also a Revans Centre at the University of Salford, where the theory and practice of action learning are particularly studied.

THE BEST SOURCES OF HELP

Revans, Reg. *Action Learning*. London: Blond & Briggs, 1974.

Administrative Behavior
by Herbert Simon

Decision-making, according to Simon, is synonymous with management. But what is decision-making, how are decisions made? Simon realised that most people's assumptions were hopelessly unrealistic. He set out to inject some realism into the subject, but not in a merely reductive way; he also elaborated a very modern concept of the organisation as an interrelated and intercommunicating body. He also said that the ability to make decisions effectively made the difference between effectiveness and ineffectiveness in organisations. On that basis alone, his book must be worth reading.

GETTING STARTED

Herbert Simon, the son of German immigrants to Milwaukee and a graduate of the University of Chicago, won the Nobel prize for economics in 1978 for his work on administrative behaviour, the subject of his doctoral thesis and this book. He is said to have been inspired to write it by observations made while working part-time for the Milwaukee local authority while a student. He is also said to have told the Nobel committee, when collecting his award, that his real interest was in artificial intelligence—the field into which his interest in how decisions and choices are made ultimately led him.

In *Administrative Behavior: A Study of Decision-making Processes in Administrative Organization* (to give the book its full title), he developed a theory of human choice or decision-making that aimed to be sufficiently broad and realistic to accommodate both the rational views of economists and the human concerns of psychologists and practical decision-makers.

CONTRIBUTION

The problems of organisational theory. According to *Administrative Behavior*, the way in which administration is usually described suffers from superficiality, over-simplification, and a lack of realism. Theorists have refused to undertake the tiresome task of studying the actual allocation of decision-making functions. Instead, they have been satisfied with talking loosely about authority, centralisation, span of control, function, and the like, without seeking operational definitions of these terms.

Classic economic theory also suggests that decisions are made by obtaining all the available information, assessing it, and coming to an objective and rational conclusion as to how the best result can be achieved. In reality, nobody has the time and the mental resources to do this. Instead of aiming for 'the best', administrative man is content with what is 'good enough', a solution that is 'satisficing' (that satisfies and suffices).

Organisation is important. Organisation is important, first, because in our society, people spend most of their waking adult lives in organisations, and this environment provides much of the force that moulds and develops personal qualities and habits.

Second, it is important because it provides those in responsible positions with the means for exercising authority and influence over others.

The complexity of organisational interaction. It is not sufficient to regard organisational behaviour as a matter of understanding people or measuring the performance of people more effectively. Each act in an organisation exists in a complex interaction with the organisational system as a whole.

Understanding decision-making. A complex decision is like a great river, drawing from its many tributaries the innumerable component premises of which it is constituted.

Many individuals and organisation units contribute to every large decision, and the problem of centralisation and decentralisation is a problem of arranging the complex system into an effective scheme.

The importance of relationships. An organisation is not an organisational chart, but a complex pattern of communications and other relationships in a group of human beings.

This pattern provides the members of the group with much of the information, assumptions, goals, and attitudes that enter into the decisions made by each and every one of them. It also provides them with a set of stable and comprehensible expectations as to what the other members of the group are doing and how they will react to what any individual says and does.

CONTEXT

Simon later observed that he must have had a prophetic gift when he included the words 'behavior', 'decision-making', and 'organization' in the book's full title as they quickly became the fashionable phrases of social science.

Organisational theory had remained deeply bedded in vagueness before the publication of *Administrative Behavior*. Its clearest proponent up to that time had been Chester Barnard, who contributed the foreword to Simon's book.

> Organisational theory had remained deeply bedded in vagueness before the publication of *Administrative Behavior*.

In response, Simon developed a theory of human choice or decision-making that aimed to accommodate:

- the rational aspects of choice that have been the principal concern of the economist
- the properties and limitations of the human decision-making mechanisms that have attracted the attention of psychologists and practical decision-makers

He thus formed a bridge between the humanists and engineers in management thinking.

His views were ahead of their time. For the next 40 years, organisation, in the West at least, continued to be seen as an act of ordering, simplifying, and categorising rather than as a powerful dynamic and ever-changing force.

Only in the early 1990s, partly through the success of Senge's *The Fifth Discipline*, did systems thinking make the leap from academic obscurity to the executive agenda.

THE BEST SOURCES OF HELP

Simon, Herbert. *Administrative Behavior: A Study of Decision-making Processes in Administrative Organization*. New York: Macmillan, 1947.

The Age of Discontinuity
by Peter Drucker

Drucker predicted the rise of the knowledge worker long before the term came into common usage. His definition is much broader than the IT-led version that is currently used. The book gives a valuable insight into the changing nature of management roles and responsibilities in the knowledge economy.

GETTING STARTED

According to Drucker, the manager as knowledge worker was a new breed of thoughtful, intelligent executive. The manager was reincarnated as a responsible individual, paid for applying knowledge, exercising judgement, and taking responsible leadership.

The knowledge worker sees him or herself as another professional. While dependent on the organisation for access to income and opportunity, the organisation equally depends on him or her.

In this book we read that knowledge, rather than labour, is the new measure of economic society—and the knowledge worker is the true capitalist in the knowledge society. Knowledge is not only power, but also ownership of the means of production.

CONTRIBUTION

The manager as knowledge worker. Drucker coined the term 'knowledge worker'. This was a new breed of executive—a highly trained, intelligent managerial professional who realised his or her own worth and contribution to the organisation. Drucker bade farewell to the concept of the manager as mere supervisor or paper shuffler. The manager was reincarnated as a responsible individual.

Though the knowledge worker is not a labourer, and certainly not proletarian, he or she is not a subordinate (in the sense that he or she can be told what to do). The knowledge worker is paid, on the contrary, for applying his or her knowledge, exercising judgment, and taking responsible leadership.

The nature of the knowledge worker. According to Drucker, the knowledge worker sees him or herself just as another professional, no different from the lawyer, the teacher, the preacher, the doctor, or the government servant of yesterday. He or she has the same education, but more income—and probably greater opportunities as well.

The knowledge worker may well realise that he or she depends on the organisation for access to income and opportunity, and that without the organisation, there would be no job. But there is also the realisation that the organisation depends equally on him or her.

Drucker effectively wrote the obituary for the obedient, grey-suited, loyal, corporate man and woman. The only trouble was, it took this corporate creature another 20 years to die.

The impact of knowledge workers. The social ramifications of this new breed of corporate executive were significant. If knowledge, rather than labour, was the new measure of economic society then the fabric of capitalist society had to change. The knowledge worker is both the true capitalist in the knowledge society and dependent on his or her job.

Collectively the knowledge workers—the employed, educated middle class of today's society—own the means of production through pension funds, investment trusts, and so on. Knowledge was not only power, but it was also ownership.

CONTEXT

The book effectively mapped out the demise of the age of mass, labour-based production and the advent of the knowledge-based, information age. Drucker's realisation that the role of the manager had fundamentally changed was not a sudden one. The foundations of the idea of the knowledge worker can be seen in his description of management by objectives in *The Practice of Management* (1954). Knowledge management, intellectual capital and the like are now the height of corporate fashion. The modern idea of the knowledge worker is a creature of the technological age, the mobile executive, the hot-desker. Drucker provided a characteristically broader perspective. He placed the rise of the knowledge worker in the evolution of management into a respectable and influential discipline.

Drucker has since developed his thinking on the role of knowledge, most notably in his 1992 book, *Managing for the Future*, in which he observed, 'From now on the key is knowledge. The world is becoming not labour intensive, not materials intensive, not energy intensive, but knowledge intensive'.

The Age of Discontinuity was startlingly correct in its predictions. Much of it would fit easily into business books of today.

Management guru Gary Hamel said, 'Peter Drucker's reputation is as a management theorist. He has also been a management prophet. Writing in 1969, he clearly anticipated the emergence of the knowledge economy. I'd like to set a challenge for would-be management gurus: try to find something to say that Peter Drucker has not said first, and has not said well. This high hurdle should substantially reduce the number of business books clogging the bookshelves of booksellers, and offer managers the hope of gaining some truly fresh insights'.

THE BEST SOURCES OF HELP

Drucker, Peter. *The Age of Discontinuity*. Oxford: Butterworth-Heinemann, 1969.

In the Age of the Smart Machine
by Shoshana Zuboff

This is a book written in the 1980s about the way technology will impact on the structure of business. It covers a number of themes, such as empowerment and knowledge management, that are still extremely relevant and may be useful to companies considering their strategic direction.

GETTING STARTED

The author asserts that information technology can transform work at every organisational level, and technology will surrender knowledge to anyone with the requisite skills. It can automate or empower people, and has the capacity to change where knowledge and power reside in the organisation. It also changes the concept of the 'working day' and the speed of competition. However, for every empowered worker doing valuable work, there is another who has lost his or her job.

The 'informated' workplace is an arena through which information circulates. The informated organisation is a learning institution, and learning is the new form of labour.

CONTRIBUTION

The impact of technology on business life. Information technology can transform work at every organisational level. It has the potential to give all employees a comprehensive view of the entire business, and will surrender knowledge to anyone with the requisite skills. This contrasts with earlier generations of technological advance, where the primary impact of new machines was to decrease the complexity of tasks.

Increasing the intellectual content of work. Information technologies can potentially increase the intellectual content of work at all levels.

Work involves an ability to understand, respond to, manage and create value from information. The most effective organisations will be those that achieve a more equitable distribution of knowledge and authority.

Automation or empowerment. Information technology presents a difficult choice: do we use it to continue automation (at the risk of robbing workers of gratification and self image), or should it be used to empower ordinary working people to make judgements?

Changing organisational structures. Unlocking the promise of information technology depends on dismantling managerial hierarchies that all too often seek to block the ready flow of information.

Information technology has the capacity to change where knowledge and power reside in the organisation, and offers the possibility of restructuring whole industry sectors.

Traditional value-chain structures are fragmenting and reforming, and 'virtual' organisations are emerging.

Changing the concept of time. The 'working day' has less meaning in a global village where communication via e-mail, voice mail and facsimile can be sent or received at any time of day or night. As the working day has expanded, so time has contracted. Companies compete on speed, using effective co-ordination of resources to reduce the time needed to develop new products, deliver orders or react to customer requests.

Winners and losers in the new economy. If a company can replace an employee with a computer program that does not demand an ever-increasing salary, a pension, cheap mortgage or insurance, the danger is that it will.

As a consequence, people can lose their outdated jobs almost overnight and remain unemployable because they lack the variety of skills and mental flexibility to adjust. For every empowered worker doing valuable work, there is another who has lost their job, and another putting in longer and longer hours doing more of the same work.

The result could be a world where some people are permanently overworked, while others are permanently underworked.

How humans relate to technology. Technology's potential is limited primarily by the power of the human imagination. Technological capability has moved ahead of our ability to cope because so far, patterns of morality, sociality, and feeling are evolving much more slowly than technology.

The 'informated' workplace. The informated workplace is an arena through which information circulates, to which intellectual effort is applied. The quality, rather than the quantity, of effort will be the source from which added value is derived. Traditional economic measures do not relate to what is most valuable in the informated organisation.

A learning organisation. The informated organisation is a learning institution. One of its principal purposes is the expansion of knowledge—not knowledge for its own sake (as in academic pursuit), but knowledge that resides at the core of what it means to be productive.

The behaviours that define learning and the behaviours that define being productive are one and the same. Learning is not something that requires time out from being engaged in productive activity; it is the heart of productive activity. Learning is the new form of labour.

Empowerment in a learning organisation. The precise contours of a new division of learning will depend upon the business, products, services and markets that people are engaged in learning about.

The empowerment, commitment and involvement of a wide range of employees in self-managing activities means that organisational structures are likely to be both emergent and flexible. The structures will change as members continually learn more about how to organise themselves for learning about their business.

CONTEXT

In the Age of the Smart Machine is based on research carried out in the United States by Shoshana Zuboff during the late 1970s and early 1980s. The book concentrates less on the technology itself and more on its meaning and potential.

It sets out to document the pitfalls and promise of computerised technology in business life. Perhaps the most crucial point the author raised revolves around how humans relate to technology.

Other authors have argued whether technology's potential is limited primarily by the power of the human imagination. B.F. Skinner, for example, wrote, 'The real question is not whether machines think, but whether men do'.

THE BEST SOURCES OF HELP

Zuboff, Shoshana. *In the Age of the Smart Machine: The Future of Work and Power.* New York: Basic Books, 1988.

The Age of Unreason
by Charles Handy

Written in 1989, this book includes a number of incisive predictions about the way work would develop. The author provides valuable insights into changing organisational structures and developments such as knowledge working, outsourcing, and strategic alliances—the hallmarks of the new economy.

GETTING STARTED

In the author's view, the age of unreason is a time when the future is shaped by us and for us. At such a time, a number of organisational forms will emerge, as will new working patterns such as outsourcing, telecommuting, the intellectual capital movement, and the rise of knowledge workers.

The portfolio worker will become more important, contributing to a greater work/life balance. A work portfolio is a way of describing how the different bits of work in our lives fit together to form a balanced whole. Portfolio work includes wage work and fee work, home work, gift work, and study work.

Handy goes on to state that the social changes resulting from these developments will be reflected in changing patterns of business, with a mix of small enterprises and large conglomerates. There will also be temporary alliances of large and small organisations to deliver a particular project.

CONTRIBUTION

The concept of an age of unreason. The age of unreason is a time when the future, in so many areas, is to be shaped by us and for us. The only prediction that will hold true is that no predictions will hold true. It will be a time for thinking the unlikely and doing the unreasonable.

New organisational forms. The author suggests that a number of organisational forms will emerge in an age of unreason:

- the shamrock organisation
- the federal organisation
- the Triple I organisation

> The age of unreason is a time when the future, in so many areas, is to be shaped by us and for us.

The shamrock organisation is a form of organisation based around a core of essential executives and workers supported by outside contractors and part-time help.

The federal organisation is a form of decentralised set-up, in which the centre's powers are given to it by the outlying groups; the centre therefore co-ordinates, advises, influences, and suggests rather than directs or controls. Federalism is the way to combine the autonomy of individual parts with the economics of co-ordination.

The Triple I organisation is based on Information, Intelligence, and Ideas. This type of organisation will resemble a university and will seek to make added value out of knowledge. To achieve this, the Triple I organisation increasingly uses smart machines, with smart people to work with them.

New working patterns. Handy anticipated the growth of outsourcing, telecommuting, the intellectual capital movement, and the rise of knowledge workers. He also foresaw how these developments might impact on the individual. His concept of the portfolio worker helped redefine the nature of work, as well as questions of work/life balance.

Portfolio working. A work portfolio is a way of describing how the different bits of work in our lives fit together to form a balanced whole. There are five main categories of portfolio work:

- wage work and fee work, which are both forms of paid work
- home work, gift work, and study work, which are all free work

Wage (or salary) work represents money paid for time given.

Fee work is money paid for results delivered. Employees do wage work; professionals, craftspeople, and freelancers do fee work. Fee work is increasing as jobs move outside the organisation. Some employees now get fees (bonuses) as well as wages.

Home work includes that whole catalogue of tasks that go on in the home, from cooking and cleaning, to children and carpentry. Done willingly or grudgingly, it is all work.

Gift work is work done for free outside the home, for charities and local groups, for neighbours or for the community.

Study work done seriously is a form of work, not recreation.

A broader portfolio. In the past, for most people, the work portfolio has had only one item in it—their career. This was a risky strategy. Few people would put all their money into one asset, yet that is what most people were doing with their lives. The career had to provide many things at once—interest or satisfaction in the work, interesting people and good company, security, money, and the opportunity for development.

Funding the portfolio. Portfolio people think in terms of portfolio money, not salary money. Money comes in fits and starts from different sources, for example a bit of a pension, some part-time work, some fees to charge or things to sell. They lead cash-flow lives not salary lives, planning always to have enough in-flows to cover out-flows.

Portfolio people think in terms of barter and know that most skills are saleable if you want to sell them.

Changing patterns of business. It will be a world of 'fleas and elephants'—large conglomerates and small individual entities, or large political and economic blocs and small countries.

A small enterprise can be global as easily as a large conglomerate, but can more easily be swept away. Conglomerates are a guarantee of continuity, but small enterprises provide the innovation.

There will also be ad hoc organisations, temporary alliances of large and small organisations to deliver a particular project.

CONTEXT

The book predicted many of the important changes in working patterns which are now commonplace, including outsourcing, telecommuting, and virtual project teams from different organisations. It also recognised the growing importance of knowledge workers and intellectual capital.

THE BEST SOURCES OF HELP

Handy, Charles. *The Age of Unreason*. London: Hutchinson, 1989.

All the Right Moves
by Constantinos Markides

Bill Gates once remarked that though his firm did good work, the problem was that products aged so quickly. It is plain from this that innovative strategies are vital for survival in business; organisations must differentiate themselves clearly from their competitors. They must also develop strategies that enable them to find and occupy a unique position within their own industry, while at the same being constantly on the watch for new strategic positions. In this book, Constantinos Markides guides readers towards discovering the breakthrough strategy that will work best for them.

GETTING STARTED

Markides describes what makes a strategic position distinctive and how a business can make sure it occupies a unique strategic position within its industry. He demonstrates how established companies can discover and work on new strategic positions in parallel to their old position. On the basis of examples drawn from actual practice, he presents a guide to how a firm can allow an old strategy that obviously no longer has a future to 'run out' and, simultaneously, prepare the ground for a new one.

CONTRIBUTION

No strategy without innovation. According to the author, a successful business needs a strategy that enables it to find and occupy a unique position within its own branch of industry. But no position is made to last for ever. Ambitious competitors not only copy attractive positions, they create new ones and these, over time, can become so successful that they endanger established positions. A company that is not permanently striving to discover new positions in its field encourages the competition to do precisely that.

> A company that is not permanently striving to discover new positions in its field encourages the competition to do precisely that.

Building a unique strategic position. Markides suggests that in order to create a unique strategic position and make the best use of it, a company must first define what business it is in. It must then decide what customers it wishes to appeal to and what products or services it intends to offer. The task then is to build up an organisational environment in which these decisions can be implemented. In his view, all this involves looking at the following areas:

- Core business: Defining one's own business is the starting point for any strategy. As soon as a definition is arrived at, actions follow from it automatically. But after it has been accepted, it has nevertheless to be questioned again and again, and one must always be on the lookout for better alternatives.
- Customers: In deciding who its customers are and what it is selling, the company at the same time marks out the terrain that it does not intend to enter: the customers it is not setting out to attract, the investments it is not going to action. In this way the company protects itself against squandering its limited resources through not having a clear focus or not following a clearly-defined path.

- Activities and achieving objectives: The company must try to reach a dynamic under-standing with its workforce. It can, for example, encourage internal diversity to develop competences that it then has 'in stock' and promote a type of culture in which changes are welcomed.
- Values and capabilities: The values and capabilities that can give a company a lasting advantage are those that it is difficult for a competitor to achieve. They are rare, they cannot be copied, and there is no substitute for them.
- Organisation: A company's organisational environment is made up of four elements: culture, structure, incentive systems, and workforce. If all these are to function as desired, then the company must ensure that it shapes the environment in such a way as to support their proper functioning.
- Strategy development: The development of a new strategy involves planning and trial and error. The planning is necessary to identify the parameters within which the experiments can take place. The process of strategy formation is made up of two parts: first, the production of ideas; second, assessment, experimentation, learning, and modification.

Preparing strategic innovations. The book then goes on to say that, as soon as a company occupies a unique position within an industry, it must try to improve it. While improving its current position, it must be vigilant for new and potentially dangerous positions that its competitors may be adopting.

Since it cannot be taken for granted that new positions will harmonise with previously existing ones, it is often a good idea for established firms to set up their own units for that purpose. When a company takes over a new position and intends to concentrate on it entirely at some time in the future, it should separate itself from its old position through a gradual process of transition.

In developing its strategy, a company must be able to envisage itself going through the following cycle:

- First, it identifies a distinctive strategic position within its industry and occupies it.
- Then it does so well in that position that the position becomes more attractive than any other in the industry.
- While carrying the fight to its competitors from its present position, it constantly looks around for new strategic positions in the industry.
- Once it has identified another more promising position, it attempts to maintain the old position and the new one simultaneously.
- As it gradually removes itself from the old position, it completes the transition to the new one and begins the cycle over again.

CONTEXT

The book is based on numerous case studies of companies from different countries over a period of three years. The author has supplemented the results of these with material from other firms as well as generally available information. It is written from a management perspective and describes the thought processes that a manager has to go through to find a new and innovative strategy.

THE BEST SOURCES OF HELP

Markides, Constantinos C. *All the Right Moves: A Guide to Crafting Breakthrough Strategy.* Boston, Massachusetts: Harvard Business School Publishing, 1999.

The Art of Japanese Management
by Richard Pascale and Anthony Athos

This book was one of the first business bestsellers. It played a crucial role in the discovery of Japanese management techniques. In its comparisons of Japanese and US companies, it provides rare insights into the truth behind the mythology of Japanese management and the inadequacy of much Western practice.

GETTING STARTED

By the late 1990s, growing Japanese superiority threatened the United States' dominant position in world markets. In the authors' view, a major reason for the superiority of the Japanese is their managerial skill. Japanese managers have vision, something notably lacking in the West. In Japan, visions are dynamic, rather than generic statements of corporate intent. US managers are constrained by their beliefs and assumptions. The seven S framework (strategy, structure, skills, staff, shared values, systems, and style) represents the key categories requiring managers' attention. The Japanese succeeded through attention to the 'soft' Ss—style, shared values, skills, and staff, while the West remained preoccupied with the 'hard' Ss of strategy, structure, and systems.

CONTRIBUTION

Growing Japanese superiority. In 1980, Japan's GNP was third highest in the world. Extrapolating trends at the time, it looked likely to be the highest by the year 2000.

For the US readership, *The Art of Japanese Management* contains some hard-hitting truths.

If anything, the extent of Japanese superiority over the United States in industrial competitiveness is underestimated.

> In Japan, managers enhance their modus operandi via dynamic visions rather than pallid or generic statements of corporate intent.

Managerial skills. A major reason for the superiority of the Japanese is their managerial skills. Among the key components of Japanese management is vision, something they found to be notably lacking in the West, where the tools are there but vision is limited.

Beliefs, assumptions, and perceptions about management frequently constrain US managers. The Western vision of management circumscribes our effectiveness.

In Japan, managers enhance their modus operandi via dynamic visions rather than pallid or generic statements of corporate intent.

The seven S framework. The book is best known for its central concept: the seven S framework.

As a generic statement of the issues facing organisations the seven S framework is unremarkable, though it did gain a great deal of attention. It simply lists the seven important categories that managers should take into account—strategy, structure, skills, staff, shared values, systems, and style.

According to Pascale, the value of a framework such as the seven Ss is that it imposes an interesting discipline on the researcher.

Comparing management styles. The seven Ss presents a framework for comparing Japanese and US management approaches.

The Japanese succeeded largely because of the attention they gave to the 'soft' Ss—style, shared values, skills, and staff.

The West remained preoccupied with the 'hard' Ss of strategy, structure, and systems.

Since the book's publication, the general trend of Western managerial thinking has been directed towards the soft Ss.

CONTEXT

The book played a crucial role in the discovery of Japanese management techniques. Its roots lie in Pascale's work with the US National Commission on Productivity. Having initially thought that lessons from Japan were limited for cultural reasons, Pascale decided it would be more productive to look at Japanese companies in the United States. The research for the book eventually covered 34 companies over six years.

The authors' championing of vision proved highly influential. It was Athos who really started the entire 'visioning' industry in the United States. Soon after *The Art of Japanese Management*, a flurry of books appeared highlighting so-called visionaries. Today, corporate visions are a fact of life.

Leading author Gary Hamel commented, 'Japan-phobia has subsided a bit, helped by a strong yen, inept Japanese macroeconomic policy, and the substantial efforts of many Western companies to rebuild their competitiveness. While Pascale and Athos undoubtedly overstated the unique capabilities of Japanese management (is Matsushita really that much better managed than Hewlett-Packard?), they successfully challenged the unstated assumption that the United States was the font of all managerial wisdom. Since *The Art of Japanese Management* hit the bookstores, US companies have learned much from Japan. Pascale and Athos deserve credit for setting the learning agenda.'

THE BEST SOURCES OF HELP

Pascale, Richard Tanner, and Anthony Athos. *The Art of Japanese Management*. London: Penguin, 1981.

The Art of the Long View
by Peter Schwartz

It may be impossible to predict the future, but it *is* possible to prepare for it and lessen the degree of any shocks it may bring. The 'scenario method', presented in this book by Peter Schwartz, enables managers to cover the possible outcome of their actions and take account of external events outside their control. It has been widely used in major corporations to prevent problems caused by unexpected developments.

GETTING STARTED

The book describes the use of scenarios to investigate and test decisions about the future. A scenario is a way of looking ahead, a description of how the world might turn out to be in the future, if certain events take place. Schwartz believes that scenarios enable an organisation to plot routes through necessarily uncertain terrain. They are not predictions—accurate predictions are impossible. Nor are they extrapolations of trends. Scenarios, according to the author, are an approach to making better decisions about the future.

CONTRIBUTION

What type of scenario? The author highlights three possible scenarios for the future:
- more of the same, but better
- worse, leading to decay and depression
- different but better, with profound social changes

It is possible to identify what types of business would succeed in each of those scenarios.

The problem of denial. Schwartz explains that some scenarios predict situations that people are not prepared to contemplate. He refers to this as a state of denial. Scenarios, he suggests, need to be treated as stories to overcome the problem of denial. Putting figures in the scenario makes them believable. With stories, readers can suspend belief.

Responses to scenarios. People have different mindsets and so respond to scenarios differently. Schwartz puts people into three main categories: optimists, pessimists, and people who prefer the status quo. Some commentators dismiss scenarios as impossible dreams, but the author believes it is important to ask awkward questions and be prepared for the unexpected.

The right perspective. Schwartz recommends changing focus between the broad picture and the specific area of concern. For someone looking at the future prospects for an industry, it is important to take account of global developments as well as industry trends.

Wide-ranging research. Research into areas such as science, technology, politics, and economics underpins the development of scenarios, but conventional research sources may simply point to the continuation of the status quo. The author believes that 'fringe research' may be equally important.

Certainty and uncertainty. The author explains how the building blocks of scenarios are society, technology, economics, politics, and the environment. Looking at developments in each area gives the scenario builder a series of useful perspectives. The author describes how Shell set up the Global Business Network to bring together people with different perspectives. Scenario builders use multiple perspectives to create a series of challenges and possible responses, and identify potential winners and losers.

CONTEXT

The book draws on the author's wide-ranging experience in scenario development within Shell. He uses real-life examples to demonstrate the importance of scenarios in an industry like energy that is influenced by technology, politics, and economic and environmental factors. He explains how unexpected events such as war or major political change could have had a significant impact on the industry if it had not prepared for change through the use of scenarios.

Schwartz is careful to highlight the difference between scenarios and predictions about the future. His book is not a prediction about the way the world might look, but a method for assessing what might change if unforeseen circumstances occur. In that sense, the book is a valuable complement to books on strategy development based on 'business as usual'.

THE BEST SOURCES OF HELP

Schwartz, Peter. *The Art of the Long View*. Chichester: John Wiley, 1997.

The Art of War
by Sun Tzu

When the post-war achievements of Japanese industry began to make a significant impression in the West, and Western business people began to inquire into the thinking that underlay the success of their Eastern counterparts, Sun Tzu's *The Art of War* was a book that was often mentioned. This may seem surprising as it was probably written some 2,500 years ago. But military language and imagery have played an important role in the development of management thinking, and if you wish to gain an insight into strategy, leadership, and survival in a hostile, competitive environment, who better to turn to than a general whose name is a byword for sagacity?

GETTING STARTED

Sun Tzu is thought to have lived over 2,400 years ago, at roughly the same time as Confucius. Historians are generally agreed that he was a general who led a number of successful military campaigns in present-day Anhui Province; the state of Wu, under whose sovereign he served, became a dominant power at that time. Since then, it has become standard practice for Chinese military chiefs to familiarise themselves with his writings.

The Art of War (the book's actual title is *Sun Tzu Ping Fa*, literally 'The Military Method of Mr Sun') is a compilation of the legendary general's thinking on the strategies that underlie military success. His anecdotes and thoughts, which fill no more than about 25 pages of text in all, are divided into 13 sections. Not all of them are relevant to modern-day concerns, but some strike a significant chord. Rather like a proponent of judo, Sun Tzu particularly recommends using the momentum of your enemy's own moves to defeat him.

CONTRIBUTION

Get the strategy right. Sun Tzu, like most good and seasoned generals, is anything but an adventurer and anything but gung-ho. 'Why destroy', he asks, 'when you can win by stealth and cunning? To subdue the enemy's forces without fighting is the summit of skill.'

His advice shows subtlety and restraint: 'A sovereign should not start a war out of anger, nor should a general give battle out of rage. While anger can revert to happiness and rage to delight, a nation that has been destroyed cannot be restored, nor can the dead be brought back to life.'

He continues: 'The best approach is to attack the other side's strategy; next best is to attack his alliances; next best is to attack his soldiers; the worst is to attack cities.'

Get information from the right sources. Sun Tzu also gives sound advice on knowing your markets, saying: 'Advance knowledge cannot be gained from ghosts and spirits, but must be obtained from people who know the enemy situation.'

Stay focused. His view on strategy leaves no room for sentiment or distraction.

'Deploy forces to defend the strategic points; exercise vigilance in preparation, do not be indolent. Deeply investigate the true situation, secretly await their laxity. Wait until they leave their strongholds, then seize what they love.'

CONTEXT

So what does *The Art of War* have to offer the manager of a small components factory in, say, Peoria or Nottingham? Sun Tzu's admirers argue that his pithy sayings encapsulate basic and eternal truths. According to Gary Hamel, 'Strategy didn't start with Igor Ansoff; neither did it start with Machiavelli. It probably didn't even start with Sun Tzu. Strategy is as old as human conflict . . . '. Anyone, therefore, who has to devise a plan, anyone who has to give a lead, can do with all the help they can get.

Hamel goes on to add ' . . . and, if the stakes are high in business, they're rather higher in the military sphere'. One of the attractions of the military analogy and the military role model in business is that they elevate proceedings to a loftier plane. Not only are the issues larger, and the scale more heroic, but it is clear who your enemy is, and when your enemy is clear, the world appears clearer whether you are a military general or a managing director.

Embattled managers, in particular, may benefit from the stimulus that military authors, like Sun Tzu, Clausewitz, or Liddell-Hart, and the writings of modern military leaders, like Colin Powell or Norman Schwarzkopf, can give to their civilian imaginations.

Finally, as has often been pointed out, Sun Tzu has long been revered in the East. He is said to be required reading not only for Eastern military tacticians but also for Eastern business people. To know your enemies—or indeed to know your friends, partners, and colleagues—it is useful to have read what they read.

THE BEST SOURCES OF HELP

Sun Tzu. *The Art of War*. (Trans. Griffith.) Oxford: Oxford University Press, 1963.

A Behavioral Theory of the Firm
by Richard Cyert and James March

The book is a powerful introduction to the complex world of decision-making. One of its authors, James March, is one of the foremost decision-making theorists of the 20th century. The book evaluates traditional approaches to decision-making and puts forward real-world alternatives.

GETTING STARTED

An entire academic discipline, decision science, is devoted to understanding management decision-making. Early thinkers believed that the decision process could be rationalised and systematised, and that decision-making can therefore be distilled into a formula. However, reality is often more confused and messy, and managers make decisions based on a combination of intuition, experience, and analysis.

CONTRIBUTION

The evolution of decision-making theory. Early theories were based on the premise that, under a given set of circumstances, human behaviour is logical and therefore predictable— so the decision process can be rationalised and systematised.

A profusion of models, software packages, and analytical tools followed, seeking to distil decision-making into a formula. The danger is in concluding that the solution provided by a software package is the answer.

The rational theory of decision-making. The authors suggest that the rational, or synoptic, model of decision-making involves a series of steps:

- identifying and clarifying the problem
- prioritising goals
- generating and evaluating options
- comparing predicted outcomes of each option with the goals
- choosing the option that best matches the goals

These models rely on a number of assumptions about the way in which people will behave when confronted with a set of circumstances. The assumptions allow mathematicians to derive formulae based on probability theory. The decision-making tools include such things as cost/benefit analysis, which aims to help managers evaluate different options.

Problems in the rational theory. Reality is often more confused and messy than a neat model can allow for. Underpinning the mathematical approach are a number of flawed assumptions. The model assumes that decision-making is:

- consistent
- based on accurate information
- free from emotion or prejudice
- rational

Real-world decision-making. According to the authors, the reality is that managers make decisions based on a combination of intuition, experience, and analysis. As intuition and experience are impossible to quantify, the temptation is to focus on the analytical side of decision-making—the science rather than the mysterious art.

The relevance of decision-making models. This does not mean that decision theory is redundant or that decision-making models should be cast to one side.

A number of factors mean that decision-making is becoming ever more demanding. The growth in complexity means that companies no longer encounter simple problems. Complex decisions are now not solely the preserve of senior managers but the responsibility of many others too. Managers are having to deal with a flood of information: a 1996 Reuters survey of 1,200 managers worldwide found that 43% thought important decisions were delayed and their ability to make decisions affected as a result of having too much information.

Decision theory and the use of models is reassuring, as they lend legitimacy to decisions that may be based on prejudices or hunches. However, no models are foolproof; none is universally applicable, and none can yet cope with the idiosyncrasies of human behaviour.

The challenge for organisational decision-making. Business decision-making theory faces a crucial and immediate problem: individuals have goals; collective groups do not. The need, therefore, is to create useful organisational goals, while not believing there is such a thing as an organisational mind.

Organisations should be regarded as coalitions that negotiate goals.

Creating goals requires three processes:

- bargaining, which establishes the composition and general terms of the coalition
- internal organisational control, which clarifies and develops the objectives
- the process of adjustment to experience, which alters agreements in accord with changing circumstances

Goals are inconsistent for three reasons:

- decision-making being decentralised
- short-term goals taking most managerial attention
- the resources available to the organisation being insufficient to maintain the coalition

A new decision-making model. The authors assert that the five principle goals of the modern organisation are production, inventory, sales, market share, and profit. There are nine steps in the decision process: forecast competitors' behaviour; forecast demand; estimate costs; specify objectives; evaluate plans; re-examine costs; re-examine demand; re-examine objectives; select alternatives. To work successfully, this decision-making model demands that there are standard operating procedures. The procedures can be divided into general ones based on avoiding uncertainty, maintaining the rules, and using simple rules. There are also specifics, such as task performance rules, continuing records and reports, information-handling rules, and plans. These procedures are the link between the individual and organisation. They are the means by which organisations make and implement choices.

CONTEXT

Much of decision science is built on the foundations set down by early business thinkers, such as computer pioneer, Charles Babbage, and scientific management founder, Frederick W. Taylor, who believed that, under a given set of circumstances, human behaviour was logical and therefore predictable. Based on this premise, models emerged to explain the workings of commerce which, it was thought, could be extended to the way in which decisions were made.

THE BEST SOURCES OF HELP

Cyert, Richard, and James March. *A Behavioral Theory of the Firm.* Harlow: Prentice Hall, 1963.

Being Digital
by Nicholas Negroponte

This book explains why knowledge is more important than physical commodities. Although it argues that organisations of any size can break into the new economy, this is not a book that offers practical guidelines.

GETTING STARTED

Negroponte was a regular contributor to *Wired* magazine and provided many insights into the digital world. He introduced the terms 'bits' and 'atoms' that are used to describe the elements of the digital world. He explains that most information, despite being digital, is delivered to us in the form of atoms, that is to say, as newspapers, magazines, and books.

Economists still measure trade and write balance sheets with atoms in mind, he points out. But looking ahead, he explains why bits are easy to make and keep. They can travel easily around the world, he argues, and they are the basis of a global economy that allows the smallest company to participate.

CONTRIBUTION

The concept of 'bits' and 'atoms'. According to Negroponte, the best way to appreciate the merits and consequences of being digital is to reflect on the difference between 'atoms' and 'bits'. Atoms, he explains, are the elements of the old economy. Bits are digital. However, he points out that, while we are undoubtedly in a new digital age, most information is still delivered to us in the form of atoms: newspapers, magazines, and books.

The author argues that, although the economy may be moving toward an information economy, we measure trade and we write our balance sheets in the traditional way, using atoms as the measure.

Describing the digital world. According to Negroponte the bits and atoms distinction has improved, not weakened, over time. He claims that people quickly grasp the idea of bits that have no weight, no size, no shape, no colour, and can travel at the speed of light.

The value of bits. Bits are the key elements of the new information economy. Negroponte explains how the marginal cost of making more bits is zero, and you need no inventory. It is possible to sell bits and keep them for yourself at the same time because the originals and the copies are indistinguishable.

Towards a global marketplace. The author believes that bits will form the basis of a global marketplace that is accessible to even the smallest company. That is because bits don't stop at customs. Governments cannot tell where they are, and regulators cannot determine their appropriate jurisdiction.

CONTEXT

The book consists of a 're-purposing' of many of the themes first visited in the author's monthly *Wired* column in the early- to mid-1990s. The book offers practical insights into the future of communications, but allows little opportunity for considered reflection of big-picture issues.

According to critics, Negroponte seems content to describe rather than to analyse, and the book lacks an incisive conclusion bringing together the key themes that he touches on but never really makes explicit.

THE BEST SOURCES OF HELP

Negroponte, Nicholas. *Being Digital.* London: Coronet, 1996.

Blur
by Stan Davis and Christopher Meyer

Blur is a book about the future, but the authors do not offer prescriptions. Instead they offer a starting point: provocative ideas, observations, and predictions to get you to think creatively about your business and your future.

GETTING STARTED

At the heart of *Blur* are three forces—connectivity, speed, and intangibles—that are redefining businesses and destroying solutions that worked for the industrial world. The forces are known as the blur of desires, the blur of fulfilment, and the blur of resources.

A product offer and exchange were once clear cut, but buyers and sellers are now in a constantly evolving relationship. The entire theory and practice of competitive strategy is changing, and intellectual capital has emerged as the key resource.

Change no longer carries the huge weight it did only a few years ago, and connectivity is speeding the economy up and changing the way it works.

CONTRIBUTION

The nature of *Blur*. At the heart of the authors' Blur theory are three forces: connectivity, speed, and intangibles. These forces are blurring the rules and redefining our businesses and our lives. They are destroying solutions, such as mass production, segmented pricing, and standardised jobs, that worked for the relatively slow, unconnected industrial world.

> Intellectual capital has emerged as the key resource. Hard assets have become intangibles; intangibles have become your only assets.

The three forces are shaping the behaviour of the new economy and are affecting what Davis and Meyer label the blur of desires, the blur of fulfilment, and the blur of resources.

The blur of desires. The blur of desires has two central elements— the offer and the exchange that were once clear cut.

In the product-dominated age, a company offered a product for sale. Money was exchanged and the customer disappeared into the distance. Now, however, products and services are often indistinguishable from each other. Buyers and sellers are in a constantly evolving relationship—a mutual exchange—which is driven by information and emotion as well as by money.

The blur of fulfilment. As organisations change to meet changing demands, so too must the entire theory and practice of competitive strategy.

Connectivity produces different forms of organisation operating to different first principles.

The blur of businesses has created a new economic model in which returns increase rather than diminish; supermarkets mimic stock markets, and you want the market, not your strategy, to price, market, and manage your offer.

The blur of resources. Intellectual capital has emerged as the key resource. Hard assets have become intangibles; intangibles have become your only assets.

Change is less critical. The authors assert that 'built to last' now means 'built to change'. However, change, and the ambiguity it brings, no longer carries the huge weight it did only a few years ago.

The impact of connectivity. In the information economy, small things are connected in myriad ways to create a complex adaptive system.

Instantaneous, myriad connections are speeding the economy up and changing the way it works. The problem is that the connections are so many and so complex, that they can bring things to a grinding, inexplicable halt.

CONTEXT

From Dale Carnegie to Stephen Covey, Frederick Taylor to Michael Porter, business book readers have been weaned on a diet of prescriptions for success. Books are distilled down to a handful of key points or simple models. The trouble is that lists of the essential ingredients for success are becoming increasingly more questionable.

Uncertainty is uncharted territory and *Blur* is a book of the new breed. *Blur* would not even have been considered as a possible title even ten years ago when blind faith and certainty ruled. It would have been too weak, too suggestive of managerial confusion and impotence, too realistic.

THE BEST SOURCES OF HELP

Davis, Stan, and Christopher Meyer. *Blur: The Speed of Change in the Connected Economy.* Oxford: Capstone, 1997.

The Book of the Five Rings
by Miyamoto Musashi

Emerging victorious from combat is not a matter of fighting skill, but rather of attitude. Miyamoto Musashi, a 17th-century master samurai swordfighter, says that the fighter's attitude should be characterised by open-mindedness, uprightness, equanimity, and relaxation. The principles he enunciates also apply to managers in modern businesses. From them the perceptive manager can derive useful strategy concepts and rules of conduct for modern business life.

GETTING STARTED

Musashi's work offers the Western reader access to, and an understanding of, the thought, attitudes, and traditions of Japan; and it attempts to show how to achieve and preserve individuality in today's mass society. It is divided into five 'books', each assigned to one of the five elements in Japanese tradition and each showing, on the basis of simple principles, how a samurai can defeat an opponent.

CONTRIBUTION

The Book of the Earth. Those who wish to learn the art of swordfighting, says Musashi, must follow these rules:

- never have malicious thoughts
- practise constantly to follow the Way
- make yourself familiar with all the arts and techniques required
- study the ways of all occupations and professions
- learn to distinguish between profit and loss in all things
- develop your ability to see through things at first glance
- endeavour also to perceive the nature of things that remain invisible
- never let your attention slip, even when dealing with the smallest things
- do not waste time on useless activities

Only those, Masushi says, who strictly follow these rules, consider each situation in its totality. Constant practice will enable them to control their bodies so that they defeat their opponent physically, and if they have steeled their minds, they will be able to overcome their opponent psychologically as well. If there is a way that leads to invincible self confidence, that helps the individual to overcome all manner of difficulties, and brings fame and honour, that way is the Way of the Warrior.

The Book of Water. Masushi stresses that in combat your inner attitude should be the same as it usually is. Take good care, he advises, that you are always the same in fight as you are in everyday life. If your body is at rest, do not let your mind remain inactive, but if your body is in violent motion, let your mind remain calm.

In order to defeat an opponent in the correct way, you must first learn the five fighting positions and the corresponding tactics for attack. In this way, he argues, you will develop your judgment and your understanding of rhythm.

The Book of Fire. Masushi lists three methods of seizing the initiative:

- Attacking before your opponent does. This is called *Ken-no-sen* (leading by making the first move).
- Seizing the initiative at precisely the moment when the opponent launches an attack. This is *Tai-no-sen* (leading by waiting).
- Still seizing the initiative though both attack at the same time. This is *Tai-tai-no-sen* (leading in a tie).

If you have seized the initiative, says Masushi, victory is as good as assured.

Turning to the broader military picture, Masushi teaches that it is important to recognise the situation and judge whether your opponent is in full command of his forces or already beginning to falter. That involves assessing the fighting spirit of his troops and the positions they have taken up and thus establishing a clear picture of the state he is in, so that you can deploy your own troops accordingly. If you use this strategy, victory is in your hands, because you fight with foresight.

The Book of the Wind. He who relies solely on the power of his sword to beat down an opponent, according to Masushi, will strike with unreasonable force and not be in a position to finish the opponent off.

No matter what opponent you are in life-and-death combat with, do not consider whether your blows are strong or weak; your mind must be set solely on killing him. The Book of the Wind says you should think about nothing else but his death.

All other tricks to bring down an opponent, by winding the body, leaping away, or twisting the hand, do not belong in the true art of swordsmanship, according to Masushi.

The Book of the Void. The void is that in which nothing exists; it is that which it is impossible for humans to know. If, says Masushi, you know that which exists, you will also be capable of knowing that which does not exist. If, as a samurai, you understand precisely the way of swordsmanship, if daily and hourly you are diligent in training yourself, if you sharpen your wisdom and the power of your mind and learn judgment and vigilance, this will bring you to a state of true emptiness, understood by Masushi in the Buddhist sense as the state of ultimate fulfilment.

CONTEXT

Miyamoto Musashi (1584–1645) was a famous samurai. His *Gorin-no-sho*, or *Book of Five Rings* is a manual of swordsmanship, and, in contrast to other samurai texts like the *Hagakure*, it contains little information on the ethical and philosophical principles of the 'Way of the Warrior'. Musashi was a 'masterless', or independent, samurai. For him, there was no superior authority apart from the Way. He remained undefeated throughout his life and shortly before his death withdrew to a cave as a hermit in order to write down his experiences.

Reviews describe Musashi as a cult figure, as a guru, whose disciples now fight in world markets on the same principles that once guided the samurai. Musashi's guide to strategy is treated with great respect in internal seminars held by large Western companies. Japanese business people use it as a handbook for planning sales campaigns.

THE BEST SOURCES OF HELP

Miyamoto Musashi. *The Book of Five Rings*. (Trans. Wilson.) London: Kodansha Europe, 2002.

Hagakure: The Book of the Samurai
by Yamamoto Tsunetomo

It should take no more than seven breaths to make a decision—so wrote Yamamoto Tsunemoto 300 years ago. His book, the *Hagakure*, is the code of honour of the samurai of old Japan. The key virtues it commends are: assertiveness and integrity, determination and sympathy, courage and loyalty.

GETTING STARTED

Hagakure ('In the Shadow of Leaves') is a spiritual guide to professional and private success for an 18th-century samurai. It shows the way to resolution and loyalty, and sharpens understanding of, and trust in, one's own abilities. Inner peace is a decisive factor in asserting oneself in conflicts, remaining calm when making personal decisions, and achieving wisdom in the conduct of life.

CONTRIBUTION

Fearless devotion to one's lord. 'The warrior must above all things honour his lord and be unfailingly devoted to him in spirit. This makes him supremely valuable as a follower.'

Know the limits of your own wisdom. 'If no worthwhile idea comes into one's own head, it is better to ask a wise man for advice. The wise man, who is not personally involved, can make a candid and disinterested judgment of the case.'

Be careful in criticising others. 'Reproaching others in order to correct their faults, which is a highly gracious and sympathetic act, is one of the most important services a follower can render. It does, however, demand extraordinary tact.'

Be prepared for any situation. 'Military tactics and strategy reveal both capable and incapable men. The former are not only wise through experience, but also ready, at the decisive moment, to solve any problem admirably, guided by their previous study of a great variety of cases. They are prepared for any situation. The latter, on the other hand, have not considered the possibilities in advance. If they solve a problem, it is by sheer good luck.'

Matters of great importance should be approached calmly. In this rule, Yamamoto Tsunetomo advises that one should formulate a response to serious issues in advance, so that when one faces a crucial situation it is easy to make a decision.

Learning through following the example of others. 'Students in all disciplines are more inclined to imitate their teachers' imperfections than their strengths. This is unprofitable. Find out other people's strong points and copy them. This way, anyone, no matter who he is, can become a good example and teacher.'

Watch what you say. 'Others can easily draw a man of weak convictions over to their side. If at a gathering one is fascinated by another man, one sometimes hears oneself cry out "Precisely!", even though he is speaking carelessly about something he has not considered deeply. A third party will surely take such an exclamation for assent. Be on your guard, therefore, whenever you meet with others.'

Be decisive. An old proverb says: 'Consider quickly and decide inside seven breaths'. Prince Takanobu once commented: 'Long consideration blunts the sharp edge of a decision'. Prince

Naoshige said: 'In seven out of ten cases, things that are delayed over turn out wrong. Swift action is expected from a samurai in everything he undertakes'.

Avoid promotion while you are young. 'To be promoted when young cannot lead to good results for those who wish to be useful samurai. It is therefore better to rise gradually at around the age of 50.'

Throw away petty logic. Yamakzi Kurando once remarked: 'A follower who tries too hard to get to the bottom of things is not an asset'. Such a man's mind is obsessed with questions: is this or that action loyal, justified, appropriate for a follower or not? Things are then analysed from the standpoint of reason and justice, which the author advises against.

How one helps one's lord. 'One should praise a calm and cheerful master without reserve and ensure he can do his duty without failing—with the long-term objective of cultivating the positive sides of his character.'

How to settle a dispute. 'Before considering a matter in conference, the chairman should discuss the case in detail with the person directly involved. Afterwards he should hear the opinions of others present, and then make his decision. Otherwise everyone feels insulted.'

How to win in discussions. If one is pressed to give a definite answer in a lawsuit or controversy, Tsunetomo says one should gain time by saying: 'I shall give you my answer after due reflection'. One can also add, 'I should like to give the matter further thought', in order to gain breathing space.

CONTEXT

The book contains the lesson, rules, and stories of the Japanese samurai Yamamoto Tsunetomo. He became a Zen Buddhist monk, being forbidden by a decree of his lord from committing *seppuku* (or *harakiri*) when the latter died. Yamamoto dictated *Hagakure* to the scribe Tashiro Tsuramoto between 1710 and 1716. It was produced during the Genroku era, considered a period of decadence. The Tokugawa shogunate had pacified the country and suppressed uprisings by the feudal lords. The philosophy contained in *Hagakure* is a counterblast on behalf of the mighty warrior to the Confucianist academic rhetoric of the shogunate.

Hagakure is also presented as an alternative to today's advisors and seminars on power and careers. While the preoccupations of modern managers are clearly different from those of the author, the book nonetheless offers an insight into the life and thought of another culture and another age.

THE BEST SOURCES OF HELP

Yamamoto Tsunetomo. *Hagakure: The Book of the Samurai.* (Trans. Wilson.) London: Kodansha Europe, 2000.

The Borderless World
by Kenichi Ohmae

Like *The Mind of the Strategist*, the book gives valuable insights into the strategic thinking behind Japanese corporate success. The author adds new elements to the structure of business strategy, showing how it operates on a global scale.

GETTING STARTED

According to Ohmae, in the global marketplace, the concepts of country and currency are important to business strategy. Fluctuations in trade policy or exchange rates can affect an otherwise brilliant strategy. Strategy is about more than being better than the competition. Big companies must relearn the art of invention in global industries. Customers are not driven to purchase things through nationalistic sentiments, therefore strategy should be formulated around a determination to create value for customers. Global business balances world-scale economies with products tailored to key markets. The role of central governments must change to allow individuals access to the best and cheapest goods and services from anywhere in the world.

CONTRIBUTION

The key elements of business strategy. To the three Cs of his previous works (commitment, creativity, and competitiveness), Ohmae adds:

- country—the government-created environments in which every global organisation must operate
- currency—the exposure of such organisations to fluctuations in foreign exchange rates

These two additional elements are now key to the formulation of any strategy.

An otherwise brilliant strategy can be ruined by a sudden fluctuation in trade policy or exchange rates, leading to a seemingly irreparable haemorrhage of cash.

Making arrangements to deal with fluctuations must lie at the very heart of strategy.

Strategy is creating sustained values for the customer more effectively than do your competitors.

Invention is critical. In the author's view, invention and the commercialisation of invention are essential. Most people in big companies have forgotten how to invent, but they must relearn the art of invention. This time they must learn to manage invention in industries or businesses that are global, where it is necessary to achieve world-scale economies and yet tailor products to key markets.

Going beyond the competition. Strategy is about more than simply being better than the competition, which only encourages companies to become fixated on the competition. This fixation drives them to formulate their strategy according to the strategy of their competitors.

Possible strategies should be tested against competitive realities.

Tactical responses to what competitors are doing may be appropriate, but they should come second to your real strategy.

Before you test yourself against the competition, your strategy should encompass the determination to create value for customers.

The interlinked economy. In the author's view, countries are merely government creations.

In the interlinked economy (made up of the triad of the United States, Europe, and Japan) consumers are not driven to purchase things through nationalistic sentiments, no matter what politicians may say.

At the cash register, people don't care about country of origin or country of residence. They don't think about employment figures or trade deficits.

This also applies to industrial consumers.

Declaration of interdependence. The role of central governments must change to:

- allow individuals access to the best and cheapest goods and services from anywhere in the world
- help corporations provide stable and rewarding jobs anywhere in the world, regardless of the corporation's national identity
- co-ordinate activities with other governments to minimise conflicts arising from narrow interests
- avoid abrupt changes in economic and social fundamentals

Governments must deal collectively with traditionally parochial affairs, including taxation.

CONTEXT

The Borderless World explores the new logic of the global marketplace, as well as what Ohmae calls power and strategy in the inter-linked economy.

This manifesto for the future is as broad-ranging as it is, in political reality, unlikely.

The Borderless World has, however, fuelled debates about the role of governments, as well as the relationship between governments and the business world, which have yet to be resolved.

Ohmae has since gone on to explore the role of nations still further and now suggests that we have reached a time when the end of the nation state is imminent (see *The End of the Nation State*, Free Press, 1996, and *The Invisible Continent*, HarperBusiness, 2001).

Gary Hamel, author of *Leading the Revolution*, commented, 'So the world is becoming interdependent. Hardly news to companies like Dow Chemical, IBM, Ford, or Nestlé. But in 1990 this was still news to Japanese companies (and politicians) who typically defined globalisation as big open export markets, and maybe a factory in Tennessee. Kenichi challenged Japanese companies, and myopic executives elsewhere, to develop a more sophisticated view of what it means to be global. Just what balance will ultimately be struck between the forces of globalisation and the forces of nationalism and tribalism remains to be seen.'

THE BEST SOURCES OF HELP

Ohmae, Kenichi. *The Borderless World: Power and Strategy in the Interlinked Economy*. London: William Collins, 1990.

Built to Last
by James Collins and Jerry Porras

According to the authors, companies that enjoy enduring success have core values and a core purpose that remain fixed, while their business strategies and practices endlessly adapt to a changing world. The book shows the importance of developing and sticking to a set of guiding principles, and identifies the qualities essential to building a great and enduring organisation.

GETTING STARTED

Values are important in the context of business and corporations, and many companies have long recognised the importance of possessing a set of guiding principles.

In the authors' view, enduring organisations with strong guiding principles have out-performed the general stock market by a factor of 12 since 1925.

Core values are the organisation's essential and enduring tenets, and drive the way the company operates at a level that transcends strategic objectives. Such values don't change, although strategies and practices adapt endlessly to change.

Core ideology defines what the company stands for and why it exists. It complements the envisioned future—what the company aspires to become. Any effective vision must embody the core ideology of the organisation.

CONTRIBUTION

The importance of corporate values. Honesty, integrity, wealth, fairness are all values that we may be able to relate to on an individual personal basis. But what about values in the context of business and corporations?

> Honesty, integrity, wealth, fairness are all values that we may be able to relate to on an individual personal basis. But what about values in the context of business and corporations?

While the term 'corporate values' is a relative newcomer to the business lexicon, the concept of values as an important aspect of corporate life is not. Many companies have long recognised the importance of possessing a set of guiding principles, and the evolution of the concept can be traced through some of the most influential business books over the last 50 years.

Thomas Watson Jr, CEO of IBM, observed that any great organisation that has lasted over the years owes its resilience to the power of its beliefs and the appeal these beliefs have for its people.

The qualities of an enduring organisation. The book sets out to identify the qualities essential to building a great and enduring organisation—the successful habits of visionary companies.

The 18 companies chosen as subjects had outperformed the general stock market by a factor of 12 since 1925.

Core values are the organisation's essential and enduring tenets. These are a small set of guiding principles (not to be confused with specific cultural or operating practices) which are never to be compromised for financial gain or short-term expediency.

Values are timeless guiding principles that drive the way the company operates at a level that transcends strategic objectives. For Hewlett-Packard, for example, values include a strong sense of responsibility to the community. For Disney, they include creativity, dreams, imagination, and the promulgation of wholesome American values.

Core values don't change. Companies that enjoy enduring success have core values and a core purpose that remain fixed while their business strategies and practices endlessly adapt to a changing world. This is a key factor in the success of companies such as Hewlett-Packard, Johnson & Johnson, Procter & Gamble, Mercke, and Sony.

A model for core values. The authors recommend a conceptual framework to cut through some of the confusion swirling around the issues.

In their model, vision has two components—core ideology and envisioned future. Core ideology, the Yin in their scheme, defines what the company stands for and why it exists. Yin is unchanging and complements Yang, the envisioned future.

The envisioned future is what the company aspires to become, to achieve, to create—something that will require considerable change and progress to attain. Core ideology provides the glue that holds an organisation together through time.

An effective vision. Any effective vision must embody the core ideology of the organisation. This has two components—core values (a system of guiding principles and tenets) and core purpose (the organisation's most fundamental reason for existence).

CONTEXT

Built to Last set out to identify the qualities, or corporate values, essential to building a great and enduring organisation.

The evolution of the concept of corporate values can be traced through some of the most influential business books over the last 50 years.

In *A Business and Its Beliefs*, published in 1963, Thomas Watson Jr observed, 'Consider any great organisation—one that has lasted over the years—I think you will find it owes its resiliency not to its form of organisation or administrative skills, but to the power of what we call beliefs and the appeal these beliefs have for its people'.

In the early 1980s, Tom Peters and Robert Waterman thought corporate values important enough to warrant an entire chapter in *In Search of Excellence*.

THE BEST SOURCES OF HELP

Collins, James, and Jerry Porras. *Built to Last*. New York: HarperBusiness, 1994.

A Business and Its Beliefs
by Thomas Watson Jr

A Business and Its Beliefs: The Ideas that Helped Build IBM was written by the son of the founder of IBM's commercial greatness, who himself led the company into the computer age. It describes the origins of one of the world's most successful corporations and shows how its achievements were built on a strong corporate culture and a passionate commitment to customer service.

GETTING STARTED

Thomas Watson Jr went to work for IBM in 1946 as a salesman. He was appointed chief executive in 1956 and retired in 1970, after presiding over IBM's rise to international pre-eminence at the beginning of the computer age.

IBM's origins lay in the Computing-Tabulating-Recording Company, which Thomas Watson Sr joined in 1914. The company initially made everything from butcher's scales to meat slicers, but gradually concentrated on tabulating machines that processed information mechanically on punched cards. It changed its name to International Business Machines in 1924.

IBM's development was helped by the 1937 Wages-Hours Act, which required US companies to record hours worked and wages paid. The existing machines couldn't cope; Watson Sr developed a solution, the Mark 1, followed by the Selective Sequence Electronic Calculator in 1947. By then IBM's revenues were $119 million and it was set to make the great leap forward to become the world's largest computer company.

As far as management thinking is concerned, what IBM stood for is more important than what it did. Thomas Watson Jr took on a hugely successful company with a strong corporate culture built around salesmanship and service. Thomas Watson Sr had emphasised people and service obsessively. IBM was a service star in an era of machines that performed badly. This is where the heart of the message of *A Business and Its Beliefs* lies.

CONTRIBUTION

Core values are critical. A company's central beliefs (what would now be called its core values) are central to its success. Watson believed that these beliefs help people find common cause with each other, and sustain this common cause and sense of direction through the many changes that take place from one generation to another.

> A company's central beliefs (what would now be called its core values) are central to its success.

Success, in his view, comes through a sound set of beliefs, on which the corporation premises all its policies and actions. Beliefs must always come before policies, practices, and goals. The latter must always be altered if they are seen to violate fundamental beliefs.

Not only should the beliefs be sound, they should be stuck to through thick and thin. The most important single factor in corporate success is faithful adherence to those beliefs. Beliefs never change. Change everything else, but never the basic truths on which the company is based.

However, Watson argued for flexibility in all other areas. If an organisation, he asserted, is to meet the challenges of a changing world, it must be prepared to change everything about itself except beliefs as it moves through corporate life. The only sacred cow in an organisation should be its basic philosophy of doing business.

Develop a corporate culture. The beliefs that mould great organisations frequently grow out of the character, the experience, and the convictions of a single person. In IBM's case that person was Thomas Watson Sr.

The Watsons created a corporate culture that lasted. IBM, Big Blue, became the archetypal modern corporation and its managers the ultimate stereotype, with their regulation sombre suits, white shirts, plain ties, zeal for selling, and company song.

A passion for competing. Behind the corporate culture lay a belief in competing vigorously and providing quality service. Later, competitors complained that IBM's sheer size won it orders. This was only partly true. Its size masked a deeper commitment to managing customer accounts, providing service, building relationships, and to the values laid out by the Watsons.

People matter. The real difference between success and failure in a corporation can very often be traced to the question of how well the organisation brings out the great energies and talents of its people. Giving full consideration to the individual employee was one of the enduring beliefs on which IBM's success was built.

CONTEXT

In this book, the author codified and clarified what IBM stands for. The book is a statement of business philosophy, an extended mission statement for IBM.

Though it was published in the same year as Alfred P. Sloan Jr's *My Years with General Motors* it could not be more different. While Sloan sidelines people, Watson celebrates their potential; while Sloan espouses systems and structures, Watson talks of values.

Guru Gary Hamel commented, 'Never change your basic beliefs, Watson argued. He may be right. But the dividing line between beliefs and dogmas is a fine one. A deep set of beliefs can be the essential pivot around which the company changes and adapts; or, if endlessly elaborated, overly codified, and solemnly worshipped, the manacles that shackle a company to the past.'

THE BEST SOURCES OF HELP

Watson, Thomas Jr. *A Business and Its Beliefs: The Ideas That Helped Build IBM*. New York: McGraw-Hill, 1963.

Business @ the Speed of Thought
by Bill Gates

This is a very practical book that shows how to make better use of information inside an organisation. It shows how networks and technology can be used to capture, store, and distribute information in a way that improves many different business processes.

GETTING STARTED

The author asserts that technology can radically change in business and corporate evolution. A digital nervous system is a key tool uniting all systems and processes. It provides an integrated flow of information to the right part of the organisation at the right time.

A digital nervous system improves business processes and responsiveness. It offers accuracy, immediacy, and richness of information to knowledge workers, and also improves insight and collaboration.

CONTRIBUTION

Technology transforms businesses of all sizes. Technology has a transformative power in business. It also plays a key role in corporate evolution, not just for corporate giants but for small businesses as well.

Concept of a digital nervous system. A digital nervous system requires a combination of hardware and software and unites all systems and processes under one common infrastructure.

> Technology has a transformative power in business.

It is the corporate, digital equivalent of the human nervous system, providing a well-integrated flow of information to the right part of the organisation at the right time.

Improving business processes. A digital nervous system consists of the digital processes that enable a company to:

- perceive and react to its environment
- sense competitor challenges and customer needs
- organise timely responses

It is distinguished from a mere network of computers by the accuracy, immediacy, and richness of the information it brings to knowledge workers. It also improves the insight and collaboration made possible by the information.

CONTEXT

Gates and his company are significant global players, and what Gates says will happen in the world of technology has more than a fair chance of coming to pass. *Business @ the Speed of Thought* uses case studies from around the world to demonstrate the impact of technology in business. Gates also provides readers with his view on technology's role in corporate evolution, not just for rival corporate giants but for small businesses as well.

Gates has a world view that puts the technology itself in pole position—there is no consideration of the new economy's wider issues.

It is not a particularly rounded view of the technology scene, and there is a sense of 'if Microsoft isn't doing it, it's not worth talking about' here. Nevertheless, Gates's position as head of the world's biggest and arguably most powerful IT company makes his viewpoint a unique and challenging one.

THE BEST SOURCES OF HELP

Gates, Bill. *Business @ the Speed of Thought*. New York: Warner Books, 1999.

Website: **www.Speed-of-Thought.com**

Capital
by Karl Marx

In the capitalist world, human labour itself becomes a commodity. *Capital*, the major work by the social philosopher Karl Marx (1818–83), is a thoroughgoing critique of capitalism. Marx recognised the dynamics of the economic process, foresaw economic cycles, and developed a closed theory of economic activity. He was also the first economist to bring economics and history into relation with each other and *Capital* was the book in which he did it.

GETTING STARTED

Marx describes the capitalist method of production in its overall context. He follows Ricardo in positing that only labour can produce value, then develops a theory of added value as the difference between the use value and the exchange value of labour as a commodity. Workers do only a portion of their work for themselves; a large portion goes to create added value, which falls entirely to the capitalist. Capitalists, Marx suggests, attempt to increase added value either by making their workers work longer or by reducing the amount of working time necessary for their workers' subsistence. Workers, therefore, have to earn their livelihoods in a shorter time, so that they can produce more added value. This leads to the exploitation of the working class.

CONTRIBUTION

Volume one: the production process of capital. Volume one deals with the development of the laws of added-value production. This is the part of *Capital* that has always played the largest role in public discussion of the book.

Capitalist production, for Marx, is the production of goods, that is, production for the market. It is not carried out by small independent producers such as craftspeople, but by non-working entrepreneurs, who control the means of production and who therefore have the ability to make others work for them and to exploit them.

Every commodity, Marx argues, has two characteristics: usefulness (equivalent to its use value), and the property of being produced by human labour. Since use value varies, depending on persons, time, and circumstances, it cannot be the basis of price. Labour must therefore be the criterion of value.

With the development of the exchange of goods, Marx continues, trade emerges as an independent function. In trade, consumption is not the purpose of the act of exchange, as it is in a simple exchange of goods, but profit.

The following paradox, according to Marx, then emerges. The law of value regulating the exchange of goods knows only the exchange of equal values. But in exchange transactions in trade, on the other hand, an inequality must come into play. This can only stem from production. For this to be possible, the capitalist must discover a commodity whose use value is that it creates more value than it actually possesses. That commodity is labour.

Volume two: the circulation process of capital. In the second volume, Marx deals with the circulation of capital as it passes through various stages. Capital must, he says, continually take on and then divest itself of three separate forms in order to be able to function and be of use: money capital, productive capital, and commodity capital. Money capital constantly transforms itself into the elements of the production process—labour and the means of production—and the result of its functioning appears in the form of commodities, endowed with added value, which are once again transformed into money. Acts involving the circulation of commodities take place continually, sales and purchases are always being transacted, goods and money are constantly brought into conjunction. But it is, says Marx, the fact that these acts are transition stages in the circulatory process of capital that makes them functions of capital; it is precisely that that transforms a sum of money into money capital, that makes commodities either productive capital or commodity capital. It is not their material nature that gives them this character, but the economic and historical conditions under which the process takes place. Commodities are not by nature capital, any more than workers are.

Volume three: the overall process of capitalist production. In this volume, Marx brings volumes one and two into unity. The theoretical category of value, he asserts, is of interest to the capitalist. What the capitalist looks at is the capital advance that must be made to bring about production of a particular commodity. The advance is made up of constant and variable capital and represents, for the capitalist, the cost of the commodity. Capitalists do not calculate added value achieved in relation to the capital used, they simply calculate the surplus achieved against aggregate costs when the goods are sold, the profit.

Added value, says Marxist, interests capitalists as little as does value per se. They expect a gain not on the variable capital they advance, but on aggregate capital. The added value on aggregate capital is profit; the numerical relationship of the one to the other is the profit rate.

CONTEXT

Marx came to economics after his political party failed to achieve power in the revolution of 1848/49. *Capital*, published in 1867, became the cornerstone of Marxism, the political doctrine and system named after him. It is, of course, more than pure economic theory. It is a mighty intellectual construct made up of historical, sociological, and economic ideas and propaganda. It was to provide the groundwork for socialism and give a theoretical basis to Marx's other major work, the *Communist Manifesto*. Marx's guiding light was the classless society, communism. As a result, while some honour him as the prophet and advocate of the working

> It is a mighty intellectual construct made up of historical, sociological, and economic ideas and propaganda.

class, others refuse to take him seriously as an economist. He has also been blamed for the fact that, while concerned in theory with the working class, he avoided actual contact with the object of his investigations and never once saw a factory from the inside.

THE BEST SOURCES OF HELP

Marx, Karl. *Capital: A Critique of Political Economy.* (Trans. Fernbach.) Harmondsworth: Penguin, 1992.

The Change Masters
by Rosabeth Moss Kanter

This book is regarded as an authoritative work on the factors behind successful corporate change. Kanter's work takes a human relations perspective, and was one of the earliest books to focus on the importance of empowerment.

GETTING STARTED

According to the author, 'change masters' are adept at anticipating the need for, and leading, productive change. Companies with a commitment to human resources were significantly ahead in long-term profitability and financial growth.

Kanter goes on to suggest that growth problems in American companies are due to suffocation of the entrepreneurial spirit—innovation is the key to growth. New skills are required to manage effectively in innovation-stimulating environments: power skills, the ability to manage employee participation, and an understanding of how change is managed. Empowerment is critical to corporate success.

CONTRIBUTION

The nature of change masters. Change masters are those people and organisations adept at the art of anticipating the need for, and leading, productive change. Change resisters are intent on reining in innovation.

The importance of managing people. A research programme asked 65 human resource directors in large organisations to name companies that were progressive and forward-thinking in their systems and practices, in relation to people. Forty-seven companies emerged as leaders in the field. They were then compared to similar companies. The companies with a commitment to human resources were significantly ahead in long-term profitability and financial growth.

> The message is that if you manage your people well, you are probably managing your business well.

The message is that if you manage your people well, you are probably managing your business well.

Innovation as the key to growth. Kanter places responsibility for company growth problems on the quiet suffocation of the entrepreneurial spirit in segmentalist companies. She identifies innovation as the key to future growth. The way to develop and sustain innovation is to adopt an integrative approach rather than a segmentalist one.

Three new sets of skills are required to manage effectively in such integrative, innovation-stimulating environments:

- the ability to persuade others to invest information, support, and resources in new initiatives driven by an entrepreneur
- the ability to manage problems associated with increased use of teams and employee participation
- an understanding of how change is designed and constructed in an organisation: how the microchanges introduced by individual innovators relate to macrochanges or strategic re-orientation

The importance of empowerment. The extent to which individuals are given the opportunity to use power effectively influences whether a company stagnates or innovates. In an innovative company, people are at centre stage.

CONTEXT

Rosabeth Moss Kanter began her career as a sociologist before her transformation into international business guru. *The Economist* (15 October 1994) commented, 'Kanter-the-guru still studies her subject with a sociologist's eye, treating the corporation not so much as a micro-economy, concerned with turning inputs into outputs, but as a mini-society, bent on shaping individuals to collective ends.'

Kanter's work is a development of the Human Relations School of the late 1950s and 1960s. Through *The Change Masters* (1983) and *When Giants Learn to Dance* (1989), she was partly responsible for the increased interest in empowerment, if not its practice.

The Change Masters has been called 'the thinking man's *In Search of Excellence*'.

Gary Hamel said: 'In a turbulent and inhospitable world, corporate vitality is a fragile thing. Yesterday's industry challengers are today's laggards. Entropy is endemic. Certainly *The Change Masters* is the most carefully researched, and best argued, book on change and transformation to date. While Rosabeth may not have discovered the eternal fountain of corporate vitality, she certainly points us in its general direction.'

THE BEST SOURCES OF HELP

Kanter, Rosabeth Moss. *The Change Masters*. London: Allen & Unwin, 1983.

The Changing Culture of a Factory
by Elliott Jaques

This book is based on an extensive study of industrial democracy in practice at the United Kingdom's Glacier Metal Company between 1948 and 1965. The company introduced a number of highly progressive changes in working practice that were ahead of their time and set a pattern for future practice.

GETTING STARTED

The Glacier Metal Company introduced a number of highly progressive changes in working practice, resulting in a form of industrial democracy that was ahead of its time. According to the study, the emphasis was on granting people responsibility and giving them a say in every problem. The project highlighted the shortcomings of conventional industrial relations practice, and showed that managers should be measured by the long-term impact of their decisions.

CONTRIBUTION

Introducing industrial democracy. The Glacier Metal Company introduced a number of highly progressive changes in working practice:

- a works council was introduced. This was far removed from the usually toothless attempts at worker representation
- no change of company policy was allowed unless all members of the works council agreed. Any single person on the council had a veto
- 'clocking on', the traditional means of recording whether someone had turned up for work, was abolished

Contrary to what experts and observers anticipated, the company did not grind to an immediate halt.

> The project was a decade ahead of any form of organisational development.

Increasing personal responsibility. The emphasis was on granting people responsibility and of understanding the dynamics of group working. Everybody should be encouraged to accept the maximum amount of personal responsibility, and should be allowed to have a say in every problem in which they could help.

Anticipating organisational developments. The project was a decade ahead of any form of organisational development. It highlighted a number of issues:

- the redundancy of conventional organisation charts
- the potential power of corporate culture (a concept then barely understood)
- the potential benefits of running organisations in a fair and mutually beneficial way

Theory of the value of work. 'The manifest picture of bureaucratic organisation is a confusing one', according to Jaques. 'There appears to be no rhyme or reason for the structures that are developed, in number of levels, in titling, or even in the meaning to be attached to the manager–subordinate linkage'.

A solution, labelled 'the time span of discretion', contended that levels of management should be based on how long it was before their decisions could be checked. Managers should be paid in accordance with that time, and measured by the long-term impact of their decisions.

CONTEXT

The practices introduced at the Glacier Metal Company were almost a decade ahead of their time. However, they did not ensure the company's survival.

The study's progressive views on the importance of motivation at work have undoubtedly influenced other management writers and practitioners, such as Mary Parker Follett and Frederick Herzberg. Jaques' work was based on long-term scientific observation, in contrast to what he terms the 'fantasy fads', the 'waffle and fiddling around' of management consultants.

THE BEST SOURCES OF HELP

Jaques, Elliott. *The Changing Culture of a Factory*. London: Tavistock Publications, 1951.

The Cluetrain Manifesto
by Rick Levine, Christopher Locke, Doc Searls, and David Weinberger

This book sets out the opinions of a number of commentators who believe that the Internet is being hijacked by business for the wrong reasons. It provides an alternative point of view which is more in line with Tim Berners-Lee's original vision for the Internet.

GETTING STARTED

In the authors' view, new, networked markets have emerged—and networked markets can change suppliers overnight. The Internet is enabling conversations among human beings that were simply not possible in the era of mass media, and the current homogenised 'voice' of business will seem contrived and artificial in the future.

Companies can now communicate with their markets directly, and company positioning should relate to something their market actually cares about. Customers want open access to corporate information and genuine knowledge—and it is essential that businesses take the new markets seriously.

CONTRIBUTION

The new markets. According to the book, markets are conversations, consisting of human beings, not demographic sectors. Networked markets can change suppliers overnight.

> Companies that assume online markets are the same markets that used to watch their ads on television are kidding themselves.

The voice of business. Conversations among human beings sound human. They are conducted in a human voice. The Internet is enabling conversations among human beings that were simply not possible in the era of mass media.

In just a few more years, the current homogenised 'voice' of business—the sound of mission statements and brochures—will seem as contrived and artificial as the language of the 18th-century French court.

Communicating with the new market. Companies that assume online markets are the same markets that used to watch their ads on television are kidding themselves. Companies can now communicate with their markets directly. If they do not make the most of this opportunity, they may not get another.

Companies attempting to 'position' themselves need to take a Position. Optimally, it should relate to something their market actually cares about.

'Public Relations' do not relate to the public. Companies are deeply afraid of their markets.

Brand loyalty is the corporate version of going steady, but the breakup is inevitable—and coming fast. Because they are networked, smart markets are able to renegotiate relationships with blinding speed.

Open access. The authors assert that customers want access to a company's corporate information, its plans and strategies, its best thinking, and its genuine knowledge. They will not settle for visually attractive but essentially useless publications and websites.

Taking the new markets seriously. Maybe you're impressing your investors. Maybe you're impressing Wall Street. You're not impressing your customers. They want you to take 50 million of them as seriously as you take one reporter from the *Wall Street Journal*.

Customers' allegiance is to themselves—their friends, their new allies and acquaintances, even their sparring partners. Companies that have no part in this world also have no future.

CONTEXT

The book is a manifesto for the Internet generation. It is a series of charges against the corporate sector and represents a declaration of human rights for inhabitants of the business and technology world.

The Cluetrain Manifesto began in early 1999 when the authors decided to use a website as a forum for articulating 'a set of 95 principles we believe will determine the future experience of both individuals and organisations online'. They invited visitors to the site to sign up to it. Word about the site spread virally through corporate America, and the site rapidly attained a cult status. The book gave the authors the opportunity to expand and augment the contents of the manifesto.

THE BEST SOURCES OF HELP

Levine, Rick, Christopher Locke, Doc Searls, and David Weinberger. *The Cluetrain Manifesto: The End of Business as Usual*. London: FT.com, 2000.

Website: **www.cluetrain.com**

Competing for the Future
by Gary Hamel and C.K. Prahalad

Competing for the Future, named by *BusinessWeek* as the best management book of 1994, is regarded as the definitive book on strategy for contemporary business. It criticises the narrow mechanistic view of strategy and calls for a broader approach that recognises a company's core competencies.

GETTING STARTED

This book argues that traditional strategy is too narrow in its perspective. Few managers spend enough time looking to the future. They should adopt 'strategising'—a new approach for developing complex, robust strategies, focusing on core competencies.

Today the onus is on transforming not just individual organisations, but entire industries. The true challenge is to create revolutions when you are large and dominant. Small entrepreneurial offshoots are not the route to organisational regeneration. Downsizing is an easy option—growth comes from creating a difference, and vitality comes from within, if only executives would listen.

CONTRIBUTION

The narrow focus of traditional strategy. The authors assert that strategy has tied itself into a straitjacket of narrow, and narrowing, perspectives:

- a huge proportion of strategists, perhaps 95%, are economists and engineers who share a mechanistic view of strategy
- strategy is multi-faceted, emotional as well as analytical, concerned with meaning, purpose, and passion
- strategy should be looked on as a learning process
- today, the onus is on transforming not just individual organisations but entire industries

Strategy is not simple. In the authors' view, executives perceive that the problem with strategy is not creating it, but implementing it. Strategy is not a ritual or a once-a-year exercise. As a result, managers are bogged down in the nitty gritty of the present—spending less than 3% of their time looking to the future.

Adopt strategising. Instead of talking about strategy or planning, companies should talk of strategising and ask, 'What are the fundamental preconditions for developing complex, variegated, robust strategies?'

Strategising is part of the new managerial argot of strategic intent, strategic architecture, foresight (rather than vision), and the idea of core competencies.

Focus on core competencies. Core competencies represent the collective learning in the organisation, especially how to co-ordinate diverse production skills and integrate multiple streams of technologies.

Organisations should see themselves as a portfolio of core competencies, as opposed to business units. Core competencies are geared to growing opportunity share, whereas business units are narrowly focused on market share.

Different approaches to strategy. There is a thin dividing line between order and chaos. Neither Stalinist bureaucracy nor Silicon Valley provides an optimal economic system. Silicon Valley is good at creating new ideas, but in other ways is extraordinarily inefficient.

Small or large organisations? Small entrepreneurial offshoots are not the route to organisational regeneration. They are too random, inefficient, and prone to becoming becalmed by corporate indifference. Smaller companies have had a revolutionary impact (IKEA, Body Shop, Swatch, and Virgin), but the true challenge is to create revolutions when you are large and dominant. American companies such as Motorola and Hewlett-Packard are more successful at this than their European counterparts. We are moving to more democratic models of organisation, to which US corporations appear more attuned. In Europe and Japan there is a more elitist sense of knowledge residing at the top—a hierarchy of experience, not of imagination.

Rules for success.

- A company surrenders today's businesses when it gets smaller faster than it gets better.
- A company surrenders tomorrow's businesses when it gets better without getting different.
- Downsizing is an easy option.
- Growth (the authors prefer to talk of vitality) comes from difference, though there are as many stupid ways to grow as there are to downsize.
- The pressure for growth is usually ignited by a crisis.
- Vitality comes from within, if only executives would listen.
- Companies will pay millions of dollars for the opinions of McKinsey's bright 29-year-old, but ignore their own bright 29-year-olds.

CONTEXT

The debate on the meaning and application of strategy is long-running. The 1960s gave us the resolutely analytical Igor Ansoff; the 1970s Henry Mintzberg with his cerebral and creative crafting strategy; the 1980s, Michael Porter's rational route to competitiveness.

Nominations for the leading strategic thinkers of the 1990s would certainly include Gary Hamel and C.K. Prahalad. *Competing for the Future* has been called the blueprint for a new generation of strategic thinking. *BusinessWeek* (19 September 1994) said: 'At a time when many companies continue to lay off thousands in massive re-engineering exercises, this is a book that deserves widespread attention. It's a valuable and worthwhile tonic for devotees of today's slash-and-burn school of management.'

The surge of interest in core competencies has tended to enthusiastic oversimplification. Commentators believe companies need to be cautious about where core competencies will lead. They are a very powerful weapon, but can encourage companies to get into businesses simply because they see a link between core competencies rather than ones where they have an in-depth knowledge.

The authors' strategic prognosis falls between two extremes. At one extreme are the archrationalists, insisting on a constant stream of data to support any strategy. At the other is the thriving-on-chaos school, with its belief in strategy as a moveable feast.

THE BEST SOURCES OF HELP

Hamel, Gary, and C.K. Prahalad. *Competing for the Future.* Boston, Massachusetts: Harvard Business School Press, 1994.

The Competitive Advantage of Nations
by Michael Porter

Many consider *The Competitive Advantage of Nations* to be one of the most ambitious books of our times. Said to do 'for international capitalism what Marx did for the class struggle', it re-examines the nation state, suggesting that its basic role today is an economic one, and that, even in a global economy, it has a key role to play by ensuring the competitiveness of the companies operating within its borders who are the actual wealth producers for the population.

GETTING STARTED

Michael Porter, author of the modern business classic *Competitive Strategy*, has a good deal of experience as a consultant to national governments. *The Competitive Advantage of Nations* emerged from his work on US President Ronald Reagan's Commission on Industrial Competitiveness. The research for the book encompassed ten countries: the United Kingdom, Denmark, Italy, Japan, Korea, Singapore, Sweden, Switzerland, the United States, and Germany (then West Germany).

The book can be read on three levels:

- as a general inquiry into what makes national economies successful
- as a detailed study of ten of the world's main modern economies
- as a series of prescriptions about what governments should do to improve their country's competitiveness

It asks crucial questions. What makes a nation's firms and industries competitive in global markets and what propels a whole nation's economy to advance? Why are firms based in a particular nation able to create and sustain competitive advantage against the world's best competitors in a particular field? Why is one nation often the home for so many of an industry's world leaders? Why, for example, is Switzerland the home base for international leaders in pharmaceuticals, chocolate, and trading?

At its heart is a radical new perspective on the role of nations. From being military power-houses they are now economic units whose competitiveness is the key to power.

CONTRIBUTION

Nations, competition, and productivity. According to the author, 'Nations don't compete. Companies compete. Nations can make it hard or easy for them to do so.' When governments deliberately set out to help companies compete, however, their efforts are often counterproductive. The principal economic goal of a nation is to produce a high and rising standard of living for its citizens. The ability to do so depends not on the amorphous notion of competitiveness, but on the productivity with which a nation's labour and capital resources are employed.

The paradox of globalisation. Companies and industries have become globalised and more international in their scope and aspirations than ever before. This would appear to suggest that the nation has lost its role in the international success of its firms. Companies, at first glance, seem to have transcended countries.

While the globalisation of competition might appear to make the nation less important, instead it seems to make it more so. With fewer impediments to trade to shelter uncompetitive domestic firms and industries, the home nation takes on growing significance because it is the source of the skills and technology that underpin competitive advantage.

In addition, it is the intensity of domestic competition that often fuels success on a global stage.

The national diamond. To make sense of the dynamics behind national or regional strength in a particular industry, Porter developed the concept of the national diamond.

This is made up of four forces.

- Factor conditions—these would once have been largely restricted to natural resources and plentiful supplies of labour; now they also embrace data communications, university research, and the availability of scientists, engineers, or experts in a particular field.
- Demand conditions—if there is strong national demand for a product or service, this can give the industry a head start in global competition. The United States, for example, is ahead in health services due to heavy national demand.
- Related and supporting industries—industries which are strong in a particular country are often surrounded by successful related industries.
- Firm strategy, structure, and rivalry—domestic competition fuels growth and competitive strength.

Together, these four determine whether a nation has competitive advantage or not.

Clusters. 'Nations succeed not in isolated industries, but in *clusters* of industries connected through vertical and horizontal relationships.' Groups of interconnected firms, suppliers, and related industries arising in particular locations contribute substantially to national success. Porter shows how such clusters come into being.

CONTEXT

According to *The Economist* (8 October 1994), 'The book that projected Mr Porter into the stratosphere, read by aspiring intellectuals and despairing politicians everywhere, was *The Competitive Advantage of Nations*.'

Not everyone, however, agrees with Porter on the relationship between the nation and the globalised economy. Kenichi Ohmae believes that the nation state is on its way out, and Gary Hamel commented: 'While *The Competitive Advantage of Nations* provides a good account of why particular industry clusters emerged in some countries and not others, it is essentially backward-looking. In a world of open markets, and mobile capital, technology, and knowledge, no firm need be the product of its geography. That a German company, SAP, can succeed in the software industry; that a Japanese company, Yamaha, can lead the world in making grand pianos, and a Korean company, Samsung, can become number one in the world in memory semiconductors suggests that geography is having less and less to do with firm competitiveness. *The Competitive Advantage of Nations* . . . told us almost nothing about the future of competitiveness, a future in which companies from one part of the world can access and internalise the competitive advantage of far distant geographies.'

Yet on balance, readers around the world have embraced the challenges outlined in Porter's book, and its status and impact as a classic business text cannot be underestimated.

THE BEST SOURCES OF HELP

Porter, Michael. *The Competitive Advantage of Nations*. New York: Free Press, 1990.

Competitive Strategy
by Michael Porter

Competitive Strategy is a modern classic. It claims to provide a solution to a long-running strategic dilemma, and certainly put strategy at the forefront of management thinking.

GETTING STARTED

In 1973 Michael Porter became one of the youngest professors ever at the Harvard Business School. He has since acted as a strategy counsellor to many leading US and international companies, besides playing an active role in economic policy with the US Congress, business groups, and as an advisor to foreign governments.

Competitive Strategy is one of those books that bases its message around significant numbers—in this case three and five, the three generic strategies (every company must adopt one or lose out to its competitors), and the five competitive forces (that determine what a company must do to remain competitive). Over 20 years after its first publication, the current critical consensus seems to be that the competitive forces are truer to reality than the generic strategies. But strategy, having gone out of fashion in the 1980s and 1990s, may be making a comeback.

CONTRIBUTION

Resolving the strategy dilemma. *Competitive Strategy* presents a rationalist's solution to a long-running strategic dilemma. At one end of the spectrum are the pragmatists, who contend that companies have to respond to their own specific situations. Competitive advantage emerges from immediate, fast-thinking responsiveness. There is no pat formula for achieving sustainable competitive advantage.

At the other end are those who, like the Boston Consulting Group, think that market knowledge is all-important. Any company that masters the intricacies of a particular market can reduce prices and increase market share. Porter proposes a logical compromise, arguing that there are three generic strategies for dealing with competitive forces: differentiation, overall cost leadership, and focus.

Differentiation. Differentiation entails competing on the basis of value added to customers (quality, service, differentiation) so that customers will pay a premium to cover higher costs. It requires creative flair, research capability, and strong marketing.

Overall cost leadership. Cost-based leadership involves offering products or services at the lowest cost. Quality and service are not unimportant, but cost reduction provides focus to organisation.

Focus. Focus involves combining elements of the previous two strategies and targeting a specific market intensively.

Combining the strategies. Companies with a clear strategy outperform those whose strategy is unclear or those that attempt to achieve both differentiation and cost leadership.

Sometimes the firm can successfully pursue more than one approach, though this is rarely possible. Effectively implementing any of these generic strategies usually requires total commitment, and organisational arrangements are diluted if there is more than one primary target.

The risks of ignoring generic strategies. If a company fails to focus on any of the three generic strategies, it is liable to encounter problems. The firm stuck in the middle is almost guaranteed low profitability. It either loses the high-volume customers who demand low prices or must bid away its profits to get this business away from low-cost firms. It also loses high-margin businesses, the cream, to the firms who are focused on high-margin targets. In addition, it will also probably suffer from a blurred corporate culture and a conflicting set of organisational arrangements and motivation systems.

The five competitive forces. In any industry, whether domestic or international or product- or service-oriented, the rules of competition are embodied in five competitive forces.

- The entry of new competitors. New competitors necessitate some competitive response, which will inevitably use resources and reduce profits.
- The threat of substitutes. If there are viable alternatives to your product or service in the marketplace, the prices you can charge will be limited.
- The bargaining power of buyers. If customers have bargaining power they will use it. This will reduce profit margins.
- The bargaining power of suppliers. Given power over you, suppliers will increase their prices and adversely affect your profitability.
- The rivalry among the existing competitors. Competition leads to the need to invest in marketing or R&D, or to price reductions. These will reduce profits.

The collective strength of these five competitive forces determines the ability of firms in an industry to earn, on average, rates of return on investment in excess of the cost of capital.

CONTEXT

When *Competitive Strategy* was published, it offered a rational and straightforward method for companies to extricate themselves from strategic confusion. The reassurance proved short-lived. Less than a decade later, companies were having to compete on all fronts. They had to be differentiated, through improved service or speedier development, and be cost leaders, cheaper than their competitors.

Porter's other contribution proved more robust. The five forces are a means whereby a company can begin to understand its particular industry. Initially passively interpreted as statements of the facts of competitive life, they are now usually seen as the rules of the game, which may have to be changed and challenged if an organisation is to achieve any impact.

Influential author Gary Hamel commented, 'In *Competitive Strategy*, Michael Porter did a masterful job of synthesising all that economists know about what determines industry and firm profitability. While *Competitive Strategy* isn't much help in discovering profitable strategies, it is an unfailing guide to whether some particular strategy, once articulated, can be counted on to produce worthwhile profits. What distinguishes *Competitive Strategy* from many other contemporary business books is its strong conceptual foundation. Every MBA graduate in the world can remember Porter's five forces. How many can recall the eight rules of excellence?'

THE BEST SOURCES OF HELP

Porter, Michael. *Competitive Strategy*. New York: Free Press, 1980.

Complexity
by Mitchell Waldrop

The science of complexity is now recognised as important to the study and development of economics and business strategy. This book is regarded as one of the most influential in the field. Complexity is based on mathematical theories that show how random events can quickly organise into complicated structures. In a business context, the theory can be used to gain an insight into the interdependencies of an organisation and the potential impact of change.

GETTING STARTED

The science of complexity shows how, in any system, there are a vast number of independent agents interacting with each other in different ways. In many cases, the author claims, individual elements are interdependent. In a simple model of a market, for example, there may be thousands of buyers and sellers.

According to the author, the complexity theory also indicates that these systems are self-organising and adaptive. In the market example, groups or sectors will emerge and these groups will change or adapt to external conditions. Waldrop explains that the order emerging from these groupings can be contrasted with a state of chaos, where there is no interaction or dependency.

The complexity theory also suggests that a random event, such as a fall in the price of a single stock or share, can impact on the whole market. In that particular example, a single share price change has the potential to trigger a stock market crash because of the interdependencies in the market.

CONTRIBUTION

Complexity in economics. An economy, according to the author, is a web of transformations among goods and services. A producer extracts raw materials and converts them into a useful product. As an economy grows more complex, he explains, the number of possible combinations expands.

New technologies can accelerate the process even more. However, economies that depend on a single industry are likely to stagnate and decline. The author also describes a process called 'economic take-off' where an economy reaches a critical point of complexity. Trade and mergers, he explains, can stimulate the complexity of different countries or organisations. The process can also lead to the phenomenon of 'boom and bust'.

The problem of predictability. Waldrop introduces game theory and chess analogies to describe economics. Players in a market, he explains, will not necessarily take predictable positions. They may change their roles. He points out that this runs counter to traditional economic theories that players make decisions based on analytical reasoning.

Traditional theory suggests that stock exchange behaviour should be predictable. Prices should move up and down in line with the laws of economics. On that basis, he argues, crashes and booms should not occur. The new theory of economics, based on complexity, says that the stock market is a living thing. It would adapt to new pricing levels.

The end of equilibrium. The author argues that it is hard to follow economic theory when things are not in equilibrium, because change is occurring all the time. This means that:

- problems are not well defined
- the environment is not well defined
- the environment might be changing
- changes are totally unknown

The implication, according to Waldrop, is that an economy can never be in equilibrium. The real world is never that well defined.

A new approach to economics. Waldrop uses the terms 'evolutionary economics' or 'increasing return economics' to describe a new approach based on complexity theory. He points out that traditional economic theory is based on equilibrium, the balance of supply and demand in the marketplace. New economics looks at the phenomenon of increasing returns—the more you have, the more you'll get. This is in stark contrast to the traditional theory of diminishing returns.

Increasing returns. The author cites examples of increasing returns such as Silicon Valley, Microsoft Windows, or VHS video technology. Silicon Valley attracts more technology start-ups because the early technology companies are established there. Companies build to the Microsoft Windows standard because it is so widely adopted by computer users. VHS eliminated the technically-superior Betamax video format because more people were buying VHS.

This is also known as positive feedback. Waldrop shows how new technology developments emerge from an interconnected web of dependencies. A new technology spawns other new developments and the market becomes a self-organising entity.

CONTEXT

Complexity theory has many other applications beyond economics. However, it is beginning to be accepted as part of mainstream management thinking.

Richard Pascale is another author to apply the theory to business. In a *Sloan Management Review* article, 'Surfing the edge of chaos', he looks at the challenges posed to organisations by continuous change. Pascale uses complexity theory to explain why it is important for companies to increase the number of winning business strategies they pursue.

Pascale seeks to explore the process of change by trying to understand its complexities and interrelationships. He argues:

- complex adaptive systems cannot be directly controlled
- a complex adaptive system is at risk when it is interfered with and controlled
- complex adaptive systems are capable of self-organisation and of generating new methods of operating

Kevin Kelly's 1994 book, *Out of Control: The New Biology of Machines*, explores the organic nature of human-made systems. Kelly's view is that our technological future is headed towards a neo-biological civilisation.

The concept of positive feedback and the interdependencies among technology companies is also explored in *Information Rules* by Carl Shapiro and Hal Varian. The authors describe the development of networks fuelled by positive feedback, though they base their views on observation, rather than complexity theory.

THE BEST SOURCES OF HELP

Waldrop, Mitchell. *Complexity*. New York: Simon & Schuster, 1992.

Co-opetition
by Barry Nalebuff and Adam Brandenburger

The authors claim that this is the first book to adapt game theory to business strategy. Combining co-operation with competition to produce 'co-opetition' is, they claim, an innovative business strategy that will give companies a winning advantage. It is a technique for making the right strategic decisions in complicated business situations.

GETTING STARTED

The authors explain why game theory provides a valid basis for thinking about business. The theory states that nothing is static; markets are dynamic and evolutionary. Companies can create new models or take on different roles to succeed. Nothing is taken as given. According to the authors, players in the game of business can change the rules to succeed. *Co-opetition* uses game theory to show how companies who co-operate can influence each other's success. Software, for example, becomes more valuable when a complementary company produces more powerful computers. Co-opetition strengthens the interdependence between companies.

CONTRIBUTION

The game of business. Nalebuff and Brandenburger believe that co-opetition depends on complementary activities. When products stimulate demand for complementary products, companies should co-operate.

> To succeed in a game, companies must be able to offer added value.

They show how the game of business includes customers, suppliers, competitors, and complementors. These organisations form part of a value net with integral dependencies. The value net expands the concept of a company's customers. By taking a multiple perspective, they argue, companies can redefine the role of a customer in a value net.

The authors explain how film companies initially saw video as a threat to their business. Now, they recognise video as complementary to film distribution. Similarly, computers did not create a paperless office, they made it easier to create paper.

The importance of added value. To succeed in a game, companies must be able to offer added value. However, say the authors, this must represent what a customer or competitor regards as valuable. If the value is not sufficient, the company can change the game by playing a different role or changing the rules. Perception therefore plays an important part in co-opetition; recognising what other people believe is important.

Companies must recognise the boundaries of their business. According to the authors, companies operating in a lower segment can easily harm their core business by attempting to move into a higher segment.

Changing the rules. The authors suggest a number of ways to change the rules.

A company entering a monopoly market may create competition, but if the incumbent has strong brand values, the new entrant may not gain sales. In those circumstances they recommend 'getting paid to play'. The new entrant should gain some benefit from entering a market, rather than just acting as a makeweight competitor.

The authors suggest that a company needing sales of complementary products to boost its own sales can influence a market by negotiating favourable prices for its own customers.

As the authors point out, a dominant supplier can exercise a monopoly position: limiting development and supplies to keep customers and suppliers hungry strengthens its own position.

Changing the game. Nalebuff and Brandenburger recommend an action plan for bringing about change:

- look at your own value net
- identify opportunities for co-operation and competition
- change the players
- identify the implications if the players change
- identify added value
- see how you can add further value
- identify the other players' added value
- see which roles are hindering or helping you
- identify roles you would like to adopt
- work out whether you can change the rules
- work out how other players perceive the game

CONTEXT

Game theory began in the 1950s with the publication of the book *Theory of Games and Economic Behaviour* by Neumann and Morgenstern. Their theories were applied to economics, military strategy, computer science, and evolutionary biology. Game theory has been used more widely in business since the 1990s.

Co-opetition is the first book to use game theory to demonstrate business strategy. Its publication is timely as industry commentators from leading companies believe that the idea of complementary business is still not widely understood.

THE BEST SOURCES OF HELP

Nalebuff, Barry J., and Adam M. Brandenburger. *Co-opetition.* London: Profile Business, 1997.

Corporate Strategy
by Igor Ansoff

In *Corporate Strategy*, Ansoff codifies and generalises his experiences as a strategist at Lockheed. The book develops a series of concepts and procedures that managers can use to develop a practical method for strategic decision-making within an organisation.

GETTING STARTED

Corporate Strategy integrated strategic planning concepts invented independently in leading American firms. The book provided a powerful, rational model by which strategic and planning decisions could be made. Ansoff saw strategic planning as a complex sequence, or cascade, of decisions and defined two main concepts which are essential to understanding its nature, and therefore to implementing it successfully. The first of these was 'gap analysis'—the 'gap' being the difference between the current position of an organisation and its strategic objectives. The second was 'synergy'—the concept that $2 + 2 = 5$.

CONTRIBUTION

Integrating strategic planning concepts. *Corporate Strategy* integrated strategic planning concepts which were invented independently in a number of leading US firms, including Lockheed.

> *Corporate Strategy* provided a rational model by which strategic and planning decisions could be made. The model concentrated on corporate expansion and diversification, rather than on strategic planning as a whole.

Ansoff saw strategic management as a powerful applied theory, offering a degree of coherence and universality lacking in the functionally-dominated management theorising.

New theoretical concepts. The book presented several new theoretical concepts such as partial ignorance, business strategy, capability and competence profiles, and synergy. One particular concept, the product-mission matrix, became very popular, because it was simple and—for the first time—codified the differences between strategic expansion and diversification.

A rational model for planning decisions. *Corporate Strategy* provided a rational model by which strategic and planning decisions could be made. The model concentrated on corporate expansion and diversification, rather than on strategic planning as a whole.

The Ansoff Model of Strategic Planning was a complex sequence, or cascade, of decisions. The decisions started with highly aggregated ones and proceeded towards the more specific.

The introduction of gap analysis. Central to the cascade of decisions is the concept of gap analysis, which can be summarised as: see where you are, identify where you wish to be, and identify the tasks that will take you there.

The procedure within each step of the cascade is similar:

- a set of objectives is established
- the difference (the gap) between the current position of the organisation and the objectives is estimated

- one or more courses of action (strategy) is proposed
- these are tested for their gap-reducing properties

A course is accepted if it substantially closes the gap; if it does not, new alternatives are tried.

The concept of synergy. *Corporate Strategy* introduced the word 'synergy' to the management vocabulary. Although the term has become overused, Ansoff's explanation (2 + 2 = 5) remains memorably simple.

CONTEXT

Corporate Strategy was published at a time of widespread enthusiasm for strategic planning, and an increasing number of organisations were joining the ranks of its users. Until its publication, strategic planning was a barely-understood, ad hoc concept. It was practised, while the theory lay largely unexplored. Ansoff also examined corporate advantage long before Michael Porter's dissection of the subject in the 1980s.

While *Corporate Strategy* was a remarkable book for its time, its flaws have been widely acknowledged, most honestly by Ansoff himself. It is highly prescriptive and advocates heavy reliance on analysis.

Some companies have encountered what Ansoff calls 'paralysis by analysis'—the more information they possess, the more they think they need. This vicious circle dogs many organisations that embrace strategic planning with enthusiasm.

Ansoff regards strategic planning as an incomplete invention, though he is convinced that strategic planning was an inherently useful management tool. He has spent the last 40 years attempting to prove that this is the case and that, rather than being prescriptive and unwieldy, strategic management can be a dynamic tool able to cope with the unexpected twists of turbulent markets.

Business guru Gary Hamel described Ansoff as 'Truly the godfather of corporate strategy', and said, 'Though Ansoff's approach may now appear overly-structured and deterministic, he created the language and processes that, for the first time, allowed modern industrial companies to explicitly address the deep questions of corporate strategy: how to grow, where to co-ordinate, which strengths to leverage, and so on'.

THE BEST SOURCES OF HELP

Ansoff, Igor. *Corporate Strategy*. McGraw-Hill, New York: 1965.

Corporate-level Strategy
by Michael Goold, Marcus Alexander, and Andrew
Campbell

Although large conglomerates claim to add value through synergy and economies of scale, the authors suggest this is not the case. They recommend that multibusiness organisations should aim for a tighter fit between individual company strategies and the overall corporate strategy. The book introduces the concept of heartland businesses and shows how it can help corporations improve their overall performance.

GETTING STARTED

The authors argue that most large companies are now multibusiness organisations. Research indicates that the benefits of economies of scale and synergy do not, in reality, exist.

Whilst individual businesses within the organisation often have strategies, the corporation as a whole may not. Only a tight fit between the parent organisation and its businesses will add value.

There must be a clear insight about the role of the parent organisation. 'Parents' must concentrate on heartland businesses that they understand. The parent must only intervene on limited issues, and corporate strategy should be driven by parenting advantage.

CONTRIBUTION

The value of multibusiness organisations. Multibusiness companies, by virtue of their very size, should offer economies of scale and synergy between the various businesses, which can be exploited to the overall good. The authors' research suggests that in reality this is not the case.

They calculate that in over half of multibusiness companies, the whole is worth less than the sum of its parts. Instead of adding value, the corporation actually detracts from its value. Its influence, though pervasive, is often counter-productive.

This condemnation is not restricted to conglomerates. The influence of the corporate parent is also felt in companies with portfolios in a single industry, or in a series of apparently related areas.

Lack of overall strategy. A primary cause of this phenomenon is that while individual businesses within the organisation often have strategies, the corporation as a whole may not. The proclaimed strategy is often an amalgam of the individual business strategies given credence by general aspirations.

Need for a tight fit. According to the authors, if corporate-level strategy is to add value, there needs to be a tight fit between the parent organisation and its businesses.

Successful corporate parents focus on a narrow range of tasks and create value in those areas, and align the structures, processes, and central functions of the parent accordingly. Rather than being all-encompassing and constantly interfering, the centre is akin to a specialist medical practitioner—intervening in its areas of expertise when it knows it can suggest a cure.

Success factors for multibusiness organisations. From their analysis of 15 successful multi-business corporations, the authors identify three essentials for successful corporate strategies:

- there must be clear insight about the role of the parent. If the parent does not know how or where it can add value, it is unlikely to do so.
- the parent must have distinctive characteristics. It, too, has a corporate culture and personality.
- it must be recognised that each parent will only be effective with certain sorts of business—described as its 'heartland'.

The importance of heartland businesses. 'Heartland businesses are well understood by the parent; they do not suffer from inappropriate influence and meddling that can damage less familiar businesses,' say the authors. 'The parent has an innate feel for its heartland that enables it to make difficult judgements and decisions with a high degree of success.'

> The concept of heartland businesses is distinct from core businesses.

Heartland businesses are broad ranging and can cover different industries, markets, and technologies. Given this complexity, the ability of the parent to intervene on a limited number of issues is crucial.

Core businesses. The concept of heartland businesses is distinct from core businesses. 'A core business is often merely a business that the company has decided to commit itself to', they say. Though core businesses may be important and substantial, the parent may not be adding a great deal to them.

Building parenting advantage. The authors continue: 'In contrast, the heartland definition focuses on the *fit* between a parent and a business: do the parent's insights and behaviour fit the opportunities and nature of this business? Does the parent have specialist skills in assisting this type of business to perform better?'

Corporate strategy should be driven by 'parenting advantage' to create more value in the portfolio of businesses than would be achieved by any rival. To do so requires a fundamental change in basic perspectives on the role of the parent and of the nature of the multibusiness organisation.

CONTEXT

Most large companies are now multibusiness organisations. The logic behind this fact of business life is generally assumed rather than examined in depth.

The authors' research runs counter to the findings of authors such as Alfred Chandler in *Strategy and Structure* and Peter Drucker in *The Practice of Management*.

Gary Hamel said: 'Chandler and Drucker celebrated large multi-divisional organisations, but as these companies grew, decentralised, and diversified, the corporate centre often became little more than a layer of accounting consolidation. In the worst cases, a conglomerate was worth less than its break-up value. In writing the definitive book on corporate strategy, Goold, Alexander, and Campbell gave hope to corporate bureaucrats everywhere. Maybe it really was possible for the corporate level to add value'.

THE BEST SOURCES OF HELP

Goold, Michael, Marcus Alexander, and Andrew Campbell. *Corporate-level Strategy*. New York: John Wiley, 1994.

The Death of Distance
by Frances Cairncross

The book sets out the ways in which converging communications technology will reshape business, politics and economics. It is ideal for someone looking to understand 'the bigger picture', but is not a practical, 'how to survive the new economy' book.

GETTING STARTED

In this book, the author states that distance will no longer determine the cost of doing business, and location will become less important, particularly for screen-based activities. Size will no longer be relevant to business success and individuals will be able to order customised 'content for one'.

The value of strong brands will increase greatly in line with huge global markets. Communities of practice will become more common, and companies will be based on networks of independent specialists.

Lower start-up costs will mean more new small companies; larger companies will leverage the power of networks to increase brand strength. Information will travel faster to the remotest corners of the world, resulting in a shift from government policing to self-policing.

Redistribution of wages will follow the restructuring of business, which will mean there is less need for immigration and emigration. Countries will compete on tax rates, and there will be a rebalance of political power. Global peace should follow.

CONTRIBUTION

The death of distance. According to Cairncross, distance will no longer determine the cost of communicating electronically. Companies will organise certain types of work in three shifts, according to the world's three main time zones.

Freedom of location. Companies will locate any screen-based activity wherever they can find the best bargain of skills and productivity.

The irrelevance of size. Small companies will offer services that, in the past, only giants could provide. Individuals with valuable ideas will attract global venture capital.

More customised content. Improved networks will allow individuals to order 'content for one'.

A deluge of information. Because people's capacity to absorb new information will not increase, they will need filters to sift, process, and edit it.

Increased value of brands. The author suggests that strong brands—such as products, personalities, sporting events, or the latest financial data—will attract greater rewards because the potential market will increase greatly. This will create a category of global super rich, many of them musicians, actors, artists, athletes, and investors.

Communities of practice. Common interests, experiences, and pursuits—rather than proximity—will bind communities together.

Changing industrial structure. Many companies will become networks of independent specialists; more employees will therefore work in smaller units or alone.

More business diversity. The cost of starting new businesses will decline, and companies will more easily buy in services so that more small companies will spring up. Global communications will also favour giants by amplifying the strength of brands and the power of networks.

Greater proliferation of ideas. New ideas and information will travel faster to the remotest corners of the world. Third-world countries will have access to knowledge that the industrial world has long enjoyed.

The shift from government policing to self-policing. As content sweeps across national borders, it will be harder to enforce laws banning child pornography, libel, and other criminal or subversive material, as well as those protecting copyright and other intellectual property.

Redistribution of wages. Low-wage competition will reduce the earning power of many people in rich countries employed in routine screen-based tasks, but the premium for certain skills will grow. People with skills that are in demand will earn broadly similar amounts wherever they live in the world. Income differences within countries will grow; income differences between countries will narrow.

Less need for immigration and emigration. Poor countries with good communications technology will be able to retain their skilled workers. These workers will be less likely to emigrate to countries with higher costs of living if they can earn rich-world wages and pay poor-world prices for everyday necessities at home.

A market for citizens. The greater freedom to locate anywhere and earn a living will hinder taxation, claims Cairncross. Countries will compete to bid down tax rates and attract businesses, savers, and wealthy residents.

Rebalance of political power. Rulers and representatives will become more sensitive to lobbying and public-opinion polls, especially in established democracies.

Global peace. As countries become even more economically interdependent, people will communicate more freely and learn more about the ideas and aspirations of human beings in other parts of the globe. The effect will be to increase understanding, foster tolerance, and ultimately promote worldwide peace.

CONTEXT

The Death of Distance maps out how converging communications technology will reshape the economic, commercial, and political landscape over the next few years.

It considers the practical ramifications of these advances for the way in which we work and live, and looks at the changing nature of organisations, communities, government authority, and culture and languages.

The author outlines 30 developments in information and communication technology that will impact on industry and society in the not-so-distant future.

Since the book was published some of the specific, technology-based phenomena that she predicted have come to pass. Some developing countries, for example, now provide online services for the rest of the world, such as monitoring security screens, running help-lines and call centres, and writing software.

Much of the social and political change she anticipated, however, has yet to show through at any meaningful level.

THE BEST SOURCES OF HELP

Cairncross, Frances. *The Death of Distance*. London: Orion Publishing, 1997.

The Dilbert Principle
by Scott Adams

A comic book as a source of advice for companies? Well, more a source of anti-advice. Scott Adams offers the employee who has been the victim of restructuring, relayering, or Total Quality Management, a few strategies for self-defence. And he shows management how not to do it!

GETTING STARTED

Writing with a well-sharpened pen and plenty of irony, Adams analyses the stuff of everyday office life: meetings, downsizing, teamwork, management pronouncements, budgeting, project management, marketing, and ISO 9000. His satirical observations are enlivened cartoons featuring Dilbert, who personally suffers the consequences of modern management methods, and the dog, Dogbert. Adams rounds off all 26 chapters with letters from long-suffering employees recounting their own real-life experiences.

CONTRIBUTION

The Dilbert Principle. We systematically promote the people with the least ability, says Adams. If nature went about organising things the way modern businesses do, a group of mountain gorillas would have an 'alpha' squirrel as their leader.

Humiliation. The frame of mind most conducive to employee productivity can be described, according to Adams, as happy, but with low self-esteem. The annual performance review is a particularly humiliating experience, he says elsewhere. Your boss's strategy is to get you to admit your inadequacies. These are then documented and for the rest of your life they serve as a justification for giving you measly salary increases.

Business communication. The true object of communication is furthering your own career. An unambiguous communication can get you into trouble, because it's only when you tie yourself down to something that you can turn out to be wrong.

Great lies of management. These include 'The employees are our greatest asset', 'People who take risks, get rewarded', and 'Your contribution is very important to us'. The following equation, says Adams, applies to management: employee suggestions = more work = bad!

Machiavellian methods. Give bad advice, says devil's advocate Adams. That's your opportunity to push people who ask you for advice off the career track you're both running on.

Marketing and communications. Good advertising will induce people to buy your product even if it is unsuitable for them. A dollar spent on brainwashing, says Adams, is more cost-effective than a dollar spent on improving your product.

Business consultants. Think hard about signing up a consultant who will take your money, get on your employees' nerves, and come up with innumerable strategies for extending his or her consultancy contract.

The business plan. In Adams's world, the business plan lies somewhere in between the boss's hallucinations and the reality of the market. It's made in two stages. First, you collect data. Second, you ignore them.

Changes. First, says Adams, you need consultants who tell you how to make changes. Then you need consultants who tell you that the environmental conditions have altered and that you ought to make more changes.

Financial planning. If you change the budget often enough, Adams points out, the employees become frightened of making any moves that might draw attention to themselves. Where fear rules, outgoings are low. Where outgoings are low, there are share options for management, followed by the collapse of the business.

Selling. If your firm's products are overpriced and faulty, do not worry, says Adams. This can be compensated for by buyer motivation. Emphasise the 'intangible' economic benefits offered by your company. In selling, confusion is your friend.

Conferences. The secret of success at conferences, according to Adams, is a combination of arrogance and honesty. Your audience has to believe that you are giving serious thought to the problems of other people.

Projects. The success of a project depends mainly on two things: luck and a fantastic name for the project.

ISO 9000. Adams explains it like this. A group of bored Europeans had drunk too much beer and decided to play a trick on the world's companies. They understood that any crazy management method can become an international mania.

Downsizing. The most intelligent people are the ones who are the first to turn their backs on a shrinking organisation, because they take compensation packages with them. The stupid ones, who stay on, offset that by working longer hours.

How to tell if your company is doomed. Ominous signs of approaching disaster are such things as open-plan offices, teamworking, presentations by management, reorganisation, and process management.

Re-engineering. Re-engineering was invented, Adams suggests, by a bacteriologist as an antidote to quality programmes. In re-engineering all of the natural incompetence stored in the firm is unleashed on a monumental scale.

Team-building exercises. Exercises designed to strengthen team spirit, says Adams, can take many forms. A typical team-building exercise exposes the employees to unpleasant situations for so long that they end up either as sworn brothers and sisters or a bunch of car thieves.

Managers. A manager is someone who prevails on people to do something for his or her benefit. The most important ability of a manager is to be able to claim the credit for something that happens of its own accord.

New company model: OA5. This chapter contains a serious suggestion, says Adams. The only problem with it is that in today's business world an employee who leaves at five o'clock gets little respect. The most important task of an OA5 firm is to acknowledge that the employees have done valuable work.

CONTEXT

This work is one of the best-selling business books of all time and has attained cult status. Satire and humour are a means here of dispelling employee anxiety in the face of management decisions. Adams attacks management eccentricity, useless bureaucracy, and sadistic supervisors, and makes them look ridiculous in words and pictures.

THE BEST SOURCES OF HELP

Adams, Scott. *The Dilbert Principle: A Cubicle's Eye View of Bosses, Meetings, Management Fads, and Other Workplace Afflictions.* London: Boxtree, 2002.

The Discipline of Market Leaders
by Michael Treacy and Fred Wiersema

The authors suggest that no company can become a market leader until it learns certain key disciplines. They provide a broad range of examples of winning companies that used these disciplines to reinvent the rules of competition in their chosen markets. The book, they claim, will make it impossible for companies to compete on the old terms.

GETTING STARTED

The authors have identified three value disciplines that they believe are essential to success—operational excellence, product leadership, and customer intimacy. By focusing on the most suitable discipline for their marketplace, a company can achieve leadership in its chosen field. That discipline, say the authors, should shape all the company's other plans and activities.

CONTRIBUTION

Improving value. According to the authors, market leaders don't excel at everything. They have achieved a level of excellence in one value discipline that puts them ahead of competitors.

Treacy and Wiersema believe that there are now new rules of competition. Successful companies must change customer expectations. They explain how customers buy different types of value, such as product quality, expert advice, or personalised service.

The authors advise companies to continue improving value year after year to meet rising customer expectations. However, producing ever-increasing value requires a superior operating model that can deliver results.

> Treacy and Wiersema show how service-driven organisations recognise and reward employees, get the supply position right, and deliver first-class service.

Winners, they suggest, concentrate on the competencies that are core to their value proposition. This determines their operating model.

Product leadership. Product leaders, say the authors, focus on investment, product development, and market exploitation. They tend to have a loose-knit organisational structure that encourages enterprise.

They believe that companies who compete on premium product performance need to have a good basis of design and quality management. They also educate and prepare the market for new products, reducing risk and uncertainty for customers.

They demonstrate how product leadership companies are driven by vision and concept. Such companies cultivate talented people who can turn ideas into marketable products. Talent is their most important asset, so they spend a great deal of time recruiting and retaining the right employees. They create a culture for innovation by giving their people personal challenges. Despite product leadership, the authors argue, companies have to adjust prices to market conditions. Brand leadership no longer provides price protection. If price is a chosen weapon, it requires an integrated system to sustain the advantage.

Service-driven organisations. Treacy and Wiersema show how service-driven organisations recognise and reward employees, get the supply position right, and deliver first-class service. Time, they believe, is critical to a market leader. Customers are no longer prepared to wait for slow service. Customers expect support as well as an excellent product, and that makes service an integral part of any market-leading offer.

Leadership through customer intimacy. The authors explain that companies who lead through customer intimacy build strong relationships and aim to achieve high levels of customer lifetime value. Their employees are empowered to deliver great levels of personal service to customers throughout the relationship.

This type of company focuses on a hierarchy of customer needs. They go beyond the product and basic service to discover underlying problems and contribute to customer success. They leverage their understanding of customer problems and offer a range of support services.

Frequently, they will manage customers' problems for them and mould their own organisations to those of their customers. The authors believe that customer intimacy requires the focus of all employees so that deep relationships can be formed throughout an organisation.

Building on operational strengths. Companies who build on their operational strengths demonstrate a number of important characteristics, according to Treacy and Wiersema. They offer standard products, services, and operating procedures. They have developed tried-and-tested formulas for success and they simplify transactions. They also make extensive use of information technology to improve their efficiency.

CONTEXT

The book is one of many that look at successful companies and try to identify a formula for success. Many of the companies given as examples are similar to those found in other 'success books'.

Tom Peters and Robert Waterman first brought the technique to prominence with the publication of *In Search of Excellence*. Unfortunately, many of their excellent companies failed in subsequent years, but that did not prevent other authors from following similar investigations.

Treacy and Wiersema focus on three strands—operational excellence, product leadership, and customer intimacy. The themes of product leadership and customer intimacy are well covered by other authors.

Operational excellence is less of a recurring theme. However, the authors acknowledge a debt to Hammer and Champy's *Reengineering the Corporation* for examples of operational excellence at work.

THE BEST SOURCES OF HELP

Treacy, Michael, and Fred Wiersema. *The Discipline of Market Leaders: Choose Your Customers, Narrow Your Focus, Dominate Your Market*. Cambridge, Massachusetts: Perseus, 1997.

Dynamic Administration
by Mary Parker Follett

The book provides one of the earliest perspectives on business from the point of view of human relationships. It was written at a time when workers were seen simply as part of the mass-production process. The book provides useful background on the development of concepts such as empowerment and visionary leadership.

GETTING STARTED

In the author's view, management is a social process and should have a special human dimension. The process is based in human emotions and in the interrelations created by working. The working environment has human problems, with psychological, ethical, and economic dimensions.

She goes on to say that workers should be given greater responsibility, which is the great developer of people—and successful leaders must offer a vision of the future and train followers to become leaders.

Relationships, not just transactions, are important in organisations. Knowing this involves recognising that conflict is a fact of life that we should use to work for us—but integration is the only positive way forward.

CONTRIBUTION

Management as a social process. 'We can never wholly separate the human from the mechanical sides', says Follett. The study of human relations in business and the study of the technology of operating are bound up together. The everyday incidents and problems of management reflect the presence or absence of sound principle.

> Follett advocated giving greater responsibility to people at a time when the mechanical might of mass production was at its height. 'Responsibility is the great developer of men', she said.

Management has a special human character. Its nature as a social process is deeply embedded in the emotions of man and in the interrelations to which the everyday working of industry necessarily gives rise—both at manager and worker levels and, of course, between the two.

Towards empowerment. Mary Parker Follett believed that, 'we should undepartmentalise our thinking in regard to every problem that comes to us'.

She continued, 'I do not think that we have psychological and ethical and economic problems. We have human problems, with psychological, ethical, and economical aspects, and as many others as you like.'

Follett advocated giving greater responsibility to people at a time when the mechanical might of mass production was at its height. 'Responsibility is the great developer of men', she said.

Leadership through vision. The most successful leader of all is one who sees another picture not yet actualised—who sees the whole rather than the particular, organises the experiences of the group, offers a vision of the future, and trains followers to become leaders.

Leading should be a two-way, mutually beneficial process. 'We want worked out a relation between leaders and led which will give to each the opportunity to make creative contributions to the situation', Follett wrote.

Relationships matter. Relationships, not just transactions, are important in organisations. The reciprocal nature of relationships means that a mutual influence is developed when people work together, however formal authority is defined.

Conflict is a fact of life that we should use to work for us. There are three ways of dealing with confrontation: domination; compromise; or integration. Integration is the only positive way forward. This can be achieved by first uncovering the real conflict and then taking the demands of both sides and breaking them up into their constituent parts.

Outlook is narrowed, activity is restricted, and chances of business success largely diminished when thinking is constrained within the limits of what has been called an either-or situation. 'We should never allow ourselves to be bullied by an either-or', said Follett. There is often the possibility of something better than either of two given alternatives.

CONTEXT

Published eight years after her death, *Dynamic Administration* is a collection of Mary Parker Follett's papers on management gathered from 12 lectures given between 1925 and 1933. Her work stands as a humane counterpoint to that of Frederick Taylor and the proponents of scientific management. Follett was a female, liberal humanist in an era dominated by reactionary males intent on mechanising the world of business.

Bearing in mind she was speaking of America in the early 1920s, her thinking can be described as little less than revolutionary, and certainly a generation ahead of its time. During her life, Mary Parker Follett's thinking on management was generally ignored— though in Japan there was a great deal of interest in her perspectives.

Leading commentator Gary Hamel said, 'The work of Mary Parker Follett is refreshingly different from that of her peers. She was the first modern thinker to get us close to the human soul of management. She had the heart of a humanist, not an engineer.'

To some, Follett remains a utopian idealist, out of touch with reality; to others, she is a torchbearer of good sense whose ideas have sadly not had significant impact on organisations.

Henry Mintzberg commented, 'Integration requires understanding, in-depth understanding. It requires serious commitment and dedication. It takes effort, and it depends on creativity. There is precious little of all of these qualities in too many of our organisations today.'

THE BEST SOURCES OF HELP

Follett, Mary Parker. *Dynamic Administration*. New York: Harper & Bros, 1941.

Emotional Intelligence
by Daniel Goleman

Daniel Goleman challenges traditional thinking, which claims that a high IQ is essential for success. He provides examples of people with high IQs and considerable academic achievement who have failed in business and in life, and, conversely, of those who, though apparently less gifted intellectually, were able to manage and harness their emotional intelligence in order to succeed. Although the book does not specifically relate to behaviour in business, its conclusions highlight patterns that can be used to improve personal performance at work. Emotional intelligence is also referred to as the 'soft skills', and these are increasingly regarded as important in business, particularly for people in sales, supervisory, or customer service roles.

GETTING STARTED

Goleman describes the evolution of the brain and explains how the two main brain functions that influence behaviour—emotion and intelligence—are situated in different parts of the brain. The part of the brain that controls emotions receives external signals before the intelligence functions, and that means that initial reactions to events may be emotional rather than rational. Goleman explains that the brain still retains a primitive 'survival mode' that may trigger reactions and responses that are inappropriate. To succeed, he advises, we need to understand those reactions and learn how to control them.

CONTRIBUTION

Overcoming impulses. According to Goleman, emotions have a wisdom of their own that can be harnessed. Although our natural reaction is to respond emotionally, it is important to make use of emotional intelligence to develop more positive responses.

A framework of emotional intelligence. Goleman has developed a framework that explains emotional intelligence in terms of five elements:

- self-awareness
- self-regulation
- motivation
- empathy
- social skills

> By looking at your strengths and weaknesses and learning from your experiences, you can gain self-confidence and certainty about your capabilities, values, and goals.

Self-awareness. According to Goleman, this element enables you to develop a better understanding of the way emotions affect your performance. You can also use your values to guide your decision-making. By looking at your strengths and weaknesses and learning from your experiences, you can gain self-confidence and certainty about your capabilities, values, and goals.

Self-regulation. Goleman describes how this element can help you control your temper and reduce stress by acting in a more positive and action-orientated way. This enables you to retain your composure and improves your ability to think clearly under pressure. Through self-regulation, he claims, you can handle your impulses effectively and exercise self-restraint.

Motivation. According to the author, by harnessing this aspect of emotional intelligence, you can enjoy challenge and stimulation, and strive for achievement. You will be committed to the cause and seize the initiative. You will also be guided by your personal preferences in following one set of goals, rather than another.

Empathy. Empathy is the characteristic that enables you to understand other points of view, and behave openly and honestly.

Social skills. Goleman describes how social skills such as persuasion, communication, listening, negotiating, and leading can be honed.

Emotional intelligence and management. Goleman claims that people with a higher degree of emotional intelligence are more likely to succeed in senior management. He also believes that emotional intelligence can be developed over a period of time, although this is disputed by a number of commentators.

CONTEXT

Daniel Goleman has built on the work in this book to research leadership styles based on different characteristics of emotional intelligence. These range from coercive leaders who are self-motivated and driven to succeed, to democratic leaders who are good at communication and listening, and coaching leaders who listen well and motivate others. The research is reported in the March–April 2000 edition of the *Harvard Business Review*.

Commentators point out a possible contradiction in Goleman's work. He claims that emotional intelligence is inherent, yet suggests that it can be developed.

Other studies of leaders have pointed out the relationship between high achievement and characteristics such as self-awareness and empathy. In *Emotional Intelligence*, Goleman does not specifically deal with the relationship between leadership and emotional intelligence. His subsequent research does, however, analyse the relationship further.

THE BEST SOURCES OF HELP

Goleman, Daniel. *Emotional Intelligence.* London: Bloomsbury, 1995.

The End of Work
by Jeremy Rifkin

Since the beginning of the modern age, the value of human beings has been measured by the market value of their labour. Since this commodity is coming to seem superfluous in today's automated world, the human individual's relationship to society has to be redefined. This is the task that crusading journalist Jeremy Rifkin set himself in this book.

GETTING STARTED

According to the author, unemployment is the most urgent problem facing our society. There are more than 800 million people worldwide who are jobless, and another upturn in the world economy is unlikely to create more employment opportunities. The Third Industrial Revolution has been underway for some time. Millions of employees are being replaced by computers and machines that can work more profitably and efficiently. Rifkin appeals to us to give up our fixation on the market and the state and instead to construct a 'third sector'. There are tens of thousand of non-profit-making organisations across the world. They provide a model for a field of 'social' work that would help the unemployed find new occupations.

CONTRIBUTION

Underemployment and overproduction. New technologies increase productivity, lower costs, and extend the range of low-priced goods: purchasing power and markets grow as a consequence. The economic policies of industrial countries have hitherto rested on this central assumption. But, Rifkin claims, the true consequences of this logic are now becoming apparent: unemployment on an enormous scale, a stark decline in purchasing power, and a dangerously high level of overproduction.

The Third Industrial Revolution. There are currently, Rifkin tells us, more than a billion computers in the world. Scientists reckon that these machines will soon be intelligent enough to develop a consciousness of their own and to be able to upgrade themselves. Japanese firms have combined the lean-production method with computer and information technologies to build 'the factory of the future'—an automated production plant employing few workers. Focusing lean production on processes rather than on structures and functions created the ideal basis for the use of new technologies. Hierarchies have been flattened out, more and more work is done directly to order, and the number of employees who are surplus to requirements is growing continually.

The workless future. Technological development, Rifkin warns, is bringing a world without work nearer and nearer. New information and robot technologies are changing traditional agriculture, and replacing humans with machines everywhere. The new gene technologies will bring even more far-reaching changes, since they intervene directly in the rearing of plants and animals. The chemical industry is investing in tissue-culture production; its vision is of a landscape without soil. Even the vehicle industry and allied branches, according to Rifkin, are changing their production methods and doing away with increasing numbers of jobs. And in the end even the service sector will fall prey to automation.

The price of progress. The new economy has winners, but it also has losers. The team concept in lean production, for example, is the opposite of worker-friendly management practice, claims Rifkin. As far as employees are concerned, it is a subtle form of exploitation. The decisive factor in productivity today is no longer physical performance but mental performance. Knowledge workers are becoming more and more important to the economy, while the two groups who ruled the roost in the industrial age, workers and capitalists, are becoming less and less significant.

> The new economy has winners, but it also has losers.

The post-market era. If millions of workers have to spend less and less time in gainful employment, and the unskilled cannot find work in a globalised, automated, high-tech economy, then the question of work-free time will become a political one, says Rifkin. More attention must be paid to the third sector. This is the area of social responsibility. This, he claims, is the sector that ought to be globalised. All over the world, the social significance of non-profit-making organisations is growing. They are taking over tasks that are neglected by business and the state.

CONTEXT

Rifkin is known as one of the sharpest critics of technoscience, and is, among other things, one of the best-known and most feared journalists writing against gene technology. His book has played a large part in shaping the debate on the future of our work-orientated society. Some reviews, however, have his book as sensationalist and spoken of his 'end-of-the-world rhetoric'. Others claim that his suggested solutions remain vague and general and that he confines his attention to the United States. There is also a contradiction in his proposals. As he sees it, gainfully employed citizens must undertake voluntary work in addition to their jobs to make possible the production of goods that would not otherwise be produced. This takes it for granted that there would be a demand for these goods and somebody would be ready and willing to pay money for them. But if someone will pay for something, what need is there for voluntary work?

THE BEST SOURCES OF HELP

Rifkin, Jeremy. *The End of Work: The Decline of the Global Labor Force and the Dawn of the Post-market Economy.* Los Angeles, California: J.P. Tarcher, 1995.

The Fifth Discipline
by Peter Senge

This is the book that popularised the concept of the learning organisation. More philosophical in tone than the majority of business-oriented books, it adopts a holistic approach. Learning is an individual and a group experience, something, Senge would claim, much deeper than just taking information in. 'It is about changing individuals so that they produce results they care about, accomplish things that are important to them.'

GETTING STARTED

Peter Senge is director of the Center for Organizational Learning at MIT. *The Fifth Discipline* emerged from extensive research by Senge and his team, but Senge said the 'vision that became *The Fifth Discipline*' came to him one morning during his meditation, when he realised that 'the "learning organisation" would likely become a new management fad'.

The 'fifth discipline' of the title is systems thinking. Of the five building blocks of a learning organisation, systems thinking connects the other four and enables them to work together for the benefit of business.

CONTRIBUTION

Learning is vital. In the author's view, as the world becomes more interconnected and business becomes more complex and dynamic, work must become more 'learningful'. It is no longer sufficient to have one person learning for the whole organisation, a Ford, say, or a Sloan or a Watson. It is no longer possible to work it out from the top, and command everybody else to follow the orders of the grand strategist.

The organisations that will excel in the future will be those that can tap the commitment and capacity to learn of people at all levels within them.

Managers should therefore encourage employees to: be open to new ideas; communicate frankly with each other; understand thoroughly how their companies operate; form a collective vision, work together to achieve their goal.

The five disciplines. There are five components to a learning organisation:

- systems thinking
- personal mastery
- mental models
- shared vision
- team learning

Systems thinking. Systems thinking is a conceptual framework to make patterns clearer, claims Senge. It requires a shift of mind to see interrelationships rather than linear cause and effect. It can help managers spot repetitive patterns, such as the way certain kinds of problems persist, or the way systems have their own in-built limits to growth.

Personal mastery. This idea is based on the familiar competencies and skills associated with management. But it also includes spiritual growth—opening oneself up to a progressively deeper reality and living life from a creative rather than a reactive viewpoint.

As part of this discipline, one must continually learn to see current reality more clearly; the ensuing gap between vision and reality produces the creative tension from which learning arises.

Mental models. These are the organisation's driving and fundamental values and principles. Senge alerts managers to the power of patterns of thinking at the organisational level and the importance of non-defensive inquiry into the nature of these patterns.

Shared vision. Senge stresses the importance of co-creation and argues that shared vision can only be built on personal vision. He claims that shared vision is present when the task that follows from the vision is no longer seen by the team members as separate from the self.

Team learning. The discipline of team learning involves two practices: dialogue and discussion. Dialogue is characterised by its exploratory nature, discussion by the opposite process of narrowing down the field to the best alternative for the decisions that need to be made. The two are mutually complementary, but the benefits of combining them only come from having previously separated them.

Creating learning organisations. The author argues that transforming companies into learning organisations has proved highly problematical, principally because it involves managers surrendering their traditional spheres of power and control to the people who are learning. If people are to learn, they must be allowed to experiment and fail. In a blame-oriented culture, this requires a major change in attitude.

The learning organisation demands trust and involvement. Again, this is usually notable by its absence. Real commitment is rare in today's organisations. Experience indicates that 90% of the time, what passes for commitment is compliance. One man reported to Senge that by adopting the learning organisation model, he made what he called 'job-limiting choices'. What he meant was that he could have climbed the corporate ladder faster by rejecting Senge's theories and toeing the company line.

CONTEXT

Although the learning organisation sounds like a product, it is actually a process. Phil Hodgson of Ashridge Management College commented: 'Processes are not suddenly unveiled for all to see. Academic definitions, no matter how precise, cannot be instantly applied in the real world. Managers need to promote learning so that it gradually emerges as a key part of an organisation's culture.'

The Fifth Discipline has proved highly influential. Though the learning organisation has rarely been converted into reality, the idea has fuelled the debate on self-managed development and employability, and has affected the rewards and remuneration strategies of many organisations.

Gary Hamel observed that: 'While Professor [Chris] Argyris put organisational learning on the management agenda, Peter Senge married it with system thinking and created a language and approach that makes the whole set of ideas accessible to managers. Peter is no mere theorist, his organisational Learning Center at MIT has helped launch thousands of in-company learning experiments. *The Fifth Discipline* would certainly be on my short list of the half dozen best business books of the last 25 years.'

THE BEST SOURCES OF HELP

Senge, Peter. *The Fifth Discipline: The Art and Practice of the Learning Organization*. New York: Doubleday, 1990.

The Functions of the Executive
by Chester Barnard

Barnard is regarded as an important management thinker, who, according to Tom Peters and Robert Waterman in *In Search of Excellence*, created 'a complete management theory'. Though his language is dated, much of his thinking—particularly on the importance of communication—is relevant to modern management.

GETTING STARTED

The author asserts that an organisation allows people to achieve what they could not achieve as individuals, as they and their actions are interconnected. One essential ingredient for a successful organisation is good, short lines of communication because communication enables everyone to be tied into the organisation's objectives. It is also vital that chief executives nurture goals and values and translate them into action; executives should not just ensure conformance to a code of morals, they should create moral codes for others.

CONTRIBUTION

People are interconnected in an organisation. Barnard rejected the concept of an organisation as comprising a rather definite group of people whose behaviour is co-ordinated with reference to some explicit goal or goals. 'In a community', he argued 'all acts of individuals and of organisations are directly or indirectly interconnected and interdependent'.

> An organisation is simply a means of allowing people to achieve what they could not achieve as individuals. An organisation is a system of consciously co-ordinated activities of forces of two or more persons.

The importance of communication. Barnard highlights the need for communication. He argues that everyone needs to know what and where the communications channels are so that every single person can be tied into the organisation's objectives.

Lines of communication should be short and direct. 'The essential functions are, first, to provide the system of communications; second, to promote the securing of essential efforts; and third, to formulate and define purpose', he writes.

The need to nurture goals and values. The chief executive is not a dictatorial figure geared to simple, short-term achievements. Part of his or her responsibility is to nurture the values and goals of the organisation. Values and goals need to be translated into action, rather than meaningless motivational phraseology—'strictly speaking, purpose is defined more nearly by the aggregate of action taken than by words', he writes.

A holistic approach to management. An organisation is simply a means of allowing people to achieve what they could not achieve as individuals. An organisation is a system of consciously co-ordinated activities of forces of two or more persons.

A code of management morality. In Barnard's view, the distinguishing mark of the executive responsibility is that it requires not merely conformance to a complex code of morals, but also the creation of moral codes for others.

CONTEXT

Chester Barnard was a rarity: a management theorist who was also a successful practitioner. He won an economics scholarship to Harvard but, before finishing his degree, he joined American Telephone and Telegraph, eventually becoming president of New Jersey Bell in 1927.

The Functions of the Executive collected together his lectures on management. 'It is doubtful if any other book since Taylor's *Scientific Management* has had a deeper influence on the thinking of serious business leaders about the nature of their work,' observed Barnard's contemporary, Lyndall Urwick.

Although the language is dated, much of what Barnard argued strikes a chord with contemporary management thinking. His ideas on communication and the importance of short lines of communication remain relevant. In arguing that there was a morality to management, Barnard played an important part in broadening the managerial role from one simply of measurement, control, and supervision, to one also concerned with more abstract notions, such as values.

THE BEST SOURCES OF HELP

Barnard, Chester. *The Functions of the Executive*. Boston, Massachusetts: Harvard University Press, 1968.

Funky Business
by Jonas Ridderstråle and Kjell Nordström

The book by two Swedish academics sets out a view of the type of companies that will succeed in the new economy. The ability to manage time and people are the keys to success, together with the flexibility to adapt to constant change. The book provides a useful framework for developing a competitive strategy.

GETTING STARTED

The authors argue that the economy will be characterised by friction-free markets. Every supplier will have access to the same resources, ideas, methods and technology, and consumers will also have even greater choice.

Time and talent will be the critical differentiators. Companies that succeed will be flat, open and small; they will maintain core values but pursue constant innovation and change, entering new markets without hesitation. Successful companies will take risks and never accept that average is good enough. They will offer products and services that take the customer by surprise.

Management and leadership are keys to competitive advantage, but their nature has changed, the authors claim. How you attract, retain, and motivate a talented workforce is more important than technology.

The new economy calls for far greater flexibility in working patterns: new roles demand new skills, and work will be viewed as a series of projects.

CONTRIBUTION

Towards friction-free markets. The economy is moving towards a state of super capitalism, with near friction-free markets, say the authors. As a result, every supplier everywhere has access to the same resources, ideas, methods and technology. The problem is that every consumer now has access to fantastic choice.

Time and talent differentiate. In a friction-free market, time and talent are the two critical commodities. How companies deal with these two factors determines which fall by the wayside and which move through to the next round. The goal is to be momentarily ahead of the game.

A model for staying ahead. Funky Inc is a theoretical model for achieving this fleeting competitive advantage. The company is flat, open, and small.

Change is vital. Signal what you stand for in terms of values or branding. Maintain those values through relentless innovation and change. Bring your products to market faster than anybody else, and replace them frequently—most of Hewlett-Packard's revenues, for example, derive from products that are less than a year old.

Use your core competencies to enter new industries without hesitation.

Go beyond the average. Recognise that being average is not good enough. The goal is to be 100% completely right for a specific market, not ordinary and 95% right to everybody. Take risks; accept—even welcome—failure, and spurn all things average.

Surprise the customer. Change the frame of reference from what you are selling to what the customer is actually buying—the two are not always the same. Get on the same 'vibe' as your customer. Offer products and services that constantly take him or her by surprise.

For example, online bookseller bol.com's 'free copy for a friend' campaign increased sales three-fold.

Manage your talent. Leadership and management are more important than ever before. We are selling, exploiting, organising, employing, and packaging time and talent. In the authors' view, as a result, management and leadership are keys to competitive advantage—they differentiate you from the mass and create sustainable uniqueness.

> Leadership and management are more important than ever before.

How you attract, retain, and motivate your people is more important than technology, as is how you treat your customers and suppliers.

Changing style of management. Management and leadership have reached maturity as potent competitive weapons. Their nature has changed, and autocratic leadership is no longer effective. Management by numbers and by fear won't work. If management is people, management must become 'humanagement'.

New working patterns. The new economy calls for far greater flexibility. Throughout most of the 20th century, managers averaged one job and one career. Now, we are talking about two careers and seven jobs. The days of the long-serving corporate man are long gone. The emphasis will be on getting a life instead of a career. Work will be viewed as a series of gigs or projects.

Demand for new skills. New roles demand new skills. Thirty years ago, we had to learn one new skill per year. Now, it is one new skill per day. Tomorrow, it may be one new skill per hour.

Skills, like networking, are more important. In 1960, the average manager had to learn 25 names throughout his or her entire career; today we must learn 25 new names every single month. Tomorrow, it may be 25 new names per week.

CONTEXT

Funky Business is about how successful companies differ from their competitors. This book draws extensively from rigorously-researched data, but presents its findings with wit and intelligence, reinforced with excellent examples.

The book offers provocative ideas, but it is not a practical 'how to survive the future' road map; nor is it a set of predictions on 'what the future will be like'. It is, however, a comprehensive and coherent philosophy. Unusually, in an age of instant gurus and ready prescriptions, Ridderstråle and Nordström leave it up to the reader to embrace, integrate, and apply the thinking contained in the book.

THE BEST SOURCES OF HELP

Ridderstråle, Jonas, and Kjell Nordström. *Funky Business*. FT.com, 1999.
Website: **www.funkybusiness.com**

General and Industrial Management
by Henri Fayol

Fayol created one of the first systems of management that put management at the centre of the organisation. His system divides a company's activities into six groups, in which managerial activities are distinct from the other five. The book provides a systematic analysis of the process of management, in which he anticipated most of the more recent analyses of modern business practice. His brief résumé of what constitutes management has largely held sway throughout the 20th century.

GETTING STARTED

Fayol created a system of management in which management was the basis of the organisation. His system focused on acceptance of, and adherence to, six different functions: technical, commercial, financial, security, accounting, and managerial activities.

He believed that to manage is to forecast and plan, to organise, to command, to co-ordinate, and to control. His view of forward planning was one of the first examples of business planning in practice.

CONTRIBUTION

A system of management. Fayol created a system of management encapsulated in *General and Industrial Management*.

'Management plays a very important part in the government of undertakings; of all undertakings, large or small, industrial, commercial, political, religious, or any other', he writes.

Division by function. Fayol's system was based on acceptance of, and adherence to, different functions. He said that all activities to which industrial undertakings give rise can be divided into six groups. These are:

- technical activities
- commercial activities
- financial activities
- security activities
- accounting activities
- managerial activities

The nature of management. The management function is quite distinct from the other five essential functions. To manage is to forecast and plan, to organise, to command, to co-ordinate, and to control.

Fayol's view of what constitutes management has been highly influential throughout the 20th century and has only recently been challenged.

Principles of management. From his observations, Fayol also produces general principles of management:

- division of work
- authority and responsibility
- discipline

- unity of command
- unity of direction
- subordination of individual interest to general interest
- remuneration of personnel
- centralisation
- scalar chain (line of authority)
- order
- equity
- stability of tenure of personnel
- initiative
- esprit de corps

Forward planning. Fayol talks of ten-yearly forecasts, revised every five years—one of the first instances of business planning in practice.

The maxim 'managing means looking ahead', gives some idea of the importance attached to planning in the business world. It is true that if foresight is not the whole of management, it is at least an essential part of it.

CONTEXT

Fayol created a system that put management at the centre of the organisation in a way never envisaged by contemporaries such as Frederick W. Taylor, author of *Scientific Management*.

Fayol's championing of management was highly important. While Taylor regarded managers as little more than overseers with limited responsibility, Fayol regarded their role as critical to organisational success.

In his faith in carefully-defined functions, Fayol was systematising business organisation in ways that worked at the time, but proved too limiting and restraining in the long term.

In *The Principles and Practice of Management*, a 1953 study of early management thinking, E.F.L. Brech notes, 'The importance of Fayol's contribution lay in two features: the first was his systematic analysis of the process of management; the second, his firm advocacy of the principle that management can, and should, be taught. Both were revolutionary lines of thought in 1908, and still little accepted in 1925.'

Igor Ansoff has noted that Fayol anticipated imaginatively and soundly most of the more recent analyses of modern business practice. His brief résumé of what constitutes management has largely held sway throughout the 20th century. Only now is it being seriously questioned and challenged.

An extrapolation of Fayol's methods was later exposed by Peter Drucker who observed, 'If used beyond the limits of Fayol's model, functional structure becomes costly in terms of time and effort'.

THE BEST SOURCES OF HELP

Fayol, Henri. *General and Industrial Management*. London: Pitman, 1949.

General Theory of Employment
by John Maynard Keynes

Should the state intervene to combat unemployment? Governments today may ask themselves this question; governments were already asking themselves this question during the 1930s and had even more compelling reasons for doing so, perhaps. Keynes was the first to show convincingly why state intervention to boost employment is sensible and necessary. This book, first published in 1936, lays the foundations of Keynesianism, a demand-orientated doctrine that is still hotly debated and highly influential in both politics and economics today.

GETTING STARTED

Keynes' *General Theory* shows how economic policy can overcome periods of stagnation. He argues in favour of investment being state-directed to ensure full employment. In contrast to the exponents of classical economic theory, he does not believe in the self-healing power of the market. Demand is, for him, the lever of the economy, and in times of crisis it is the state that must operate the lever.

CONTRIBUTION

The error in classical economics. According to Keynes, Adam Smith and David Ricardo start out from the assumption that the law of supply and demand regulates the price of goods and of labour. Workers, therefore, are only dismissed when their wages are too high. If they accept lower wages, they are re-employed. The classical economic model always returns to a state of balance: anyone who is unemployed, is so voluntarily.

The world economic crisis of the 1930s could not, however, be explained in this way, Keynes thought. Millions of workers were on the streets, although wages were sinking lower and lower. The 'paradox of poverty in the midst of affluence' needed another explanation. Supply was not decisive in achieving economic success; demand was.

Aggregate demand—consumption and investment. Demand across the entire economy—the sum of expenditure on consumer and investment goods—has one essential characteristic, Keynes argues: it is unstable. Expenditure on consumption depends on income: the higher the income the more money is spent. But, above a particular level of income, the tendency to increase consumption declines. Part of the additional income is saved.

Investments are the second element in aggregate demand, because they increase the potential of businesses to produce. Investments, according to Keynes, depend on the 'marginal efficiency of capital'. If this is higher than the standard rate of interest in the market, the investor has an incentive to use credit to implement investment plans. In the opposite case, the costs of credit would be higher than the profit, and the investment would not be made.

Imbalance between the markets for goods and capital. The market interest rate for investments, says Keynes, results from the population's inclination towards liquidity, that is, their demand for cash. People save for a variety for reasons, to purchase goods, to protect themselves against hard times, or in order to speculate. Speculators keep their savings in cash until prices are low and a favourable opportunity arises to enter the stock market.

Harmonisation between the goods and capital markets is the exception; equality of savings and investments a rare and lucky chance. It is not the case, says Keynes, that people's savings decisions are solely dependent on the rate of interest and that the interest mechanism ensures that all savings are available to be loaned to businesses for the purchase of investment goods. Rather, he argues, businesses expand their production so long as they expect larger sales in the future. More and more investors try to attract the capital of the savers. Interest rates and production costs rise and reduce returns. The suppliers of capital get nervous. Panic grips the markets. The unrealistic expectations of the boom are followed by the hysteria of

> Harmonisation between the goods and capital markets is the exception; equality of savings and investments a rare and lucky chance.

crisis. Investments fall, employment drops, purchasing power disappears, future prospects become more and more dismal. Businesses do not even invest when interest rates sink to zero. The national economy is caught in the 'liquidity trap'.

The state as starter motor of the economy. To free the economy from this disastrous situation and turn it back in the direction of full employment, aggregate demand must rise, says Keynes, until increasing production by businesses offers all workers employment. If the demand for investment goods rises, this leads to more production, more work, and more income. Higher consumption boosts demand for goods and investment, which means that production and income rise further. A chain reaction begins, an 'income multiplier'—an exogenous impulse, perhaps an extra boost to investment, gives rise to a multiple increase in income.

From this, Keynes draws the following conclusion. If entrepreneurs do not invest in sufficient quantities, the state must step forward as an investor to set the economy back in motion. To produce additional investment, the public purse accepts credit and uses it to finance, for example, roads, sewage systems, schools, or hospitals.

CONTEXT

The stock market crash of 1929, the crisis in the world economy, and the Great Depression of the 1930s threw up a number of crucial economic and political questions, which Keynes attempted to answer in this book. It made him the most famous national economist of the 20th century and initiated one of the most influential strands in modern economic thought, Keynesianism. Keynesian ideas provided the framework for the post-war recovery and held sway in many countries during the middle of the last century. Even President Richard Nixon remarked, 'We are all Keynesians now'. It was only in the 1970s that the 'monetarist counter-revolution' began, eventually re-enthroning supply-side economics and the market forces whose fallibility it had been part of Keynes' purpose to demonstrate.

THE BEST SOURCES OF HELP

Keynes, John Maynard. *The General Theory of Employment, Interest, and Money.* Loughton: Prometheus Books, 1997.

Getting to Yes
by Roger Fisher and William Ury

Negotiation is an important skill in many aspects of business and personal life. The authors claim that people can become more effective negotiators by moving from adversarial haggling to constructive joint problem-solving, a solution they call 'principled negotiation'. Both Fisher and Ury have conducted negotiations at extremely high levels in business, politics, diplomacy, law, and international relations. They write with authority and have the experience to offer practical advice and insight into each stage of the negotiating process.

GETTING STARTED

The authors offer a number of negotiating principles that, they claim, will lead to successful outcomes:

- don't bargain over positions
- separate the people from the problem
- focus on interests, not positions
- invent options for mutual gain
- insist on objective criteria

CONTRIBUTION

The importance of effective negotiation. Negotiation involves everyone, the authors claim. People use negotiation to handle their differences at work and in personal life. However, they believe that standard negotiating strategies tend to leave one or both parties dissatisfied. They describe two types of negotiators:

- soft negotiators who may make easy compromises to avoid conflict
- hard negotiators who want to win at all costs

The authors propose a third way, using what they call 'principled negotiation'. Its aim is to decide issues on their merits, rather than on will.

Avoid bargaining over positions. Fisher and Ury point out that, traditionally, people take positions and defend them. The matter is only resolved through concessions. This approach can harm relationships, and that can be damaging to future negotiations. In this approach, emotions become entangled with logic, so it is important to separate people from problems.

> Fisher and Ury point out that, traditionally, people take positions and defend them.

Separate people from problems. The authors prompt us to remember that negotiators are people with emotions. Negotiators are therefore just as interested in ongoing relationships as in dealing with the immediate problem. Understanding the emotions of the other side is important, because they can act as a barrier to rational discussion. It is important to understand the other person's perspective and find out what is important to them. Listening actively and acknowledging the other party's perspective is critical.

The authors explain how successful negotiators try to make the other party own the problem so that they fully participate in reaching a satisfactory conclusion. Communication is an important part of this process, helping to build working relationships that can reduce the element of confrontation.

Focus on interests, not positions. Fisher and Ury recommend looking for the underlying interest in negotiations. Interests may not conflict, although positions do. They suggest finding out or asking why the other side takes a particular position, and acknowledging those interests as part of the problem.

Invent options for mutual gain. The aim of negotiation is a single conclusion, say the authors. Introducing other options may appear to slow down the process, but, they claim, it can make the outcome easier to achieve. Enlarging the pie can help to provide what appears to be mutual gain. They believe that brainstorming can help to determine the options because during brainstorming, no decisions have to be made and creativity is encouraged.

Insist on objective criteria. Finally, according to Fisher and Ury, it may be possible to decide on the outcome by reference to an independent or objective authority. The standards should be fair and acceptable to both sides. Comparable criteria from other negotiations may also be acceptable.

CONTEXT

Negotiation is a critical element of business. The book looks at the process of negotiation independently of business processes such as sales, customer service, or union negotiations.

The authors build on their own experience of negotiations in politics, diplomacy, and the law. Although not all of the examples relate directly to business, it is possible to apply the same principles to business situations of many types.

THE BEST SOURCES OF HELP

Fisher, Roger, and William Ury. *Getting to Yes*. London: Arrow Books, 1997.

The Goal
by Eliyahu Goldratt and Jeff Cox

What goes on in modern manufacturing businesses is highly complex, and often very frustrating. Production problems and job delays are the order of the day, and attempts to improve the situation run up against the existing organisational set-up and come to grief. This may sound like the starting point for a textbook on process optimisation, but Eliyahu Goldratt, famous for his use of the fictional format, takes an inefficient factory threatened with closure and makes it the setting for a novel as fast-paced and gripping as the average thriller. Many books are said to be entertaining as well as instructive, but Goldratt, here writing with Jeff Cox, does more than most to optimise the entertainment process.

GETTING STARTED

Plant manager Alex Rogo is handed an ultimatum by his bosses: either he makes a clear improvement in the profitability of his factory within three months, or the factory closes. For Rogo, it's then a race against time. In order not to fail, he has to change his ideas radically. He meets Jonah, the authors' spokesman in the novel, who helps him to break free of traditional ways of thinking and recognise what needs to be done. Jonah knows the solution to the factory's problems and enables Alex to discover it for himself by providing him with questions instead of guidelines. In this way the authors show that management can only learn by deductive insight.

CONTRIBUTION

Goldratt and Cox set out an important principle of product organisation in their novel. The story deals with people who want to understand how business processes function. Because they think about their problems logically, they manage to establish cause-and-effect relations between their actions and the changes that result from them. From these they gradually derive the underlying principles that enable them to turn their factory around and finally achieve success.

Alex Rogo is the novel's narrator, the 'I' of the story. It begins on the day when Bill Peach, the division vice president, walks into his factory and demands 'to be shown the status of Customer Order Number 41427'. It turns out that nobody knows anything about this order, which happens to be a fairly big one, and also a late one. Rogo sums up the situation in the factory like this: 'Everything in this plant is late. Based on observation, I'd say this plant has four ranks of priority for orders: Hot . . . Very Hot . . . Red Hot . . . and Do It NOW. We just can't keep ahead of anything'.

Rogo meets Jonah, his former maths teacher who is now a specialist in production organisation. When Jonah asks him whether productivity has risen in the plant since industrial robots were put in, he says that it has—by 36%. In response to further questions, however, Rogo reveals that the 36% increase applies only to one section. Jonah than tells him that if he hasn't slimmed down his inventory and reduced his wage costs, and if the plant is not selling more product than before, the robots cannot have increased its productivity.

Rogo speaks to Lou, the plant controller. Together they set up benchmark figures for turning the business around. These should be, they decide, the net profit, the return on investment, and cash flow, because negative cash flow would kill off the business.

But these figures are not enough in themselves. They are the ones that the people in division management use to measure progress. At the level of the individual factory, these figures do not make much sense. Jonah prompts Rogo to look at three more figures: throughput, inventory, and operating costs. Goldratt, speaking through Jonah, defines throughput as the amount of money per time unit that the system earns by sales, stressing the fact that sales are what counts, not production. Inventory, he says, is all the money that is invested in the system for the purchase of things that are intended for sale. And operating costs are all the money that the system spends to turn inventory into throughput.

Rogo starts thinking about what goes on in his factory in these terms. He then moves on to what is very much home territory for Goldratt, the exponent of the 'Theory of Constraints'. He decides that he has to find the *bottlenecks*, production units whose capacity is equal to or less than the market requirement allotted to them. He says he would like to organise everything so that the production unit with the smallest capacity has the top place in any work plans.

Eventually, Rogo gets to the point where he can go to the managing director with a five-step programme to save the plant:

1. Identify the regulating factor in the system.
2. Decide how the bottlenecks in the system can be used.
3. Make everything else subordinate to the above decision.
4. Free up the bottlenecks in the system.
5. Set the changed procedures in motion.

CONTEXT

The Goal is an economics textbook on the natural laws of business life in the form of a novel. It has attained cult status. One the two authors, Eliyahu Goldratt, has been reckoned an industrial guru and cultural revolutionary. He is an expert on production management. He created the mathematical and philosophical bases on which the OPT (Optimised Production Technology) system of planning and organising production processes is built and leads a management organisation, OPT Management Systems. Goldratt's appearances as a speaker are feared by many in business, because he tends to pillory firms and their practices in public.

THE BEST SOURCES OF HELP

Goldratt, Eliyahu, and Jeff Cox. *The Goal: A Process of Ongoing Improvement.* 2nd ed. Aldershot: Gower, 1994.

Hidden Champions
by Hermann Simon

Most business success stories concentrate on large companies. Hermann Simon took a deliberately different approach, setting out to find largely unknown businesses that have, for decades, been leaders in their markets worldwide. They exist all over the world, but Simon shows that, no matter what their location or national origins, the same principles lead to success and market leadership. For a refreshingly different take on what makes a world-beater and a celebration of the virtues of small and medium-sized businesses, this is the book to read.

GETTING STARTED
Market leadership is a goal that is within the reach of small and middle-sized businesses. This is shown by the example of the 'hidden champions', firms who hold up to 90% of world market shares and dominate their own markets worldwide. Instead of taking their cue from the giants of business, firms such as Haribo, Krones, Webasto, Brita, or Stihl prefer to shun publicity and go their own way. They thus avoid the disadvantages of 'big business syndrome', like bureaucracy, remoteness from customers, inflexibility, and excessive division of labour. Simon analyses the strategies of these companies and comes up with general recommendations for companies of any size.

CONTRIBUTION
Who are the 'hidden champions'? The unknown world market leaders are, says Simon, small and middle-sized businesses that rule world markets with low-profile products. The vast majority of them are run as family businesses. They make an important contribution to the balance of payments in their respective countries, have high export shares, and are extremely good at surviving.

Market leadership. Market leadership, Simon argues, is more than market share. It requires 'psychological' predominance, the ambition to become number one.

The market. Hidden champions define their market narrowly. As Simon describes them, they create market niches and develop unique products that define their own markets, accepting the risks of 'putting all their eggs in one basket'.

The world. Narrow specialisation is combined with global marketing. As market positions are distributed early on, it is, according to Simon, extremely important to be the first supplier to future markets.

Customers. Closeness to customers is the key factor in a market leadership strategy. Because of the distinctiveness of the products made by Simon's hidden market leaders, their customers cannot easily find substitutes for them. Conversely, however, specialisation creates a high degree of customer dependency in these companies.

Innovation. Innovation is one of the foundations of market leadership. Simon shows how many hidden champions introduced completely new products and were then able to transfer their position as pioneers into long-lasting supremacy.

Competition. The hidden leaders usually operate, says Simon, in oligopolistic markets where there is intensive competition. The competitive advantages lie more in differentiation than in cost advantages.

Partners. Leadership means not delegating the activities on which a company's dominant role is founded. It is better, in Simon's view, to retain a broad spectrum of core competences than to outsource, so that core know-how is protected and highly qualified staff are kept on board.

Employees. The culture in companies, according to Simon, should be team-oriented, dedicated to performance, and intolerant of idlers and malingerers. Acceptance of such a culture is the basis for motivation and the identification of staff with the company.

Managers. Managers should be people with energy, willpower, drive, and authority. They should, Simon suggests, be brought into the company while they are still young. Continuity is important. The average 'period in office' for leaders among the hidden champions is over 20 years.

Lessons. The hidden champions, Simon insists, are not prodigies, but they do form an elite among firms. Anyone can learn from them. Small and medium-sized businesses can recognise that many markets are by nature local or regional and that it is possible to become number one in them. Investors can realise that these businesses have clearly defined aims, are ambitious and well focused, and preserve continuity.

CONTEXT

Simon's interest in small and medium-sized companies was aroused in 1986 when he met Theodore Levitt, a professor at the Harvard Business School, for an exchange of views on German success in exports. They agreed that this success could not be put down primarily to large German companies, because these did not differ significantly from their international competitors. They concluded, therefore, that there must be a group of companies, which were hardly known, but which occupied world leadership positions in their respective markets. Because these companies frequently prefer to retain a low profile, Simon called them the 'hidden champions'.

Hermann Simon has extensive experience as a business consultant in Europe, the United States, and Asia, which enables him to approach business management questions from the perspective of a practitioner. *Hidden Champions* also has good academic credentials: Simon's practical insights are informed by his work as a professor of economics. His findings often contradict established management doctrine. This book has been published in 15 languages and had a good reception not only from the general and trade press, but in the wider business community.

THE BEST SOURCES OF HELP

Simon, Hermann. *Hidden Champions: Lessons from 500 of the World's Best Unknown Companies.* Cambridge, Massachusetts: Harvard Business School Press, 1996.

How to Win Friends and Influence People
by Dale Carnegie

Dale Carnegie was a highly successful public speaker and author of books on public speaking and confidence development. *How to Win Friends and Influence People* provides practical advice on the universal challenge of face-to-face communication. As the familiarity of the title proves, the book has had a great impact. The first edition had a print run of mere 5,000, but the book has since sold over 15 million copies.

GETTING STARTED

Carnegie holds that it is essential to handle people effectively, and to make them like you to ensure your own success. His book is littered with illustrative anecdotes from the lives of the famous—Clark Gable, Marconi, Franklin D. Roosevelt, Mary Pickford—and the not so famous.

CONTRIBUTION

Handle people effectively. Carnegie presented the fundamental techniques in handling people:
- don't criticise, condemn, or complain
- give honest and sincere appreciation
- arouse in the other person an eager want

Make people like you. He added advice on other ways to make people like you:
- become genuinely interested in other people
- smile
- remember that a person's name is to that person the sweetest and most important sound in any language
- be a good listener
- encourage others to talk about themselves
- talk in terms of the other person's interests
- make the other person feel important, and do it sincerely

CONTEXT

How to Win Friends and Influence People is the original self-improvement book, and Carnegie was the first superstar of the self-help genre. Cashing in on his success, he wrote a plethora of other titles on similar themes, including *Public Speaking and Influencing Men in Business*, *How to Stop Worrying and Start Living*, *How to Enjoy Your Life and Your Job*, and *How to Develop Self-confidence and Influence People by Public Speaking*. His successors included Anthony Robbins and Stephen Covey, who studied American success literature (of which Carnegie is a prime example) before coming up with *The Seven Habits of Highly Effective People*.

> **How to Win Friends and Influence People is the original self-improvement book, and Carnegie was the first superstar of the self-help genre.**

Carnegie had done much the same 50 years before, and his principles have a similar homely ring to those of Covey. Carnegie's books and his company's training programmes continue to strike a chord with managers and aspiring managers, because they deal with the universal challenge of face-to-face communication.

Carnegie was notable in being the first to create a credible long-term business out of his ideas. In creating a flourishing business, Carnegie ensured that his name and ideas should continue to live on and make money after his death.

THE BEST SOURCES OF HELP

Carnegie, Dale. *How to Win Friends and Influence People*. New York: Simon & Schuster, 1937.

The HP Way
by David Packard

David Packard was half of the partnership that created one of the business and management benchmarks of the 20th century—Hewlett-Packard. In 1937, with a mere $538 and a rented garage in Palo Alto, Bill Hewlett and David Packard created one of the most successful corporations in the world. This book tells the story behind the company.

GETTING STARTED

According to Packard, the HP secret lay in a simple approach to business. The HP way reflected the culture of the company and the management style used to run it. It was based on openness and respect for the individual, which was key to the company's success. Management was always available and involved, and conflict had to be tackled through communication and consensus rather than confrontation. Their commitment to people fostered commitment to the company, and HP people at all levels show boundless energy and enthusiasm. The recipe for growth was to make products leaders in their markets. They kept divisions small and didn't do anything too risky. These values worked to save the company when times were hard.

CONTRIBUTION

A simple approach to business. HP's secret lay in the simplicity of its methods.

'Professors of management are devastated when I say we were successful because we had no plans. We just took on odd jobs', said Bill Hewlett.

Their legacy lies in the culture of the company they created and the management style they used to run it—the HP way.

From the very start, Hewlett-Packard worked to a few fundamental principles:

- it did not believe in long-term borrowing to secure the expansion of the business
- its recipe for growth was simply that its products needed to be leaders in their markets
- it got on with the job

> **HP believed that management should be available and involved—'Managing by wandering about' was the motto.**

'Our main task is to design, develop, and manufacture the finest [electronic equipment] for the advancement of science and the welfare of humanity. We intend to devote ourselves to that task', said Packard in a 1961 memo to employees.

The duo eschewed fashionable management theory: 'If I hear anybody talking about how big their share of the market is or what they're trying to do to increase their share of the market, I'm going to personally see that a black mark gets put in their personnel folder.'

Respect for the individual. The company believed that people could be trusted and should always be treated with respect and dignity.

'We both felt fundamentally that people want to do a good job. They just need guidelines on how to do it.'

HP believed that management should be available and involved—'Managing by wandering about' was the motto.

Rather than the administrative suggestions of management, Packard preferred to talk of leadership.

If there was conflict, the company decided, it would be tackled through communication and consensus rather than confrontation.

Their legacy, and Packard's proudest achievement, is a management style based on openness and respect for the individual.

Keeping it small. Hewlett-Packard was a company built on very simple ideas. While competitors were turning into conglomerates, Hewlett and Packard kept their heads down and continued with their methods.

When their divisions grew too big (around 1,500 people) they split them up to ensure that they didn't spiral out of control.

They didn't do anything too risky or too outlandish. Packard was sceptical about pocket calculators though, in the end, the company was an early entrant into the market.

They didn't risk the company on a big deal or get into debt.

Commitment to values. Their values worked to save the company when times were hard. During the 1970s recession, Hewlett-Packard staff took a 10% pay cut and worked 10% fewer hours.

As the book documents, if the company hadn't had a long-term commitment to employee stock ownership, perhaps employees wouldn't have been so willing to make sacrifices. Packard claims that commitment to people clearly fostered commitment to the company.

CONTEXT

Hewlett-Packard has pulled off an unusual double—it is admired and successful. When they were assembling their list of excellent companies in the late 1970s, Tom Peters and Robert Waterman included Hewlett-Packard. When Jerry Porras and James Collins wrote *Built to Last*, their celebration of long-lived companies, there was no doubt that Hewlett-Packard was worthy of inclusion. In the same vein, in 1985, *Fortune* ranked Hewlett-Packard as one of the two most highly-admired companies in the United States. The company is ranked similarly in virtually every other poll on well-managed companies or ones that would be good to work for.

'Wherever you go in the HP empire, you find people talking product quality, feeling proud of their division's achievements in that area. HP people at all levels show boundless energy and enthusiasm', observed Tom Peters and Robert Waterman in *In Search of Excellence*.

According to Louise Kehoe in the *Financial Times*, 'Their legacy, and the achievement that Packard was most proud of, is a management style based on openness and respect for the individual.'

THE BEST SOURCES OF HELP

Packard, David. *The HP Way*. New York: HarperBusiness, 1995.

The Human Problems of an Industrial Civilization by Elton Mayo

The author was part of the team conducting the Hawthorne Studies at Western Electric's Chicago plant between 1927 and 1932, early studies into motivation in the workplace. The book shows the important link between workforce morale and organisational performance, and paved the way for policies and management theories based on teamwork and effective communication.

GETTING STARTED

The Hawthorne Studies offered important insights into the motivation of workers:

- people and their motivation were critical to the success of any business
- there was a link between morale and output—changes in working conditions led to increased output
- it is important to restore humanity to the workplace

Workers selected for a test felt that more attention was being paid to them. They felt chosen, and so responded positively. The feeling of belonging to a cohesive group led to an increase in productivity. Informal organisations between groups are a potentially powerful force.

CONTRIBUTION

The Hawthorne Studies. According to Mayo, the studies offered important insights into the motivation of workers. It was found that changes in working conditions led to increased output, even if the changes didn't obviously improve working conditions.

Whatever the dictates of mass production and scientific management, people and their motivation were critical to the success of any business.

> Mayo champions the case for teamworking and for improved communications between management and the workforce.

The link between morale and output. The researchers were interested in exploring the links between morale and output. The author documents how five women workers were removed to a test room and observed as they worked. The research was initially restricted to physical and technical variables. Sociological factors were not expected to be of any significance. The results proved otherwise.

Removed from their colleagues, the morale of the 'guinea pigs' improved. By virtue of their selection, the women felt that more attention was being paid to them.

The importance of group cohesion. Mayo reports that the feeling of belonging to a cohesive group led to an increase in productivity. 'The desire to stand well with one's fellows, the so-called human instinct of association, easily outweighs the merely individual interest and the logic of reasoning upon which so many spurious principles of management are based,' he commented.

Mayo champions the case for teamworking and for improved communications between management and the workforce.

The Hawthorne research revealed informal organisations between groups as a potentially powerful force, which companies could make use of or ignore at their peril.

Restoring humanity to the workplace. Mayo's belief that the humanity needed to be restored to the workplace struck a chord at a time when the dehumanising side of mass production was beginning to be more fully appreciated.

'So long as commerce specializes in business methods which take no account of human nature and social motives, so long may we expect strikes and sabotage to be the ordinary accompaniment of industry', Mayo notes.

The research assumed that the behaviour of workers was dictated by the 'logic of sentiment' while that of the bosses was by the 'logic of cost and efficiency.'

CONTEXT

The author is known for his contribution to the famous Hawthorne experiments into the motivation of workers.

The experiments were carried out in 1927–32 at the Chicago division of Western Electric. Although they were celebrated as a major event, their significance lay not so much in their results and discoveries but in the statement they made—that people and their motivation were critical to the success of any business.

The findings influenced the human relations school of thinkers, including Herzberg, McGregor, and Maslow, which emerged in the 1940s and 1950s.

The work of the Hawthorne researchers redressed the balance in management theorising, and the scientific bias of earlier researchers was put into a new perspective.

THE BEST SOURCES OF HELP

Mayo, Elton. *The Human Problems of an Industrial Civilization*. New York: Macmillan, 1933.

The Human Side of Enterprise
by Douglas McGregor

McGregor was a key member of the Human Relations School of Management whose work significantly influenced management styles from the 1960s on. His most famous concept is 'Theories X and Y' which describe two extreme approaches to managing people. The book highlights the potential for a more enlightened approach to human relations management and paved the way for approaches such as empowerment and the learning organisation.

GETTING STARTED

Management assumptions about controlling human resources determine an organisation's character. Theory X assumes that workers are inherently lazy, needing to be supervised and motivated. Authority is the central, indispensable means of managerial control. Theory Y assumes that people want and need to work and organisations should develop employees' commitment. McGregor argues that the average human being learns, under the right conditions, not only to accept but to seek responsibility.

CONTRIBUTION

The importance of human resources. According to the book, the assumptions management holds about controlling its human resources determine the whole character of the enterprise.

Theory X—a traditional management approach. Theory X is built on the assumption that workers are inherently lazy, need to be supervised, and motivated, and regard work as a necessary evil.

The assumptions behind Theory X.
- People inherently dislike work and will avoid it if they can.
- People need to be coerced, controlled, directed, and threatened with punishment into making adequate effort toward the organisation's ends.
- People lack ambition, preferring to be directed and to avoid responsibility. Above all they want security.

The influence of Theory X. The assumption that authority is the central, indispensable means of managerial control pervades US industry. In the author's view, this is a consequence not of man's nature, but of management philosophy, policy, and practice. It is not people who have made organisations, but organisations that have transformed the perspectives, aspirations, and behaviour of people.

Theory Y—a humanist approach. Theory Y is based on the principle that people want and need to work. An organisation needs to develop the individual's commitment to its objectives, and then to liberate his or her abilities on behalf of those objectives.

The assumptions behind Theory Y.
- Work is as natural as play or rest—the typical human doesn't inherently dislike work.
- External control and threat of punishment are not the only means for bringing about effort.
- Commitment to objectives is a function of the rewards associated with their achievement.

- The most important reward is the satisfaction of ego, which can be the direct product of effort directed toward an organisation's purposes.
- The average human being learns not only to accept, but to seek responsibility.
- The capacity to use imagination, ingenuity, and creativity in the solution of organisational problems is widely distributed in the population.

Towards the learning manager. McGregor suggests that four kinds of learning are relevant for managers:

- intellectual knowledge
- manual skills
- problem-solving skills
- social interaction

Assessing behaviour. The skills of social interaction are outside the confines of normal teaching and learning methods. 'We normally get little feedback of real value concerning the impact of our behaviour on others. If they don't behave as we desire, it is easy to blame their stupidity, their adjustment, or their peculiarities. Above all it isn't considered good taste to give this kind of feedback in most social settings. Instead, it is discussed by our colleagues when we are not present to learn about it,' says McGregor.

CONTEXT

Despite publishing little in his short life, McGregor's work remains significant. His classic study of work and motivation reflected the concerns of the middle and late 1960s, when the monolithic corporation was at its most dominant and the world at its most questioning. The common complaint against Theories X and Y is that they are mutually exclusive. To counter this McGregor was developing 'Theory Z' when he died in 1964: a theory that synthesised the organisational and personal imperatives. William Ouchi later seized on the concept of Theory Z. In his book of the same name, he analysed Japanese working methods. Here he found fertile ground for many of the ideas McGregor was proposing:

- lifetime employment
- concern for employees including their social life
- informal control
- decisions made by consensus
- slow promotion
- excellent transmittal of information from top to bottom and bottom to top with the help of middle management
- commitment to the firm
- high concern for quality

Leading author Gary Hamel commented: 'Over the last 40 years, we have been slowly abandoning a view of human beings as nothing more than warm-blooded cogs in the industrial machine. People can be trusted; people want to do the right thing; people are capable of imagination and ingenuity—these were McGregor's fundamental premises, and they underlie the work of modern management thinkers from Drucker to Deming to Peters, and the employment practices of the world's most progressive and successful companies.'

THE BEST SOURCES OF HELP

McGregor, Douglas. *The Human Side of Enterprise*. New York: McGraw-Hill, 1960.

In Search of Excellence
by Tom Peters and Robert Waterman

In Search of Excellence is the most popular management book of recent times. Appearing when Japanese competition had brought Western business low, it gave managers new heart and a new direction, reminding them, in Gary Hamel's words, 'that success often comes from doing common things uncommonly well'.

GETTING STARTED

The book emerged from research conducted by Peters and Waterman with the consulting firm, McKinsey. They identified excellent companies, then sought to distil lessons from their behaviour and performance.

The sample was eventually whittled down to 62 (which were not intended to be perfectly representative). The choices were largely unsurprising, including the likes of IBM, Hewlett-Packard, Wal-Mart, and General Electric. The emphasis was exclusively on big companies.

There is a certain irony here. Although it celebrated big manufacturing businesses, the book condemned the excesses of dispassionate modern management practice and advocated a return to simpler virtues. The authors later came to feel that their ideas were better embodied in smaller companies.

CONTRIBUTION

Success builds on first principles. The book attacks the excesses of the rational model and the business strategy paradigm that had come to dominate Western management thinking.

It counsels return to first principles:

- attention to customers
- an abiding concern for people (productivity through people)
- the celebration of trial and error (a bias for action)

'The excellent companies really are close to their customers. That's it. Other companies talk about it; the excellent companies do it.'

Achieve productivity through people. The authors quote a General Motors worker laid off after 16 years making Pontiacs: 'I guess I was laid off because I make poor quality cars. But in 16 years, not once was I ever asked for a suggestion as to how to do my job better. Not once.'

Excellent companies encourage and nurture an entrepreneurial spirit among all employees.

The management role. The real role of the chief executive is to manage the values of the organisation. Executives nurture and sustain corporate values. Rather than being distant figureheads, they should be there making things happen.

The word 'manager' in lip-service institutions often has come to mean not someone who rolls up his or her sleeves to get the job done right alongside the worker, but someone who hires assistants to do it.

Keep things simple. Excellent companies 'stick to the knitting'. They remain fixated on what they know they are good at and are not easily distracted.

One of their key attributes is that they have realised the importance of keeping things simple, despite overwhelming pressures to complicate things.

The authors explain what they call the 'smart–dumb rule' as follows.

'Many of today's managers . . . may be a little bit too smart for their own good. The smart ones . . . shift direction all the time, based upon the latest output from the expected value equation [and] have 200-page strategic plans and 500-page market requirement documents that are but one step in product development exercises. Our dumber friends are different. They just don't understand why every customer can't get personalised service, even in the potato chip business.'

Become simultaneously loose and tight. The debate about how to become loose and tight (controlled and empowered; big yet small) has dominated much subsequent business writing. The authors recommend new concepts that should be added to the management vocabulary. Each one turns the tables on conventional wisdom, implying both the absence of clear directions and the simultaneous need for action. They include:

- temporary structures
- ad hoc groups
- fluid organisations
- internal competition
- product champions
- skunk works

CONTEXT

Peter Drucker suggested that the book's simplicity explained its appeal: 'The strength of the Peters book is that it forces you to look at the fundamentals. The book's great weakness— which is a strength from the point of view of its success—is that it makes managing sound so incredibly easy.'

Gary Hamel said, 'The dividing line between simple truths, and simplistic prescription is always a thin one. For the most part, Peters and Waterman avoided the facile and the tautological. Indeed, the focus on operations research, elaborate planning systems, and (supposedly) rigorous financial analysis had, in many companies, robbed management of its soul—and certainly had taken the focus off the customer.'

For such a trailblazing book, it is surprisingly uncontroversial. Peters and Waterman admit that what they have to say is not particularly original. They commented that the ideas they were espousing had been generally left behind, ignored, or overlooked by management theorists.

The criteria for selecting excellence were debatable, as all criteria are, and set the authors up for criticism when their excellent companies fell from grace. In 1984 *Business Week* revealed that some had speedily declined into mediocrity and, in some cases, abject failure. But Peters and Waterman had already provided a warning: 'We are asked how we know that the companies we have defined as culturally innovative will stay that way. The answer is we don't.'

In Search of Excellence created the impetus for the deluge of business books and, in the business world, established customer service as a key form of differentiation and advantage.

THE BEST SOURCES OF HELP

Peters, Thomas, and Robert Waterman. *In Search of Excellence*. New York: Harper & Row, 1982.

Information Rules
by Carl Shapiro and Hal Varian

The economy is increasingly dominated by information-based products and services. There has been a tendency to believe that companies can ignore the old rules of economics and substitute new ways of marketing and doing business. The authors urge a more cautious approach, explaining that the basics of business have not changed. However, the existing rules need to be adapted to the new marketplace. They offer practical advice, backed by case studies, on ways to develop strategies for the new economy that are based on sound business principles.

GETTING STARTED

Information, according to Shapiro and Varian, is any product or service that can be digitised. It is costly to produce, but cheap to reproduce, and it has different values for different people. They believe that information has to be carefully managed to maximise its potential value. The Internet may provide the technological infrastructure needed for instant delivery to users, but there are other related technologies, such as payment mechanisms, that are essential to the profitable development of an information economy.

CONTRIBUTION

Information pricing. The cost of production, say the authors, is dominated by first-copy costs; reproduction and distribution cost very little. There are no production constraints on producing very large or very small quantities. One million copies of a software product have the same unit cost as ten million copies.

This pricing structure, they claim, leads to two business models for an information market:
- the dominant firm model
- the differential product model, where many firms produce competing versions of the same information

Companies in a dominant firm market must, they argue, strive for cost leadership. In a differentiated market, companies need to add value and protect their intellectual property rights. They point out that even a commodity product can be differentiated by organising it differently for different users. Personalising information takes this process to its logical conclusion.

They offer three approaches to information pricing:
- personalised pricing, tailored to individual users
- version pricing, where users choose their preferred version
- group pricing, aimed at discrete groups such as students or companies with large numbers of users

Personalised pricing, they claim, can be refined by the information available on customers' buying habits. Group pricing is particularly effective where a product, such as software, is sold in very large numbers and effectively creates a standard that locks customers in.

Versions of information. The authors argue that producing different versions of the same information can broaden the market. Products can be differentiated by features, availability, support levels, and quality. A 'high-end' version would have all the important features; other versions would have fewer. The authors recommend offering three versions, with the middle version likely to be the most popular.

'Bundling' is another method of versioning, where producers put together distinct but related products at a discount price. Bundling software products, experience indicates, produces more overall revenue.

Information rights management. Shapiro and Varian point out that information, or intellectual property, should be managed and protected. Free content, they say, can act as an effective method of sampling chargeable information. Many publishers, for example, provide free executive summaries and charge for access to the complete work. As most Internet users read only a few pages, free content is unlikely to reduce overall sales.

Information lock in. The authors explain how certain types of information can lock a customer in to a supplier. With products that require a great deal of training, the cost of switching supplier can be prohibitively high. They recommend building a large base of customers, putting a value on that base, and then maximising its value by offering a continuous stream of new products.

The economics of networks. The information economy is driven by the economics of networks. The authors explain how the concept of positive feedback helps to build and sustain networks. Once a product gains wide acceptance, the positive feedback encourages or forces suppliers of related products to design products that are compatible. The authors refer to this process as demand-side preference. Customers like standardisation.

Compatibility is the key factor in creating networks of suppliers developing products to the same standard. The authors explain the apparent contradiction in the importance of openness to building standards. Openness appears to open the door for competitors, but it also encourages more suppliers to join the network and add weight to the standard.

The importance of co-operation. Shapiro and Varian point out that standards and the development of networks encourage co-operation between companies who would normally be regarded as competitors. They use the term 'complementors' to describe companies who benefit from each other's products—computer manufacturers and software developers are an example. Co-operation is an important part of the information economy, and the objective of dominant firms in a network is to build strong alliances so that they can offer their customers total solutions.

CONTEXT

Media hype about digital companies led to the dot-com boom in the late 1990s, a boom that was based on the belief that the old rules of business had been blown away by new media companies. The subsequent dot-com collapse showed that basic principles still applied.

Information Rules is the first book to compare the economics of the new information economy with traditional economics. The authors take a classical economics approach to the subject, but include many practical examples of the new rules in action.

Books such as *Being Digital* by Nicholas Negroponte (Coronet, 1996) have explained the nature of digital information, while Nalebuff and Brandenberger's *Co-opetition* (Profile Business, 1997) looks at co-operation and complementary business in the information economy.

THE BEST SOURCES OF HELP

Shapiro, Carl, and Hal R. Varian. *Information Rules: A Strategic Guide to the Network Economy.* Boston, Massachusetts: Harvard Business School Press, 1998.

Innovation in Marketing
by Theodore Levitt

Levitt's views on the importance of marketing are highly regarded. His article 'Marketing myopia' (reprinted in the book) was one of the most popular *Harvard Business Review* articles ever published. It highlights how narrow perspectives result from companies focusing on production rather than customers.

GETTING STARTED

Historical success encouraged the belief that low-cost production was the key to success, but this inevitably leads to narrow perspectives. In the author's view, companies must broaden their view of the nature of their business, and should be marketing-led rather than production-led. The emphasis is on providing customer-creating value satisfactions.

There is no such thing as a growth industry: success comes from being perceptive enough to spot where future growth may lie. Companies fail because they assume continued growth, believe that a product cannot be improved, and concentrate on improved production techniques to deliver lower costs. Mass-production industries aim to produce all they can and marketing gets neglected.

CONTRIBUTION

A focus on customers. Levitt argues that the central preoccupation of corporations should be with satisfying customers rather than simply producing goods. Companies should be marketing-led rather than production-led. Management must think of itself not as producing products but as providing customer-creating value satisfactions. The lead must come from the chief executive and senior management.

Problems of production-led companies. Henry Ford's success in mass production fuelled the belief that low-cost production was the key to business success. Ford continued to believe that he knew what customers wanted, long after they had decided otherwise.

Production-led thinking inevitably leads to narrow perspectives.

Narrow perspectives. Companies must broaden their view of the nature of their business: otherwise their customers will soon be forgotten. The railways are in trouble today not because the need was filled by others, but because it was not filled by the railways themselves. They let others take customers away from them because they assumed they were in the railway business rather than in the transportation business—they were product-oriented instead of customer-oriented.

The railway business was constrained by a lack of willingness to expand its horizons. Similarly, the film industry failed to respond to the growth of television because it regarded itself as being in the business of making movies rather than providing entertainment.

Taking growth for granted. Growth can never be taken for granted, asserts the author. There is no such thing as a growth industry—growth is a matter of being perceptive enough to spot where future growth may lie.

History is filled with companies that fall undetected into decay for these reasons:

- they assume that the growth in their particular market will continue for as long as the population grows in size and wealth
- they believe that a product cannot be surpassed
- they tend to put faith in the ability of improved production techniques to deliver lower costs and, therefore, higher profits

Problems of mass-production industries. Mass-production industries are impelled by a great drive to produce all they can. The prospect of steeply declining unit costs as output rises is more than most companies can usually resist. The profit possibilities look spectacular, so all effort focuses on production.

> There is a distinction between the tasks of selling and marketing.

Concentration on the product, in Levitt's view, also lends itself to measurement and analysis. The result is that marketing gets neglected.

Distinguishing selling and marketing. There is a distinction between the tasks of selling and marketing. Selling concerns itself with the tricks and techniques of getting people to exchange their cash for your product—it is not concerned with the values that the exchange is all about. It does not, as marketing invariably does, view the entire business process as consisting of a tightly integrated effort to discover, create, arouse, and satisfy customer needs.

CONTEXT

Ted Levitt's fame was secured early in his career with 'Marketing myopia'—a *Harvard Business Review* article which enjoyed unprecedented success and attention, selling over 500,000 reprints.

It has since been reproduced in virtually every collection of key marketing texts. 'Marketing myopia' is a manifesto rather than a deeply academic article. It embraces ideas that had already been explored by others (Levitt acknowledges his debt to Peter Drucker's *The Practice of Management*).

In the 1980s when marketing underwent resurgence, companies began to heed Levitt's view that they were too heavily oriented towards production. Levitt's article and his subsequent work pushed marketing to centre stage. In some cases it led to what Levitt called marketing mania, with companies obsessively responsive to every fleeting whim of the customer.

Many of today's leading thinkers, such as Pascale and Peters, continually re-emphasise Levitt's message that there is no such thing as a growth industry.

Influential writer Gary Hamel said: 'If Ted Levitt had done nothing else in his career—and he did plenty—he would have earned his keep on this planet with the article "Marketing myopia". Managers get wrapped up inside their products (railways) and lose sight of the fundamental benefits customers are seeking (transportation). Equally provocative was Ted's 1983 *Harvard Business Review* article, "The globalization of markets". While some argue that markets will never become truly global, there are few companies that are betting against the general trend.'

THE BEST SOURCES OF HELP

Levitt, Theodore. *Innovation in Marketing*. New York: McGraw-Hill, 1962.

The Innovator's Dilemma
by Clayton Christensen

Christensen's book faces up to a fundamental problem facing innovative companies—how to deal with breakthrough technologies when customers may not be ready for them. It argues that normal practice—focusing investment and development on the most profitable products, those that are in demand among top customers—may ultimately be damaging. The risk is that companies may reject innovative products that do not meet this criterion. Christensen explains how to overcome this problem and manage breakthrough products successfully.

GETTING STARTED

Christensen examines a range of leading, well-managed companies that have failed to capitalise on innovative technologies. The dilemma is that it is often sound decisions by good managers that lead to failure. The author distinguishes between sustaining technologies, which foster improved performance, and disruptive technologies, which represent a breakthrough, but may initially lead to poorer performance. Examples of disruptive technologies include mobile telephones, digital photography, and online retailing.

Part of the problem, according to Christensen, is that the market may not be ready for the new technology. In other cases, leading customers may not be willing to risk a new product. Companies therefore focus on the safe bets, but may subsequently be overtaken by innovation.

CONTRIBUTION

Control by customers. The disk drive industry shows the dilemma in action. The author explains how the major players in the industry used sustaining technologies to offer their customers improved performance.

New entrants introduced disruptive technologies, such as smaller floppy discs that required new computer architecture. These innovations were, however, initially rejected by customers until they became a proven technology. The author concludes that, to a degree, the larger companies were controlled by their customers.

Value networks. Christensen offers a possible explanation for failure in these cases—the concept of the 'value network'. This is a technique companies can use to assess the value of a new technology in relation to their current business and customer base. It asks what rewards the company would obtain from re-allocating resources away from mainstream products.

The author believes that the problem is compounded by the scope of the company's suppliers and subcontractors. Each may have its own value network based on the needs of its own customers. Innovative ideas that come up from subcontractors may be stifled in the same way as internal ideas.

The author explains how the cost and profit structures in a value network can limit the attractiveness of an innovation. If profit margins are low, the emphasis will be on cost cutting across proven technologies. Innovation would be too risky. The other response from established companies is to move upmarket where they can earn more from existing products.

Avoiding risk. Christensen points out that new entrants have frequently forced the pace of innovation with disruptive technologies. Established companies only moved in when there was a definite market. Disruptive technologies do not initially represent large, high-margin opportunities for established companies and the decision-making structure can rule out innovative ideas.

The author cites five reasons why successful companies fail to capitalise on disruptive technologies:

- customers control the pattern of resource allocation
- small markets do not solve the growth needs of large companies
- it can be difficult to identify applications in advance
- larger organisations rely on their core competencies and values
- technology supply may not equal market demand

The importance of spin-offs. Christensen explains how companies who did harness disruptive technologies used a number of management techniques:

- projects were handled within another 'spin-off organisation' that had customers who needed the new technology
- those same project organisations could get excited about small markets and small wins
- failure was an acceptable part of the process as companies proceeded by trial and error to the right solution
- companies looked for new markets and developed the market where the disruptive technology offered value

The author gives examples of large corporations that have set up spin-off companies to exploit new technology. Frequently, the corporation pulls the spin-off back into the core business when it proves successful.

CONTEXT

The book claims that overdependence on customer needs can affect a company's success. This argument runs counter to the marketing and customer service books that put customer focus at the top of the corporate agenda.

Books such as *When Giants Learn to Dance* by Rosabeth Moss Kanter (Touchstone, 1990) have pointed out the problems faced by larger corporations who compete in fast-moving technology markets. Christensen's book is unusual in highlighting the problems inherent in what appears to be sound decision-making.

THE BEST SOURCES OF HELP

Christensen, Clayton M. *The Innovator's Dilemma: When New Technologies Cause Great Firms to Fail.* Boston, Massachusetts: Harvard Business School Press, 1997.

Intellectual Capital
by Thomas Stewart

The author is widely regarded as the world's leading authority on knowledge management, and his views are valuable to any organisation that wants to improve the return on its 'intellectual capital'. The book is a useful guide to the strategic and practical issues of identifying, capturing, and using knowledge to improve competitive advantage.

GETTING STARTED

Traditional capital had financial or physical characteristics. In the author's view, however, the emphasis now is on an intangible asset, intellectual capital, consisting of human capital, customer capital, and structural capital.

Human capital resides in the heads of employees; customer capital represents the value of a company's ongoing relationships with customers; and structural capital is the knowledge retained within the organisation. The real value comes in being able to capture and deploy intellectual capital, Stewart argues. However, you cannot define and manage intellectual assets unless you know what you want to do with them.

CONTRIBUTION

The new concept of capital. Traditionally, capital could be viewed in purely financial or physical terms. It showed up in the buildings and equipment owned, and could be found in the corporate balance sheets. The author suggests that in recent times, the emphasis has switched to an intangible form of asset, intellectual capital. Intellectual capital can be broken down into three areas: human capital; customer capital; and structural capital.

Human capital. Human capital is the knowledge residing in the heads of employees that is relevant to the purpose of the organisation.

Human capital is formed and deployed, when more of the time and talent of employees is devoted to activities that result in innovation. It can grow in two ways: when the organisation uses more of what people know; or when people know more that is useful to the organisation. Unleashing it requires an organisation to minimise mindless tasks, meaningless paperwork, and unproductive infighting.

Customer capital. This represents the value of a company's ongoing relationships with the people or organisations to which it sells. Indicators of customer capital include market share, customer retention and defection rates, and profit per customer.

Customer capital is probably the worst-managed of all intangible assets. Many businesses don't even know who their customers are.

Structural capital. Structural capital is the knowledge retained within the organisation. It belongs to the company as a whole and can be reproduced and shared.

Structural capital includes technologies, inventions, publications, and business processes.

Managing intellectual capital. The real value comes in being able to capture and deploy intellectual capital. Knowledge assets exist and are worth cultivating only in the context of strategy. You cannot define and manage intellectual assets unless you know what you want to do with them.

There are ten principles for managing intellectual capital:

- companies don't own human and customer capital. Only by recognising the shared nature of these assets can a company manage and profit from them.
- to create usable human capital, a company needs to foster teamwork, communities of practice, and other social forms of learning.
- organisational wealth is created around skills and talents that are proprietary and scarce. Companies must recognise that people with these talents are assets to invest in.
- structural assets are the easiest to manage but those that customers care least about.
- move from amassing knowledge 'just in case' to having readily-available information that customers need.
- information and knowledge can and should substitute for expensive physical and financial assets.
- knowledge work is custom work.
- every company should re-analyse its own industry to see what information is most crucial.
- focus on the flow of information not the flow of materials.
- human, structural, and customer capital work together. It is not enough to invest in people, systems, and customers separately.

Knowledge working and individual careers. Stewart argues that careers in the 21st century will have a number of characteristics:

- a career is a series of gigs, not a series of steps
- project management is the furnace in which successful careers are made
- power flows from expertise, not from position
- most roles in an organisation can be performed by either insiders or outsiders
- careers are made in markets not hierarchies
- the fundamental career choice is not between one company and another, but between specialising and generalising

CONTEXT

Thomas Stewart pioneered the field of intellectual capital in a series of articles that earned him an international reputation, with the Planning Forum calling him in 1994 'the leading proponent of knowledge management in the business press'.

Intellectual Capital has proved itself as the definitive guide to understanding and managing intangible assets. It explains not only why intellectual capital will be the foundation of corporate success in the new century, but also offers practical guidance to companies about how to make best use of their intangible assets. Since it first appeared, there have been a flood of books on knowledge management.

The term 'knowledge worker' is not a new one. In 1994, Peter Drucker wrote that, 'the true investment in the knowledge society is not in machines and tools but in the knowledge of the knowledge worker. In the knowledge society the most probable assumption for organisations . . . is that they need knowledge workers far more than knowledge workers need them.'

THE BEST SOURCES OF HELP

Stewart, Thomas. *Intellectual Capital: The New Wealth of Organizations*. New York: Doubleday, 1997.

The Knowledge-creating Company
by Ikujiro Nonaka and Hirotaka Takeuchi

The book focuses on the development of organisational knowledge in Japanese companies. The authors explain how this knowledge forms the basis of innovations that have enabled Japanese companies to become leaders in many different market sectors. They show that the ability to acquire and apply knowledge is becoming a key factor for success in the transition from an industrial economy to an information economy.

GETTING STARTED

Nonaka and Takeuchi believe that historical adversity has forced Japanese companies to pursue a policy of continuous innovation. Organisational knowledge, according to them, is the ability of a company to create new knowledge, disseminate it throughout the organisation, and embody it in innovative products, services, and systems. They distinguish between explicit knowledge, such as rules or formulas, and tacit knowledge, which is gained from experience and can rarely be learned. The Japanese, they claim, are very effective at turning tacit knowledge into explicit knowledge that can be shared throughout an organisation.

CONTRIBUTION

Characteristics of knowledge creation. According to the authors, there are three key characteristics of knowledge creation:
- metaphor and analogy
- the transition from personal to organisational knowledge
- ambiguity and redundancy

The use of metaphor and analogy helps companies to visualise difficult concepts and explain them to other people within an organisation. The transition from personal to organisational knowledge depends on the successful implementation of teamwork so that individuals can interact with each other. The concept of ambiguity and redundancy means that Japanese companies are happy to take a number of different approaches to innovation, some of which are bound to fail. They use redundancy to encourage creativity and identify what does not work in practical terms.

Knowledge management. The authors review theories of knowledge from ancient times onward. They analyse recent management writing to identify attitudes towards the question of knowledge. They cite Peter Drucker's 'knowledge worker' and Peter Senge's 'learning organisation' as important concepts in knowledge creation. They also discuss the concept of core competencies and argue that this can distract companies. Core competencies, they argue, suggest that knowledge is an existing, finite resource within a company. Knowledge creation, on the other hand, emphasises the importance of acquiring and developing knowledge from as many internal and external sources as possible.

How knowledge creation works. The authors claim that there are four key processes in knowledge conversion:

- socialisation
- externalisation
- combination
- internalisation

An example of socialisation is the brainstorming camps set up by Honda to solve difficult production problems. Externalisation is the process of using metaphors or analogies to communicate difficult concepts in product development. Combination is the process of sorting, adding, combining, and synthesising new knowledge. Internalisation is like relearning other people's experiences, or learning by doing.

The environment for knowledge creation. To create a suitable environment for knowledge creation, the authors stress the importance of vision to guide overall direction and autonomy to allow everyone in the organisation to get involved in the process.

They describe a structure called 'middle-up-down management' that underpins knowledge creation. This structure contrasts with the bottom-up or top-down management styles found in Western companies. The Japanese model puts middle managers at the heart of the process, acting between front-line workers and a visionary senior management team. The authors believe that this type of structure creates dialogue and builds relationships between the individual specialists who contribute to a development project.

Hypertext organisations. Nonaka and Takeuchi refer to the concept of a 'knowledge crew', consisting of knowledge engineers and knowledge practitioners. Underpinning this is what they call a 'hypertext organisation'. This is an organisation with multiple layers:

- a business system layer
- a project team layer
- a knowledge base layer

The business system layer and project team layer generate different types of knowledge, which are brought together in the knowledge base which can be shared throughout the organisation.

CONTEXT

A number of books have looked at the process of innovation, trying to identify the factors that distinguish a successful innovator. The authors offer both theoretical and practical insight into the way that Japanese companies use knowledge as the basis for innovation. Their findings are in contrast with the widespread Western view that Japanese success is based on access to cheap capital, lifetime employment, culture, or quality.

The authors draw on a wide range of Western management sources to highlight the differences between Japanese and Western practice. Among others, they quote Peter Drucker and Alvin Toffler on the importance of knowledge, and Peter Senge on the concept of the 'learning organisation'.

THE BEST SOURCES OF HELP

Nonaka, Ikujiro, and Hirotaka Takeuchi. *The Knowledge-creating Company: How Japanese Companies Create the Dynamics of Innovation.* Oxford: Oxford University Press, 1995.

Leaders: Strategies for Taking Charge
by Warren Bennis and Burt Nanus

Warren Bennis is an academic and regular presidential advisor who brought leadership to a new, mass audience. He is regarded as one of the most important contemporary thinkers.

Burt Nanus is the founder and director of the Center of Futures Research at the University of Southern California.

In this book, the authors use an eclectic selection of America's leaders to offer the readers key lessons on how to become successful. Their message is that leadership is open to all.

GETTING STARTED

Leaders commit people to action and convert followers into leaders. They are usually ordinary people rather than particularly charismatic, as leadership is all-encompassing and open to all.

Successful leaders also have a vision that other people believe in, and communicate it effectively. Instead of being an individual problem solver, they achieve greatness through working with groups. Devising and maintaining an atmosphere in which others can succeed is the leader's creative act.

CONTRIBUTION

The ordinary leader. In the authors' view, the new leader is one who commits people to action, who converts followers into leaders, and who may convert leaders into agents of change. Leadership is not a rare skill—leaders are made rather than born. They are usually ordinary people, or apparently ordinary, rather than charismatic. Leadership is not solely the preserve of those at the top of an organisation—it is relevant at all levels. Leadership is not about control, direction, and manipulation.

Common abilities of leaders. From a survey of 90 US leaders (including Neil Armstrong, the coach of the LA Rams, orchestral conductors, and businessmen such as Ray Kroc of McDonald's), Bennis and Nanus identified four common abilities:

- management of attention
- management of meaning
- management of trust
- management of self

Management of attention. This is a question of vision. Leadership is the capacity to create a compelling vision, translate it into action, and sustain it. Successful leaders have a vision that other people believe in and treat as their own.

Management of meaning. A vision is of limited practical use if it is encased in 400 pages of wordy text or mumbled from behind a paper-packed desk. Effective communication relies on use of analogy, metaphor, and vivid illustration as well as emotion, trust, optimism, and hope.

Management of trust. Trust is the emotional glue that binds followers and leaders together. Leaders have to be seen to be consistent.

Management of self. Leaders do not glibly present charisma or time management as the essence of their success. Instead, the emphasis is on persistence and self-knowledge, commitment and challenge, taking risks and, above all, learning. The learning person looks forward to failure or mistakes, which means that the worst problem in leadership is basically early success. There's no opportunity to learn from adversity and problems.

A positive self-regard. Leaders have a positive self-regard, known as emotional wisdom. This is characterised by an ability to accept people as they are. They also have a capacity to approach things in terms of only the present, and an ability to treat everyone, even close contacts, with courteous attention. They need an ability to trust others, and to do without constant approval and recognition.

Leaders and group working. Greatness starts with superb people. Great groups don't exist without great leaders, but they give the lie to the persistent notion that successful institutions are the lengthened shadow of a great woman or man. It's not clear that life was ever so simple that individuals, acting alone, solved most significant problems. Instead of the individual problem solver, we have a new model for creative achievement.

> Greatness starts with superb people.

Changing leadership qualities. The leader is a pragmatic dreamer, a person with an original but attainable vision. He or she knows that this dream can only be realised if others are free to do exceptional work. Typically, the leader is the one who recruits the others, by making the vision so seductive that they see it too, and eagerly sign up.

Inevitably, the leader has to invent a leadership style that suits the group. The standard models, especially command and control, simply don't work. The heads of groups have to act decisively, not arbitrarily. They have to make decisions without limiting the autonomy of other participants.

The idealistic leader. Most organisations are dull and working life is mundane, so groups can be an inspiration. Individual leaders can create a human community that will, in the long run, lead to the best organisations. 'A Great Group is more than a collection of first-rate minds. It's a miracle', say the authors. Every person has to make a genuine contribution in their lives and the institution of work is one of the main vehicles to achieving this.

CONTEXT

With the torrent of publications and executive programmes on the subject, it is easy to forget that leadership had been largely overlooked as a topic worthy of serious academic interest until it was revived by Bennis and others in the 1980s. Since then, leadership has become a heavy industry. Concern and interest about leadership development is no longer an American phenomenon: it is truly global. The book stands as a humane counter to much of the military-based hero worship which dogs the subject.

THE BEST SOURCES OF HELP

Bennis, Warren, and Burt Nanus. *Leaders: Strategies for Taking Charge*. New York: Harper & Row, 1985.

Leadership
by James MacGregor Burns

In his book *Leadership*, Burns makes an important contribution to management literature by refocusing interest on the nature of leadership. He brings practical insights from both business and politics and has used those insights to identify two key strands—transactional and transformational leadership.

GETTING STARTED

Burns believes we know too much about our leaders, but too little about leadership. It is a structure for action. It is not the preserve of the few or the tyranny of the masses.

Burns identifies two vital strands of leadership—transformational and transactional leadership. Transactional leadership is built on reciprocity—the relationship between the leader and their followers develops from the exchange of some reward. The secret of effective leadership appears to lie in combining the two elements so that targets, results, and procedures are developed and shared.

CONTRIBUTION

Problems in defining leadership. If we know all too much about our leaders, we know far too little about leadership. There are literally hundreds of definitions of leadership and, as a result, the concept 'has dissolved into small and discrete meanings', Burns claims.

> Leadership is a structure for action that engages people, to varying degrees, throughout the levels and among the interstices of society.

Leadership as a structure for action. Leadership is exercised when people with certain motives and purposes mobilise—in competition or conflict with others—institutional, political, psychological, and other resources so as to arouse, engage, and satisfy the motives of followers. Leadership is not the preserve of the few or the tyranny of the masses. The leadership approach tends often unconsciously to be elitist; it projects heroic figures against the shadowy background of drab, powerless masses. The followership approach tends to be populist or anti-elitist in ideology, perceiving the masses, even in democratic societies, as linked with small, overlapping circles of conservative politicians, military officers, hierocrats, and businessmen.

Leadership is a structure for action that engages people, to varying degrees, throughout the levels and among the interstices of society. Only the inert, the alienated, and the powerless are unengaged. It is also intrinsically linked to morality—moral leadership emerges from, and always returns to, the fundamental wants and needs, aspirations, and values of the followers.

Transformational leadership. Burns identifies two vital strands of leadership—transformational and transactional leadership.

Transformational leadership occurs when one or more persons engage with others in such a way that leaders and followers raise one another to higher levels of motivation and morality. Their purposes, which might have started out separate but related, become fused. Power bases are linked, not as counterweights, but as mutual support for common purpose. Various names are used for such leadership: elevating, mobilising, inspiring, exalting, uplifting, exhorting, evangelising.

Transformational leadership becomes moral in that it raises the level of human conduct and ethical aspiration of both the leader and the led, thus having a transforming effect on both. It is also dynamic, in the sense that the leaders throw themselves into a relationship with followers who will feel elevated by it and often become more active themselves, thereby creating new cadres of leaders.

Transformational leadership is concerned with engaging the hearts and minds of others. It works to help all parties achieve greater motivation, satisfaction, and sense of achievement. It is driven by trust, concern, and facilitation rather than direct control. The skills required are concerned with establishing a long-term vision, empowering people to control themselves, coaching and developing others, and challenging the culture to change. In transformational leadership, the power of the leader comes from creating understanding and trust.

Transactional leadership. Transactional leadership is built on reciprocity. The relationship between the leader and his or her followers develops from the exchange of some reward, such as performance ratings, pay, recognition, and praise. It involves leaders in clarifying goals and objectives, communicating well in order to plan tasks and activities with the co-operation of their employees, so that wider organisational goals are met.

The relationship depends on hierarchy and the ability to work through the mode of exchange. It requires leadership skills such as the ability to obtain results, to control through structures and processes, to solve problems, to plan and organise and work within the structures and boundaries of the organisation.

Combining transformational and transactional leadership. In their apparent mutual exclusiveness, transformational and transactional leadership are akin to Douglas McGregor's Theories X and Y. The secret of effective leadership appears to lie in combining the two elements so that targets, results, and procedures are developed and shared.

CONTEXT

Burns's book provides an important link between leadership in the political and business worlds. For all the books on leadership, the two have usually been regarded as mutually exclusive. His examination of transformational and transactional leadership also stimulated further debate on leadership at a time when it was somewhat neglected. In the 1980s, it returned to prominence in management literature as a subject worthy of study.

Business guru Gary Hamel commented, 'There is no theme in management literature which is more enduring than leadership. Among the many contributions which Burns makes to our understanding of leadership, two seem central: leadership must have a moral foundation; and the responsibility for leadership must be widely distributed. Self-interested autocrats, whether political or corporate, ignore these truths at their peril.'

THE BEST SOURCES OF HELP

Burns, James MacGregor. *Leadership*. New York: Harper & Row, 1978.

Leading Change
by John Kotter

Kotter is regarded as one of the world's leading figures in change management. His article, 'Leading change', published in the March–April 1995 *Harvard Business Review*, quickly became the *Review's* best-selling reprint. Readers commented that its analysis defined the real problem of change management. They also found the eight-stage change framework 'compelling'. The book builds on the success of the article and includes dozens of examples of effective change management in action.

GETTING STARTED

Kotter believes that successful change takes place when organisations operate an eight-stage process. The stages are:

1. establishing a sense of urgency
2. creating the guiding coalition
3. developing a vision and strategy
4. communicating the change vision
5. empowering employees for broad-based action
6. generating short-term wins
7. consolidating gains and producing more change
8. anchoring new approaches in the culture

CONTRIBUTION

Why change fails. Kotter believes that most business transformations fail because they do not meet the criteria set out in his eight-point plan. These omissions would not be important in a slower-moving world, but the volatile forces of competition mean companies must change to survive and prosper. He believes that the pace of change is driven by forces such as technological development, international economic integration, the maturation of markets, and the globalisation of markets and competition.

The result, according to Kotter, is that there are either more opportunities or more hazards, depending on whether an organisation can adapt or not. He then explains how successful change, the sort that enables companies to grasp opportunities, goes through the eight-stage process. He adds, however, that it is essential to go through all the stages in sequence. He also believes that change must be led, rather than managed.

A sense of urgency. Establishing a sense of urgency helps to get the co-operation needed for change. A committed group, Kotter argues, can drive change through. He suggests a number of approaches for increasing the urgency level:

- creating a vision
- setting targets so high they cannot be achieved through business as usual
- getting staff to talk to disgruntled customers
- showing people that great opportunities cannot be achieved by the present organisation

Building the guiding coalition. Kotter's second stage is the 'guiding coalition'. He believes that an isolated chief executive or a weak committee cannot cope with the pace of change.

The coalition must comprise people with power, expertise, credibility, and leadership. Leadership is key, because change must be led not managed. He explains why the coalition must be built on trust and a common goal, noting that team-building exercises can be an important part of that process.

Developing a vision. According to Kotter, a vision clarifies the direction of change. Other decisions must be in line with the vision. Vision also helps to align individuals and motivate them in an efficient way. He believes that a vision should be imaginable, desirable, feasible, focused, flexible, and communicable.

Communicating change. Kotter argues that a vision has real power only when it is communicated effectively. Effective communication is vital because employees receive vast amounts of information, and communications about change can easily get lost. Kotter's advice is to keep it simple, use metaphors, keep repeating the message, listen, and lead by example.

Empowering employees. Turning the vision into action means removing structural barriers to change so that employees are empowered, says Kotter. That may require training, reorganisation, aligning information and systems to the vision, and confronting people who try to restrict change.

Short-term wins. According to Kotter, short-term wins are essential. They are visible and show that change is producing results. They also help to fine-tune the change process, build momentum, and reward the people who are delivering change. Pressure and challenging targets can help to deliver the gains.

Consolidating gains. Kotter believes that all gains need to be consolidated to keep the process moving. This is particularly important in companies where there is a high level of interdependence. Maintaining momentum also requires strong leadership, effective project management, and support for the people who are effecting change.

Anchoring change in the culture. The final stage in Kotter's process is anchoring the new approaches in the corporate culture. He argues that the new behaviour should become the norm. Ideally, everyone in the organisation should have shared values. Achieving this level of acceptance depends on results. It may even require changing key people.

CONTEXT

The study of change has gained importance as competition has intensified and other structural factors impact on the business environment. Kotter's work demonstrates the positive aspects of effective change. It also shows that strong leadership is essential if change is to succeed. Rosabeth Moss Kanter's book *The Change Masters* (Allen & Unwin, 1993) puts a similar emphasis on the importance of strategic leadership. William Bridges, on the other hand, in *Managing Transitions* (Nicholas Brealey, 2002), puts more emphasis on management of the personal consequences of change, highlighting the need to reduce anxiety and manage the process he calls 'transition'.

Hammer and Champy's book *Reengineering the Corporation* (HarperBusiness, 1993) took change to a logical conclusion and showed how companies would have to transform themselves to compete effectively. Unfortunately, re-engineering has been widely associated with downsizing, and this has given change management negative connotations.

THE BEST SOURCES OF HELP

Kotter, John P. *Leading Change*. Boston, Massachusetts: Harvard Business School Press, 1996.

The Living Company: Habits for Survival in a Turbulent Business Environment
by Arie de Geus

The book looks at the problem of corporate failure, presenting alarming statistics on the relatively short life of European and Japanese enterprise. The author argues that short-term focus on profits, rather than nurturing people, is a key factor in failure. *The Living Company* is the testimony of someone who practised the human side of enterprise and who believes that companies must be fundamentally humane to prosper.

GETTING STARTED

The author argues that corporations should last as long as two or three centuries, but the reality is that companies usually die young. And focus on profits, rather than on human issues, lies behind the high failure rate. However, like all organisms, the living company exists primarily for its own survival and improvement.

A successful company is one that can learn effectively, and senior executives must dedicate a great deal of time to nurturing their people.

CONTRIBUTION

The problem of corporate morality. Companies may be legal entities, but they are disturbingly mortal. The natural average lifespan of a corporation should be as long as two or three centuries—for example, the Sumitomo Group and the Scandinavian company, Stora.

The reality is that companies usually die young. A Dutch survey indicated 12.5 years as the average life expectancy of all Japanese and European firms. The average life expectancy of a multinational corporation—Fortune 500 or its equivalent—is between 40 and 50 years.

Reasons for longevity. The high company failure rate is attributed to the focus of managers on profits, rather than on the human community that makes up their organisation.

In an attempt to get to the bottom of this mystery, de Geus and a number of his Shell colleagues carried out some research to identify the characteristics of corporate longevity. As you would expect, the onus is on keeping excitement to a minimum. The average human centenarian advocates a life of abstinence, caution, and moderation; and so it is with companies.

The research team identified four key characteristics. The long-lived companies were:
- sensitive to their environment
- cohesive, with a strong sense of identity
- tolerant
- conservative in financing

The importance of people. There is more to a company and to its longevity than mere money making. The skills, capabilities, and knowledge of people are paramount; capital is no longer king.

The learning company. A successful company is one that can learn effectively. Learning means being prepared to accept continuous change, and a company can only change if its community of people changes.

Individuals change through learning—requiring senior executives to dedicate a great deal of time to nurturing their people. The author recalls spending around a quarter of his time on the development and placement of people, while the former CEO of GE, Jack Welch, claimed to spend half of his time on such issues.

> Individuals change through learning—requiring senior executives to dedicate a great deal of time to nurturing their people.

According to de Geus, all corporate activities are grounded in two hypotheses:
- the company is a living being
- the decisions for action made by this living being result from a learning process

Like all organisms, the living company exists primarily for its own survival and improvement. It aims to fulfil its potential and to become as great as it can be.

CONTEXT

With its faith in learning, *The Living Company* represents a careful and powerful riposte to corporate nihilism.

The book proposes that the wisdom of the past be appreciated and used, rather than cast out in the manner of a cultural revolution.

Contrast this with re-engineering, which sought to dismiss the past so that the future could begin with a blank piece of paper. De Geus suggests that the piece of paper already exists, and notes are constantly being scrawled in the margins as new insights are added.

De Geus's arguments are probably at their weakest when he contemplates why companies deserve to live long lives. The average entrepreneur would probably accept a life expectancy of 12.5 years.

The Living Company is the testimony of someone who practised the human side of enterprise, and who believes that companies must be fundamentally humane to prosper—whatever the century.

THE BEST SOURCES OF HELP

de Geus, Arie. *The Living Company: Habits for Survival in a Turbulent Business Environment*. Boston, Massachusetts: Harvard Business School Press, 1997.

Living on Thin Air
by Charles Leadbetter

This book is based on the work of Demos, an independent think tank, which advises government and industry. It explains why knowledge is so important to economic success, but its message is more important to strategists or policy makers than business executives.

GETTING STARTED

The author asserts that more and more people are making a living from knowledge. Society should be organised to maximise the creation and use of knowledge capital. When financial, social, and knowledge capital work in harmony, society will be strong.

It is important to reconcile conflicts between the three types of capital, so society can then move forward. Society is currently trapped between the gridlock of the old and the chaos of the new.

CONTRIBUTION

Earning from knowledge. An increasing number of people are making a living from 'thin air', that is, from ideas and know-how—and knowledge is now the most precious resource.

Society should be organised to maximise its creation and use. Society should harness the power of markets and community to the more fundamental goals of creating and spreading knowledge.

> Society is currently trapped between the gridlock of the old and the chaos of the new.

Organising society around knowledge capital. When financial, social, and knowledge capital work in harmony, through institutions designed to reconcile their competing demands, society will be strong.

In the author's view, society will need to be organised around the creation of knowledge capital and social capital, rather than dominated by the power of financial capital.

When financial, social, and knowledge capital work in harmony, through institutions designed to reconcile their competing demands, society will be strong.

Reconciling conflicts. A society devoted to financial capitalism will be unbalanced and soulless.

A society devoted to social solidarity will stagnate, lacking the dynamism of radical new ideas and the discipline of the competitive market.

A society devoted solely to knowledge creation would be intelligent but poor, even if it did realise the value of its know-how to the full.

Moving society forward. When the three forces of the new economy work together, they can be hugely dynamic. Too often they seem in danger either of spinning out of control, or of being trapped by a society unable to stomach the institutional reforms needed to move forward. Society is currently trapped between the gridlock of the old and the chaos of the new.

CONTEXT

Charles Leadbetter believes society should harness the power of markets and community to the more fundamental goals of creating and spreading knowledge.

Society, he believes, will need to be organised around the creation of knowledge capital and social capital, rather than dominated by the power of financial capital.

To support this call to action, Leadbetter draws on research in California, Japan, Germany, and the Far East to show how his manifesto might be achieved.

'The independents: Britain's new cultural entrepreneurs' is a pamphlet from independent think tank Demos, written by Charles Leadbetter and Kate Oakley. The pamphlet explores how an increasing share of some of the fastest-growing sectors of the British economy is accounted for by a new and independent breed of cultural entrepreneurs.

This group are typically in their twenties and thirties and have emerged from a convergence of three forces:

1. Technology. This is the first generation that grew up with computers and that understands how to reap the benefits of modern computing power and communications. In earlier decades, increased computer power primarily benefited large organisations. The independents feel enabled, not threatened, by new technology.

2. Values. The independents are typically anti-establishment, anti-traditionalist, and highly individualistic. Those values predispose them to pursue self employment and entrepreneurship in a spirit of self-exploration and self-fulfilment.

3. Economics. They have entered the workforce from the late 1980s onwards, during which time self employment and entrepreneurship have become very attractive alternatives to careers in large, impersonal, frequently downsizing organisations.

THE BEST SOURCES OF HELP

Leadbetter, Charles. *Living on Thin Air*. New York: Viking, 1999.

The Machine That Changed the World
by James Womack, Daniel Jones, and Daniel Roos

Lean production was Japan's secret weapon in the trade war, and it went on to conquer the world. In 1984 a team of researchers at the Massachusetts Institute of Technology (MIT) undertook a study of the phenomenon. Within the framework of an analysis of the situation and problems of car manufacturers worldwide, Womack, Jones, and Roos examined the differences between mass production and lean production. This widely-read and wisely-praised book presents their findings.

GETTING STARTED

A new form of manufacturing—lean production—is about to supersede the mass production of goods, the authors announce. Lean production can simultaneously double productivity, improve quality, and keep costs low. The book recounts the history of the rise of lean production, describes its essential elements, and presents the prospects for the spread of this revolutionary management initiative.

CONTRIBUTION

The beginnings of lean production. In 1950 Eiji Toyoda, a Japanese engineer whose family had founded the Toyota Motor Company, and Toyota's production manager, Taiichi Ohno, visited the Ford motor works in Detroit, then the biggest and most efficient production plant in the world. The basis of the Ford system was a complete division of labour among a wide variety of specialist operatives. The conveyor belt could never be halted; faults were dealt with in post-production.

Toyoda and Ohno felt that there was waste throughout this system: wasted labour, wasted materials, wasted time. Apart from the assemblers, none of the specialists created any value for the car.

On his return, Ohno grouped his workers in teams, to whom he delegated more tasks and who were to work together on improvements. Each worker had a duty to halt the production line if a problem arose that he or she could not deal with. The whole team would then trace the fault back to its ultimate cause and then think up a solution that would ensure it never happened again. The remedial work required before dispatch was thus reduced to zero, and lean production, the authors say, was born.

The elements of lean production. The first element in lean production is the organisation of the assembly works. A lean factory, the authors report, has two main organisational characteristics. First, it allots a maximum number of tasks and responsibilities to those workers who create actual value in the product on the line. Secondly, it has a fault-detection system installed that quickly traces each fault back to its source.

The second element in lean production is product development. Lean production, the authors say, is quicker than mass production. The reason lies in basic differences in construction methods.

• Project leadership works on the *susha* system. The *susha* is the team leader, a position of great power in Japanese businesses. In mass-production companies the system is very different. The position of the development manager is too weak to push projects through. Top management often overrides his or her decisions.

- The *susha* creates a small, close-knit team, whose members are drawn from various specialist departments and who remain in contact with them. For the duration of the development project, however, they remain wholly under the control of the *susha*. In mass-production business, development teams consist of individuals on short-term secondment from specialist departments.

- Communication too is different, say the authors. In Western mass production, it is only at a late stage in the project that there is any co-ordination of different interests. In Japan, team members sign formal undertakings to do exactly what the team as a whole has decided. Any conflicts therefore show up at the very beginning of the crisis.

The third element in lean production highlighted by Womack and his co-authors is co-ordination of the supply chain. In the lean, *susha*-led product development process, all the necessary suppliers are carefully selected not on the basis of their bids, but on the basis of earlier relationships and proven performance.

Customer relations form the fourth element. Japanese car manufacturers, the authors point out, have comparatively few sales channels. These are differentiated in terms of their appealing to different types of purchaser. The aim is to establish a direct link between the production system and the customer. Employees in the sales channels are loaned to the development teams, and the dealers have a close and long-lasting relationship with the manufacturer.

The fifth major element in lean production, according to the authors, is the way the lean company is managed. Various framework conditions have to exist:

- there must be money available to finance development projects that last several years
- career ladders must be available for qualified and motivated employees
- decentralised activities must be co-ordinated worldwide

CONTEXT

The MIT investigation was at the time the most comprehensive study of a single industry ever carried out.

While it showed the undoubted successes of lean production, it also claimed to have uncovered certain deficiencies in the concept. Lean production, it suggests, overemphasises the aspects of savings and mechanisation and neglects categories such as know-how and innovation. Lean management brings about a short-term improvement in efficiency, but not a long-term increase in productivity. In addition, the authors argue, it is unsuited to dismantling complexity. Anyone, for example, who wishes to reduce the complexity of serialised production steps through individualised manufacture must understand ever more expansive processes in their entirety. In theory, the highly innovative and flexible business organisation with no hierarchy may count as the company of the future, but in everyday practice the weaknesses of lean production are clearly apparent.

THE BEST SOURCES OF HELP

Womack, James P., Daniel T. Jones, and Daniel Roos. *The Machine That Changed the World: The Story of Lean Production*. London: HarperBusiness, 1991.

Made in Japan
by Akio Morita

Made in Japan is the story of Sony and reflects the changes that took place in post-war business history. Morita and Sony's story parallels the rebirth of Japan as an industrial power. When Sony was first attempting to make inroads into Western markets, Japanese products were sneered at as being of the lowest quality. Surmounting that obstacle was a substantial business achievement.

GETTING STARTED

This book charts the re-emergence of Japan as an industrial heavyweight. It helped change the image of 'Made in Japan' from shoddy goods to high quality. Sony invented new markets with a pioneering spirit by bringing out product after product, innovation after innovation. Its most famous success was the Walkman, the development of which was based on instinct, not research. Analysis and education do not necessarily help you to reach the best business decisions; sometimes understanding must come before logic. 'Japanese people tend to be much better adjusted to the notion of work, any kind of work, as honourable,' says Morita. Recruitment is 'management's risk and management's responsibility'.

CONTRIBUTION

The Japanese renaissance. Morita and Sony's story parallels the rebirth of Japan as a major industrial power.

They helped change the image of 'Made in Japan' from something shoddy to something reputable and desirable.

> Sony's most famous success was the Walkman, the brainchild of Morita.

At the time when Sony first tried to break into the Western electronics market, Japanese products were considered fifth-rate. Morita helped Sony not only to overcome this prejudice but to reverse it.

Inventing new markets. Morita and Sony's gift was to invent new markets with a pioneering spirit. 'Sony is a pioneer and never intends to follow others,' says Morita.

'Through progress, Sony wants to serve the whole world. It will always seek the unknown. Sony has a principle of respecting and encouraging one's ability . . . and always tries to bring out the best in a person. This is the vital force of Sony.'

The power of innovation. While companies such as Matsushita were inspired followers, Sony set the pace with product after product, innovation after innovation.

Sony brought the world the hand-held video camera, the first home video recorder, and the floppy disk.

The blemishes on its record were the Betamax video format, which it failed to license, and colour television systems.

Instinct and research. Sony's most famous success was the Walkman, the brainchild of Morita. Morita noticed that young people liked listening to music wherever they went. He put two and two together and made—a Walkman.

He did not believe that any amount of market research could have told the company that this would be successful.

'The public does not know what is possible, we do,' he has famously said.

Analysis doesn't always pay. Brilliant marketing by instinct was no mere accident.

Morita believes that, if you go through life convinced that your way is always best, all the new ideas in the world will pass you by.

Analysis and education do not necessarily help you to reach the best business decisions. You can be totally rational with a machine but if you work with people, sometimes understanding has to come before logic.

Japanese culture encourages the work ethic. Morita has emphasised the cultural differences in Japanese attitudes towards work. The Japanese tend to have a much stronger work ethic, and see work as an honourable occupation.

Morita believes that management has ultimate responsibility for its staff. If a recession is looming, profit should be sacrificed rather than employees be laid off.

CONTEXT

The book tells the story of the rise of Sony and it reflects the rise of Japan as a post-war industrial power. It looks at the role of quality and innovation as key factors in the success of Japanese companies. Many Western authors have focused on the role of quality in Japan, particularly influential people like Deming and Juran.

Richard Pascale and Anthony Athos look at the phenomenon in *The Art of Japanese Management*.

Morita and Sony took the attitude that global markets were important from the outset. Ken Ohmae writes on that subject from the Japanese perspective in *The Borderless World*.

THE BEST SOURCES OF HELP

Morita, Akio. *Made in Japan*. New York: Dutton, 1986.

Management Teams: Why They Succeed or Fail
by R. Meredith Belbin

Effective teamworking is now seen as key to the success of all types of organisation. Meredith Belbin identified the characteristics of people needed to make a successful team. His recommendations are still used, and the book can therefore help anyone who needs to develop a team.

GETTING STARTED

Corporations have been preoccupied with the qualifications, experience, and achievement of individuals—but it is not the individual but the team that is the instrument of sustained and enduring success in management.

> **Unsuccessful teams can be improved by analysing their composition and making appropriate changes.**

Team performance is influenced by the kinds of people making up a group, and testing indicates that certain combinations of personality types perform more successfully than others. Nine archetypal functions make up an ideal team—plant, co-ordinator, shaper, teamworker, completer, implementer, resource investigator, specialist, and monitor evaluator. Unsuccessful teams can be improved by analysing their composition and making appropriate changes.

CONTRIBUTION

The preoccupation with individuals. Corporations have been preoccupied with the qualifications, experience, and achievement of individuals, and have applied themselves to their selection, development, training, motivation, and promotion. However commentators believe that the ideal individual for a given job cannot be found, because he or she cannot exist. It is not the individual but the team that is the instrument of sustained and enduring success in management.

The contribution of individuals in teams. Belbin was interested in group performance and how it might be influenced by the kinds of people making up a group. He asked members engaged in a business school exercise to undertake a personality and critical-thinking test and, based on the test results, discovered that certain combinations of personality types performed more successfully than others.

Belbin realised that given adequate knowledge of the personal characteristics and abilities of team members through psychometric testing, he could forecast the likely success or failure of particular teams. Unsuccessful teams can be improved by analysing their team design shortcomings and making appropriate changes.

Identifying team characteristics. A questionnaire completed by team members was analysed to show the functional roles the managers thought they performed in a team. From this research, Belbin identified nine archetypal functions which go to make up an ideal team.

Successful team composition.

- Plant—creative, imaginative, unorthodox; solves difficult problems. Bad at dealing with ordinary people.

- Co-ordinator—mature, confident, trusting; a good chairman; clarifies goals, promotes decision-making. Not necessarily the cleverest.
- Shaper—dynamic, outgoing, highly strung; challenges, pressurises, finds ways round obstacles. Prone to bursts of temper.
- Teamworker—social, mild, perceptive, accommodating; listens, builds, averts friction. Indecisive in crunch situations.
- Completer—painstaking, conscientious, anxious; searches out errors; delivers on time. May worry unduly; reluctant to delegate.
- Implementer—disciplined, reliable, conservative, efficient; turns ideas into actions. Somewhat inflexible.
- Resource investigator—extrovert, enthusiastic, communicative; explores opportunities. Loses interest after initial enthusiasm.
- Specialist—single-minded, self-starting, dedicated; brings knowledge or skills in rare supply. Contributes only on narrow front.
- Monitor evaluator—sober, strategic, discerning. Sees all options, makes judgments. Lacks drive and ability to inspire others.

CONTEXT

The explosion of interest in teamworking during the last decade has prompted greater interest in Belbin's work. The teamworking categories he identified have proved robust and are still used in a variety of organisations. Gary Hamel commented, 'High-performing companies increasingly believe that teams, rather than business units or individuals, are the basic building blocks of a successful organisation. Belbin deserves much credit for helping us understand the basic building blocks of successful teams.'

Antony Jay commented, 'Corporations have been preoccupied with the qualifications, experience, and achievement of individuals . . . it is not the individual but the team that is the instrument of sustained and enduring success in management.'

THE BEST SOURCES OF HELP

Belbin, Meredith R. *Management Teams: Why They Succeed or Fail*. Oxford: Butterworth-Heinemann, 1984.

The Managerial Grid
by Robert Blake and Jane Mouton

The book made an important contribution to the measurement of management performance. It challenged existing theories and provided organisations with a grid for assessing the types of manager they needed for different positions.

GETTING STARTED

In the early 1960s there was a sizeable gap in management theorising, especially in terms of leadership and motivation. Douglas McGregor's Theory X and Y had a number of shortcomings in reality, and Blake and Mouton found that a management performance model with three axes was a more accurate representation of reality. The important axes were concern for productivity, concern for people, and motivation. Accurate measurement is important because of managers' capacity for self-deception.

CONTRIBUTION

Challenging management performance theories. During consultancy work for Exxon, Blake and Mouton concluded that there was a sizeable gap in management theorising, especially in terms of leadership and motivation. Popular among theories of the time was that of Douglas McGregor and his motivational extremes of X and Y. However, Blake and Mouton believed that many behaviours and motivations fell in the middle of these extremes. Theories X and Y were only a part of the overall picture of organisational behaviour.

A new model of management performance. Blake and Mouton's conclusion was that a model with three axes was a more accurate representation of reality. The three crucial axes they determined were: concern for productivity, concern for people, and motivation.

Concern for production and people were both measured on a scale of one to nine, with nine being high. The reason a people axis was necessary is that managers achieve things indirectly. They don't produce nuts and bolts themselves, rather they organise others so that the production line can be productive.

Motivation was measured on a scale from negative (driven by fear) to positive (driven by desire).

Flaws in performance measurement. Blake and Mouton found that, when left to rank themselves, some 80% of people give themselves a 9.9 rating. Once this is discussed and considered, this figure is routinely reduced to 20%. Given the capacity for self-deception, it is little wonder that change programmes fail.

Key management styles. From the grid emerge five key manager styles:

- 1 (production); 1 (people): do nothing manager. The leader exerts a minimum of effort to get the work done, with very little concern for people or production.
- 1 (production); 9 (people): labelled the Country Club Manager. This manager pays a lot of attention to people, but little to production. Can be seen in small firms that have cornered the market and some public sector organisations.
- 9 (production); 1(people): this manager emphasises production and minimises the influence of human factors.

- 5 (production); 5 (people): organisation man who diligently fosters mundanity.
- 9 (production); 9 (people): managerial nirvana. The ultimate, with an emphasis on team working and team building. Personal and organisational goals are in alignment; motivation high.

CONTEXT

When Blake and Mouton examined the behaviour of people at Exxon, they concluded that there was a sizeable gap in management theorising, especially in terms of leadership and motivation. They found that many behaviours and motivations fell in the middle of Douglas McGregor's X and Y extremes. They observed that Theories X and Y were only a part of the overall picture of organisational behaviour.

Blake and Mouton's conclusion was that a model with three axes—concern for productivity, concern for people, and motivation—was a more accurate representation of reality.

THE BEST SOURCES OF HELP

Blake, Robert, and Jane Mouton. *The Managerial Grid*. Houston, Texas: Gulf Publishing, 1964.

Managing
by Harold Geneen

Geneen joined the board of ITT in 1959 and set about turning the company into the world's greatest conglomerate. Along the way he became, according to *BusinessWeek*, the legendary conglomerateur. The book relates the management style and culture that helped ITT to achieve that success. In particular, it highlights the importance of knowing the numbers in minute detail.

GETTING STARTED

Geneen's success was based on knowing every single figure possible. He did not invent the conglomerate, but he had an obsessive belief that it could be made to work. ITT bought 350 companies and appeared to be a managerial nightmare—Geneen made the nightmare work by fanatical attention to detail.

He only micro-managed the numbers; the people were generally overlooked. However, his success meant that people followed his methods without question. Over 200 days a year were devoted to management meetings held throughout the world.

Success was based on amassing all the facts so that decisions became self-evident—Geneen wanted no surprises.

CONTRIBUTION

A rigorous management style. Geneen was the archetypal workaholic. His style was unforgiving, built on a degree of intellectual rigour that bordered on ruthlessness. He pinned his managerial faith on hard work and knowing every single figure possible. For Geneen, detail was everything. Once an accountant always an accountant.

Making conglomerates work. The conglomerate was not Geneen's invention. But he brought an obsessive belief that it could be made to work. He believed that ITT could manage any business in any industry if it knew the figures.

His career with ITT, described in *Managing*, is a pageant of acquisition and diversification. Under Geneen, ITT bought companies as casually as a billionaire buys trinkets. One acquisition funded another. ITT bought 350 companies, including Avis Rent-A-Car, Sheraton Hotels, Continental Baking, and Levitt & Sons, among many others. By 1970, ITT was composed of 400 separate companies operating in 70 countries. With such huge numbers of companies in such vastly different fields, ITT was hopelessly diversified. To contemporary eyes, the company was a managerial nightmare. Yet, Geneen made the nightmare work by fanatical attention to detail.

Managing the numbers. Geneen only micro-managed the numbers; the people were generally overlooked.

'The very fact that you go over the progression of those numbers week after week, month after month, means that you have strengthened your memory and your familiarity with them so that you retain in your mind a vivid composite picture of what is going on in your company,' he wrote.

Management culture. Geneen inculcated a remarkable culture within ITT. His success meant that people followed his methods with the unquestioning faith of true believers.

Between 1959 and 1977, ITT's sales went from $765 million to nearly $28 billion. Earnings went from $29 million to $562 million, and earnings per share rose from $1 to $4.20.

As part of Geneen's formula, over 50 executives flew every month to Brussels to spend four days poring over the figures. It was calculated that over 200 days a year were devoted to management meetings held throughout the world.

> 'The highest art of professional management requires the literal ability to smell a real fact from all others,' Geneen believed.

Success based on facts. The point was to amass all the facts available so that the decisions became self-evident. If you knew everything, you would then know exactly what to do. Facts were the lifeblood of the expanding ITT.

'The highest art of professional management requires the literal ability to smell a real fact from all others,' Geneen believed. 'Managers should have the temerity, intellectual curiosity, guts and/or plain impoliteness, if necessary, to be sure that what they do have is indeed what we will call an unshakable fact.'

Geneen wanted no surprises. He also hoped to make people as predictable and controllable as the capital resources they must manage.

CONTEXT

Much of Geneen's managerial philosophy and practice would appear to be anathema to the contemporary executive.

However, his fundamentalist style of management remains. Management consultants, for example, continue to trade their rational models—pour in all the figures you can find and the right decision will emerge. There is still a temptation to manage by numbers rather than through and with people.

On the positive side, Geneen can be said to have elevated management to a new level. His system required a team of highly numerate, professional managers who had to take responsibility.

The Geneen legacy is most notably evident in the conglomerates that continue to survive. General Electric, under Jack Welch and now Jeff Immelt, may be the most lauded corporation of our age, but it is also a conglomerate with interests in everything from financial services to nuclear reactors and washing machines. Harold Geneen would have regarded the survival of such companies as vindication of his methods.

Others point to the decline of ITT on his departure as a true measure of the long-term validity of Geneen's approach to management.

THE BEST SOURCES OF HELP
Geneen, Harold. *Managing*. New York: Doubleday, 1985.

Managing Across Borders
by Christopher Bartlett and Sumantra Ghoshal

Bartlett and Ghoshal map out the new business reality of globalisation and the kinds of organisations a 'borderless' business world requires. The book is regarded as a classic, and has helped many companies to focus on the type of organisation they need for global success.

GETTING STARTED

According to the authors, changing patterns of international management have led to a new global model, in which enabling innovation and disseminating knowledge in globally dispersed organisations is a major challenge.

A number of organisational forms are now prevalent among global companies: multinational firms offer a high degree of local responsiveness; global firms offer scale efficiencies and cost advantages; international firms have the ability to transfer knowledge and expertise to overseas environments that are less advanced; and the transnational firm combines local responsiveness with global efficiency and the ability to transfer know-how better, cheaper, and faster.

Integration and the creation of coherent systems for value delivery are the new drivers of organisational structure.

CONTRIBUTION

Changing patterns of international management. The traditional international management model was simply to export your own way of doing things elsewhere, and companies believed that global operations were simply a means of achieving economies of scale. Local nuances were overlooked in the quest for global standardisation: global and local were mutually exclusive. In general, organisations either gave local operations autonomy or controlled them rigidly from a distance.

> **Global presence with local responsiveness is now key.**

A new global model. Global presence with local responsiveness is now key. Companies face the challenge of enabling innovation and disseminating knowledge in globally-dispersed organisations. Bartlett and Ghoshal identify a number of organisational forms prevalent among global companies.

Multinational companies. The multinational or multidomestic organisation offers a very high degree of local responsiveness. It is a decentralised federation of local businesses, linked together through personal control by expatriates who occupy key positions abroad.

Global companies. Global organisations offer scale efficiencies and cost advantages. With global scale facilities, the global organisation seeks to produce standardised products. It is often centralised in its home country, with overseas operations considered as delivery pipelines to tap into global market opportunities. There is tight control of strategic decisions, resources, and information by the global hub.

International companies. International companies have the ability to transfer knowledge and expertise to overseas environments that are less advanced. They are co-ordinated federations of local businesses, controlled by sophisticated management systems and corporate employees. The attitude of the parent company tends to be parochial, fostered by the superior know-how at the centre of the organisation.

The transnational companies. Global competition is forcing many businesses to shift to a fourth model, which they call the transnational. This organisation combines local responsiveness with global efficiency and the ability to transfer know-how better, cheaper, and faster. The transnational company is made up of a network of specialised or differentiated units, which focus on managing integrative linkages between local businesses as well as with the centre. The subsidiary becomes a distinctive asset, rather than simply an arm of the parent company. Manufacturing and technology development are located wherever it makes sense, and there is an explicit focus on leveraging local know-how in order to exploit worldwide opportunities.

The importance of integration. Integration and the creation of a coherent system for value delivery are the new drivers of organisational structure. Companies cannot be left to their own devices, but have to be brought within the fold—while also keeping in touch with their local business environment.

What binds the companies together is a set of explicit or implicit shared values and beliefs that can be developed and managed effectively. There are three techniques crucial to forming an organisation's psychology: 1) clear, shared understanding of the company's mission and objectives; 2) the actions and behaviour of senior managers are vital as examples and statements of commitment; 3) corporate personnel policies must be geared up to develop a multidimensional and flexible organisation process.

CONTEXT

Managing Across Borders is one of the few business books of recent years that deserves recognition as a classic. When it was published in 1989, understanding of globalisation was in its infancy. With its emphasis on networking across the global organisation and transferring learning and knowledge, the book effectively set the organisational agenda for a decade and created a new organisational model.

Bartlett and Ghoshal effectively signal the demise of the divisional organisation—which gives divisions independence—first developed by Alfred Sloan of General Motors.

THE BEST SOURCES OF HELP

Bartlett, Christopher, and Sumantra Ghoshal. *Managing Across Borders*. Boston, Massachusetts: Harvard Business School Press, 1989.

Managing on the Edge
by Richard Pascale

This book challenges traditional management thinking, which Pascale feels is too complacent for an environment driven by change. He sets out a new perspective for 'contention management' which seeks to harness the conflicting energies in an organisation to achieve positive change. The book set the management agenda for a decade after its publication.

GETTING STARTED

According to Pascale, US managerial history is largely inward-focused and self-congratulatory. Change is a fact of business life, but complacency can cause problems. It is essential to change the management perspective. The incremental approach to change is no longer effective. The new emphasis should be on asking questions. Successful organisations undergo continual renewal by constantly asking questions.

Four factors drive stagnation and renewal in organisations: fit, split, contend, transcend.

'Contention management' is essential to orchestrate tensions that arise between these four factors. Forces locked in opposition can be used to generate inquiry and adaptation and the manager's job is to maintain a constructive level of debate.

CONTRIBUTION

The dangers of management complacency. Nothing fails like success. Great strengths are inevitably the root of weakness. Of the companies listed in *Fortune 500* of 1985, 143 had been dropped by 1990. In the author's view, US managerial history is largely inward-focused and self-congratulatory.

The need for change. According to Pascale, change is a fact of business life. We are ill-equipped to deal with it and the traditional approach to managing change is no longer applicable. The incremental approach to change is effective when the goal is to obtain more of the same thing. Historically, that has been sufficient. The United States' advantages of plentiful resources, geographical isolation, and absence of serious global competition defined a league in which Americans competed with each other and everyone played by the same rules.

Growth of management fads. There have been more than two dozen management fads since the 1950s. A dozen emerged in the five years prior to 1990.

Driving stagnation and renewal. Four factors drive stagnation and renewal in organisations:
- fit—pertains to an organisation's internal consistency (unity)
- split—describes a variety of techniques for breaking a bigger organisation into smaller units and providing them with a stronger sense of ownership and identity (plurality)
- contend—refers to a management process that harnesses (rather than suppresses) the contradictions that are inevitable by-products of organisations (duality)
- transcend—alerts people to the higher order of complexity that successfully managing the renewal process entails (vitality)

Changing management perspective. Pascale calls for a fundamental shift in perspective.

Managerial behaviour is based on the assumption that people should rationally order the behaviour of those they manage. That mindset needs to be challenged.

Orderly answers are no longer appropriate. The new emphasis should be on asking questions. Strategic planning, at best, is about posing questions, more than attempting to answer them.

Successful organisations undergo a continual process of renewal. Central to achieving this is a willingness to ask questions constantly and to harness conflict for the corporate good, through systems that encourage questioning.

Companies must become engines of inquiry.

Contention management. Managers are ill-equipped to deal with the contention that arises when fundamental questions are posed.

Contention management is essential to orchestrate tensions that arise. Around 50% of the time when contention arises, it is smoothed over and avoided.

The forces that we have historically regarded as locked in opposition can be viewed as apparent opposites that generate inquiry and adaptive responses.

Each point of view represents a facet of reality, and these realities tend to challenge one another and raise questions.

If we redefine the manager's job as maintaining a constructive level of debate, we are, in effect, holding the organisation in the question. This leads to identifying blind spots and working around obstacles.

Truth—personally and organisationally—lies in the openness of vigorous debate.

Organisations are, in the last analysis, interactions among people.

CONTEXT

Managing on the Edge presents a formidably researched and argued challenge to complacency and timidity.

Pascale criticises Peters and Waterman's *In Search of Excellence* saying, 'Simply identifying attributes of success is like identifying attributes of people in excellent health during the age of the bubonic plague'.

Passions and obsessions frequently degenerate into simplistic formulae—for example, acronyms such as KISS (Keep it simple, stupid).

Managing on the Edge set the tone for much of the management thinking of the decade. Its emphasis on the need for constant change has since been developed by Pascale. He now argues that the issue of managing the way we change is a competence rather than an episodic necessity.

Influential critic Gary Hamel commented, 'In *Managing on the Edge*, Richard Pascale provides a number of useful observations on the sources of corporate vitality. One of the things I've always admired about Richard Pascale is that he focuses not on tools and techniques, but on principles and paradigms. While management bookshelves groan with the weight of simplistic how-to books (for example, *The One Minute Manager*), Pascale challenges managers to think, and to think deeply. Pascale forces managers to deconstruct the normative models on which they base their beliefs and actions.'

THE BEST SOURCES OF HELP

Pascale, Richard. *Managing on the Edge*. New York: Viking Books, 1990.

Managing Transitions
by William Bridges

This book focuses on the human aspects of change management. Change is a situation. What the author calls 'transition' is the psychological process people go through to come to terms with change. The book stresses that change involves people and that managers and leaders must help people deal with the transition. The author shows, through practical examples, how managers should make people feel comfortable during a period of change and offers advice, as well as case studies, on the best way to achieve this.

GETTING STARTED

The author believes that many companies try to impose change, but fail to manage the transition. Transition means recognising that things cannot be the same after an organisational change. People must get used to the new ways of doing things. They do this by going through a 'neutral zone' before emerging into a new beginning.

CONTRIBUTION

Letting go. The author explains that transition begins with a process of 'letting go'. However, this is a process that many people in an organisation find difficult. They are comfortable with familiar, proven ways of doing things and they fear the unknown.

> Communication is vital, claims Bridges, at this and every stage of transition.

The first stage, he suggests, is to identify who is losing what, by analysing what is going to change and identifying the impact on different groups of people. Managers should be aware that people will react in different ways. They should acknowledge the effect of the change on people and, if necessary, make some compensation for their loss. Managers should also acknowledge what was good about the existing processes and emphasise the element of continuity in the most important aspects of the new proposals.

The neutral zone. Bridges believes that the 'neutral zone' is the most difficult part of the transition process, because this is where people's uncertainties and anxieties about change are most acute. He advises managers to give people a clear sense of direction, as well as support to help them through this difficult stage. Moving from an existing routine to a new one can prove difficult without the right help.

Bridges argues that managers can reduce the damaging impact of the neutral zone by setting short-term targets that are achievable. He also believes that they should not expect or demand exceptional performance during a period of transition.

Communication is vital, claims Bridges, at this and every stage of transition. It is also important to encourage creativity during the neutral zone, particularly when there is less pressure on people to perform. Creativity can help to overcome the sense of loss people feel about leaving old routines behind.

New beginnings. When people move to the new system, uncertainties can remain, according to Bridges. There is always a risk in new ways of doing things. It is therefore essential to set out a clear plan with timings and targets. Managers should ensure that everyone has a clear part to play in the new system.

He recommends clear, regular communications to explain the aims and rationale for the new system. A vision of the future can help to paint a clear picture for people in the organisation. To reinforce the new beginning, Bridges recommends that companies should create a new identity and celebrate success.

The book also includes advice for readers on how to take care of themselves during a period of transition.

CONTEXT

This book is one of a number that deal with the subject of managing the process of change. John Kotter's *Leading Change* (Harvard Business School Press, 1996), for example, reflects on the themes of leadership, vision, and communication.

Bridges' book looks at the human perspective of change and includes a great deal of practical advice on ways of dealing with the personal issues that people face. It also contains a number of useful studies, case histories, and exercises that could be used in workshops.

As such, the book may be more suitable for people in human resources or line management roles. Senior executives who are concerned with the strategic implications of change might find more value in an author such as Kotter.

THE BEST SOURCES OF HELP

Bridges, William. *Transitions: Making Sense of Life's Changes.* London: Nicholas Brealey, 1996.

Marketing Management
by Philip Kotler

Kotler is one of the leading authorities on marketing. *Marketing Management* is the definitive marketing textbook, covering the full scope of contemporary marketing. It is the most widely used marketing book in business schools.

GETTING STARTED

Marketing continues to evolve and expand its scope exponentially. The emphasis is shifting from transaction-oriented marketing to relationship marketing—retaining customer loyalty through continually satisfying their needs. Marketing management is the process of planning and executing functions that satisfy customer and organisational objectives.

Customer-delivered value is the difference between total customer value and total customer cost.

Organisations encounter three common hurdles to marketing orientation: organised resistance, slow learning, and fast forgetting.

CONTRIBUTION

Marketing continues to evolve. The marketing discipline is redeveloping its assumptions, concepts, skills, tools, and systems for making sound business decisions.

Marketers must know when to:

- cultivate large markets or niche markets
- launch new brands or extend existing brand names
- push or pull products through distribution
- protect the domestic market or penetrate aggressively into foreign markets
- add more benefits to the offer or reduce the price
- expand or contract budgets for salesforce, advertising, and other marketing tools

The scope of marketing is expanding exponentially, as is demonstrated by the size and scope of *Marketing Management*. Its contents range over:

- industry and competitor analysis
- designing strategies for the global marketplace
- managing product life cycle strategies
- retailing, wholesaling, and physical-distribution systems

The change to relationship marketing. The emphasis is shifting from transaction-oriented marketing to relationship marketing. Good customers are an asset which, when well managed and served, will return a handsome lifetime income stream.

In the intensely competitive marketplace, the company must retain customer loyalty through continually satisfying their needs in a superior way.

Defining the role of marketing. Marketing is the social and managerial process by which individuals and groups obtain what they need and want through creating, offering, and exchanging products of value with others. A market consists of all the potential customers sharing a particular need or want, who might be willing to exchange something in order to satisfy that need or want.

Marketing management is the process of planning and executing the conception, pricing, promotion, and distribution of goods, services, and ideas, to create exchanges with target groups that satisfy customer and organisational objectives.

Analysing products. A product is anything that can be offered to a market for attention, acquisition, use, or consumption that might satisfy a want or need. It has five levels:

- the core benefit (marketers must see themselves as benefit providers)
- the generic product
- the expected product (the normal expectations the customer has of the product)
- the augmented product (the additional services or benefits added to the product)
- the potential product (all the augmentations and transformations that this product might undergo in the future)

Customer value. Customer-delivered value is the difference between total customer value and total customer cost. Total customer value is the bundle of benefits customers expect from a given product or service. It consists of product value, service value, personnel value, and image value. Total customer cost consists of monetary price, time cost, energy cost, and psychic cost. Combined, the two produce customer-delivered value.

Barriers to marketing orientation. In order to become marketing oriented, organisations encounter three hurdles:

- organised resistance—entrenched functional behaviour tends to oppose increased emphasis on marketing, as it is seen as undermining functional power bases.
- slow learning—most companies only slowly embrace the marketing concept.
- fast forgetting—companies that embrace marketing concepts tend, over time, to lose touch with the principles. Various US companies have sought to establish their products in Europe with scant knowledge of different marketplaces.

Achieving market leadership. Good companies will meet needs; great companies will create markets. Market leadership is gained by envisioning new products, services, lifestyles, and ways to raise living standards. There is a vast difference between companies offering 'me-too' products and those creating previously unimagined product and service values.

Ultimately, marketing at its best is about value creation and raising the world's living standards.

CONTEXT

Marketing Management is the definitive marketing textbook. Tightly argued and all-encompassing, its content has been expanded and updated regularly. Its 11th edition (2002) maps out the emerging challenges to all those involved in marketing.

The very size and scope of *Marketing Management* demonstrates the exponential expansion of marketing. Gary Hamel commented: 'There are few MBA graduates alive who have not ploughed through Kotler's encyclopaedic textbook on marketing, and have not benefited enormously from doing so. I know of no other business author who covers his (or her) territory with such comprehensiveness, clarity, and authority as Phil Kotler. I can think of few other books, even within the vaunted company of this volume, whose insights would be of more practical benefit to the average company than those found in *Marketing Management*.'

THE BEST SOURCES OF HELP

Kotler, Philip. *Marketing Management: Analysis, Planning, Implementation, and Control.* 11th ed. Harlow: Prentice Hall, 2002.

Maverick!
by Ricardo Semler

Maverick! describes a Brazilian success story that is genuinely extraordinary, and the ideas that underlie the success are so revolutionary it is amazing that anyone had the audacity to put them into practice (the workers hire and fire the bosses and set their own wages). In addition, the book is written by the man who had the ideas, carried through the revolution, and lived with the results—in other words it is a book about revolution written by a revolutionary, as well as that comparatively rare thing: a book about management written by a practising manager.

GETTING STARTED

Ricardo Semler took over the family business, an engineering company that he renamed Semco, from his father in 1980. The company was unexceptional in both its performance and its management.

Semler immediately set about restructuring it in a dramatic and revolutionary fashion. He fired 60% of the company's existing top management in a single day. His father's management style had been formal, traditional, and autocratic. His own was informal, unprecedented, and democratic. And he turned the standard hierarchical form of organisation on its head.

Maverick! is his own account of what he did and why he did it.

CONTRIBUTION

Democracy in the workplace. In these days of the new world order, says Semler, almost everyone believes people have a right to vote for those who lead them, at least in the public sector. But democracy has yet to penetrate the workplace. Dictators and despots are alive and well in offices and factories all over the world.

His 'revolution' consisted of introducing democracy into the workplace—and in a particularly full-blooded and thoroughgoing way. He was particularly impressed by the fact that, when the company got into trouble because the Brazilian economy went into a severe recession in the early 1990s, the workforce made a substantial and very responsible contribution to keeping it afloat. If its employees were sufficiently committed to be willing to seek out imaginative solutions to the company's problems in a crisis, he asked, why couldn't their ingenuity be harnessed all the time?

Democratic structure. Semler based his revolution on three values:
- employee participation
- profit sharing
- open information systems

Semco now has just four grades of staff.

The job of chief executive is handled by six senior managers for six months at a time. Managers set their own salaries and bonuses, and are evaluated by those who work for them. Employees are organised in autonomous teams. They decide their own working hours, set quotas, and improve products and processes. They can if they wish turn the teams into 'satellite organisations', able to make use of the resources of Semco in return for a share of their profits.

Reducing dependence on individuals. The company is organised in such a way as not to depend too much on any individual, especially Semler himself. He takes it as a point of pride that twice on his return from long trips his office had been moved, and each time it got smaller.

> The leader's role is that of a catalyst— to create an environment in which others make decisions.

Success means the leader should not make the decisions. The leader's role is that of a catalyst—to create an environment in which others make decisions.

CONTEXT

Maverick! is one of the most surprising business bestsellers of recent times. Before it was published, the idea that managerial lessons might be learnt from a Brazilian corporation was risible. Now *Maverick!* has sold a million copies, and Semler's revolutionary ideas and unique managerial style are being studied, thought about, and fought about by managers throughout the world.

Though Semler's message has received massive media attention, it is perhaps not surprising that few have been brave enough to follow Semco's lead.

Former BTR chief, Sir Owen Green, is typical of the dismissive reaction from mainstream business leaders, claiming that 'Semler's not a maverick; he is an eccentric'.

Charles Handy is more positive: 'The way that Ricardo Semler runs his company is impossible; except that it works, and works splendidly for everyone.'

Maverick! is an exception to the general run of books by successful executives. There is none of the usual corporate heroism but, instead, an acceptance that management is concerned with enabling others rather than controlling them.

Gary Hamel commented, 'Almost none of the great management books that populate this volume were written by practising managers. Why is this? Perhaps it is because managers seldom have the time, or the perspective, to generalise from their own experiences. Books by Lee Iacocca, Harold Geneen, and other management icons are typically as idiosyncratic as they are entertaining. While the managerial solutions espoused by Ricardo Semler may not be universally applicable, the set of beliefs that animate his particular approach are clearly laid out and can be debated on their own merits.'

THE BEST SOURCES OF HELP

Semler, Ricardo. *Maverick!*. London: Random House Business Books, 2001.

Megatrends
by John Naisbitt

Megatrends was written in 1982 before the technology revolution took hold. It attempts to predict the key changes in business and society. Naisbitt correctly anticipated a number of factors such as globalisation, empowerment, and the rise of an information economy.

GETTING STARTED

According to the author, we have changed to an economy based on the creation and distribution of information. Speed is a competitive weapon.

We must now acknowledge that we are part of a global economy. The bigger the world economy, the more powerful its smallest player—and in small organisations, we have rediscovered the ability to act innovatively and to achieve results from the bottom up. Big bureaucratic organisations can be beaten. Economies of scale are giving way to economies of scope. The acceleration of technological progress has created an urgent need for a return to human scale.

Empowerment, with responsibility, has become more important for every individual in an organisation. We are more self-reliant and less hierarchical. Society is moving towards much longer-term time frames.

CONTRIBUTION

Towards the information economy. Although we continue to think we live in an industrial society, we have in fact changed to an economy based on the creation and distribution of information.

In the early 1980s however, traditional issues, such as production methods, still held sway. The technological possibilities in information exchange and transfer were contemplated by a small group in laboratories on the US west coast.

Technology with a human scale. We are moving in the dual directions of high tech/high touch, matching each new technology with a compensatory human response. Heart transplants led to new interest in family doctors and neighbourhood clinics; jet aircraft resulted in more face-to-face meetings.

High touch is about getting back to a human scale. All change is local and bottom-up. If you keep track of local events, you can see the shifting patterns.

You can't stop technological progress, but by the same token, you can hardly go wrong with a high-touch response. FedEx has all the reliability and efficiency of modern electronics, but its success is built on a form of high-touch hand delivery.

The emergence of a global economy. We no longer have the luxury of operating within an isolated, self-sufficient, national economic system. We must now acknowledge that we are part of a global economy.

US business leaders have begun to let go of the idea that the United States is and must remain the world's industrial leader as we move on to other tasks.

The global paradox is that the bigger the world economy, the more powerful its smallest player.

A longer time frame. We are moving away from a society governed by short-term consider-ations and rewards to one which deals with things in much longer-term time frames.

The growth of empowerment. In cities and states, in small organisations and subdivisions, we have rediscovered the ability to act innovatively and to achieve results from the bottom up.

Naisbitt anticipated the fashion in the late 1980s and early 1990s for empowerment with responsibility being spread more evenly throughout organisations, rather than centred on a small group of managers.

Greater self-reliance. We are shifting from institutional help to more self-reliance in all aspects of our lives.

Trends in working patterns, such as employability, suggest that this is becoming the case for a select few professionals with marketable skills.

Changing framework of democracy. We are discovering that the framework of representa-tive democracy has become obsolete in an era of instantaneously shared information.

Alvin Toffler was suggesting this in his 1970 book *Future Shock*, though there are few signs of reform.

Informal networks replacing hierarchy. We are giving up our dependence on hierarchical structures in favour of informal networks. This will be especially important to the business community.

This has become one of the great trends of the last decade as networks are developed in a bewildering variety of ways—with suppliers, between competitors, internally, and globally.

Technology has enabled networks never previously anticipated, with important repercus-sions. When everyone hears about everything at the same time, we all know that everyone is equally well-informed.

Speed as a competitive weapon. Linked to this is the entire question of speed, which Naisbitt identified early on as a competitive weapon.

Economies of scale are giving way to economies of scope, finding the right size for synergy, market flexibility, and above all, speed.

More choice for society. From a narrow 'either/or' society with a limited range of personal choices, we are exploding into a free-wheeling, multiple-option society.

The power of small businesses. Naisbitt championed the role of small business in generat-ing the wealth of the future. Small companies, right down to the individual, can beat big bureaucratic companies every time.

Unless big companies reconstitute themselves as a collection of small companies, they will just continue to go out of business.

It's the small companies who are creating the global company.

CONTEXT

Megatrends identified ten critical restructurings. Some have proved accurate predictions of what has happened in intervening years, others have proved less accurate.

Naisbitt predicted the rise of the information economy when the technology was still a laboratory product and he identified the emergence of factors such as globalisation and empowerment.

Naisbitt's predictions can be compared with those of Alvin Toffler in *The Third Wave*.

THE BEST SOURCES OF HELP

Naisbitt, John. *Megatrends*. New York: Warner Books, 1982.

The Mind of the Strategist
by Kenichi Ohmae

The book illuminates the strategic thinking behind Japanese corporate success. The author shows how and why it differs from the Western approach to strategic thinking and explains that Western companies can adapt to this successful model.

GETTING STARTED

The author argues that to a large extent, Japanese success can be attributed to the nature of Japanese strategic thinking. Japanese businesses tend not to have large strategic planning staffs. The customer is at the heart of the Japanese approach to strategy. There are three main players in any business strategy—the corporation itself, the customer, and the competition—collectively called the strategic triangle. Just as events in the real world do not always fit a linear model, the Japanese approach to strategy is irrational and non-linear.

CONTRIBUTION

Strategy determines Japanese success. Japanese success can be attributed to the nature of Japanese strategic thinking. This is basically creative and intuitive rather than rational, but the necessary creativity can be learned.

Unlike large US corporations, Japanese businesses tend not to have large strategic planning staffs. Instead they often have a single, idiosyncratic, naturally-talented strategist.

From the dynamic interaction of the company, customers, and competition, a comprehensive set of objectives and plans eventually emerges.

The customer at the centre. In contrast to the West, the customer is at the heart of the Japanese approach to strategy and the key to corporate values.

Strategic triangle. In the construction of any business strategy, three main players must be taken into account: the corporation itself, the customer, and the competition. Collectively they are called the strategic triangle.

The job of the strategist is to achieve superior performance. At the same time, the strategist must be sure that his strategy matches the strengths of the corporation with the needs of a clearly-defined market. Otherwise, the corporation's long-term viability may be at stake.

Strategy is irrational. The central thrust of the book is that strategy as epitomised by the Japanese approach is irrational and non-linear.

In strategic thinking, one first seeks a clear understanding of each element of a situation, and then makes the fullest use of human brain power to restructure the elements in the most advantageous way.

Events in the real world do not always fit a linear model. Hence the most reliable means of dissecting a situation into its constituent parts, and reassembling them in the desired pattern, is not a step-by-step methodology, but the ultimate non-linear thinking tool, the human brain.

True strategic thinking thus not only contrasts sharply with the conventional mechanical systems approach, but also with the purely intuitive approach, which reaches conclusions without any breakdown or analysis.

Gaining ground through effective strategy. An effective business strategy is one by which a company can gain significant ground on its competitors at an acceptable cost to itself.

There are four main ways of achieving this:

- focusing on the key factors for success (KFS)
- building on relative superiority
- pursuing aggressive initiatives
- utilising strategic degrees of freedom

The principal concern is to avoid doing the same thing, on the same battleground, as the competition.

Focusing on key factors for success. Certain functional or operating areas within every business are more critical for success in that particular business environment than others.

If you concentrate effort into these areas and your competitors do not, this is a source of competitive advantage. The problem lies in identifying these key factors for success.

Today's industry leaders, without exception, began by bold deployment of strategies based on KFS.

Building on relative superiority. When all competitors are seeking to compete on the KFS, a company can exploit any differences in competitive conditions.

For example, it can make use of technology or sales networks not in direct competition with its rivals.

Pursuing aggressive initiatives. Frequently, the only way to win against a much larger, entrenched competitor is to upset the competitive environment, by undermining the value of its KFS.

That means changing the rules of the game by introducing new KFS.

Utilising strategic degrees of freedom. This means that the company should focus upon innovation in areas that are untouched by competitors.

CONTEXT

The author is Japan's only successful management guru. The book was published in the West at the height of interest in Japanese management methods.

Ohmae challenged the simplistic belief that Japanese management was a matter of company songs and lifetime employment. Instead, the country's success could be attributed to the nature of its strategic thinking.

Best-selling author Gary Hamel commented, 'I loved this book! At a time when most strategy savants were focused either on the process of planning (Ansoff and his followers) or on the determinants of successful, that is, profitable, strategies (Michael Porter), Kenichi Ohmae challenged managers to think in new ways. Strategy doesn't come from a calendar-driven process; it isn't the product of a systematic search for ways of earning above-average profits; strategy comes from viewing the world in new ways. Strategy starts with an ability to think in new and unconventional ways.'

THE BEST SOURCES OF HELP

Ohmae, Kenichi. *The Mind of the Strategist: The Art of Japanese Business*. New York: McGraw-Hill, 1982.

Moments of Truth
by Jan Carlzon

Jan Carlzon is a Swedish businessman who shot to international prominence by leading a turn-around at the Scandinavian airline, SAS. The turnaround was based on excellence in customer service, and the book contains many practical examples of the way this can be applied. The SAS story is one of the most frequently-used case studies in customer service training and literature.

GETTING STARTED

Carlzon used customer service as a vehicle for turning the SAS airline around. He held that quality service is built around moments of truth—the critical transactions at each stage of the ownership or use cycle. These critical transactions occur at initial contact, first use, problem-solving, on-going support, further purchases, and recommendations to others. Customer satisfaction and value are affected at different points in the cycle. They also vary by customer type.

This approach owes much to the Scandinavian management style—humane and people-centred. Scandinavian companies embraced team working and employee participation before they became fashionable: their leaders are anti-authoritarian; they make very effective use of coaching and mentoring, and they also communicate consistently and continually.

CONTRIBUTION

Making customer service work. Carlzon actually made customer service work and used it as a vehicle for turning the SAS airline—formerly an indifferent performer—into a world-class organisation.

Carlzon came up with the phrase, 'moments of truth'—the sequence of critical transactions across each stage of the ownership or use cycle. Any time a customer comes into contact with any aspect of a business, however remote, is an opportunity to form an impression.

Identifying moments of truth. The critical transactions are broken down into:

- initial contact
- first use
- problem solving
- on-going support
- further purchases
- recommendations to others

The key to understanding customer behaviour is to: 1) evaluate the degree to which satisfaction and value are affected at these different points in the cycle; 2) understand how they vary by customer type. Carlzon decided dramatically to prove the company's dedication to moments of truth by sending tens of thousands of SAS managers on training programmes.

The success of the Scandinavian approach. Like most stereotypes, the image of highly-motivated, well-rewarded, hard-working, and contented Scandinavians is only partly true. However, Scandinavian companies have a track record of managing their human resources in innovative ways. Their management style tends to be humane and people-centred, and they were champions of team working and employee participation long before they became the height of managerial fashion.

Scandinavia has a very stable political system and a fairly homogeneous society, and problems typically are solved through negotiation. Historically there has been little unrest—but the counter to this is that often, without a crisis, advancement is not achieved. The Scandinavian business culture shares some characteristics with that of the Japanese. Saving face is important and, rather than direct frontal attack, Scandinavians prefer a more obtuse and subtle approach.

A Scandinavian leadership style. Old-fashioned virtues are in. Typically, in one survey, American executives rated honesty as the prime business virtue. Swedish executives did not include honesty at all—it was assumed.

The Scandinavian leader tends to be decidedly anti-authoritarian. Highly personal and practical theories, such as coaching and mentoring, find fertile ground; being up-front and communicating openly is expected. With Carlzon and others there is a certain amount of showmanship—they play their roles to perfection. They stand in the middle of their strategy. They don't preach

> Old-fashioned virtues are in.

the strategy; they are the strategy. They communicate consistently and continually. They repeat the same messages again and again. But they never grow tired of saying them—there is no sign of boredom, no cynicism, no sarcasm. They give words real meaning. This appetite for communication is clearly linked to a more humane style of management.

CONTEXT

Carlzon set in train SAS's revival, which became a benchmark for international best practice in customer service. The achievement was celebrated, among many others, by Tom Peters in *A Passion for Excellence*.

After Carlzon left SAS, the company's halo slipped a little and Scandinavian role models were thin on the ground for a number of years. During the 1990s, however, there was a steady stream of corporate benchmarks. The new Scandinavian role models—IKEA, Skandia, Oticon, and ABB—remain indebted to Carlzon's example.

THE BEST SOURCES OF HELP

Carlzon, Jan. *Moments of Truth*. New York: HarperBusiness, 1987.

Motivation and Personality
by Abraham Maslow

Maslow introduced the concept of a hierarchy of needs which has formed an integral part of marketing, human resource, motivational, and management literature ever since. The book makes an important contribution to the emergence of human relations as a professional discipline.

GETTING STARTED

There is an ascending scale of needs that provides the basis for motivation. Basic physiological needs come first; once these are met, other needs dominate. At the top of the scale is self-actualisation, where individuals achieve their personal potential. Also high up are social or love needs, and ego or self-esteem needs. The hierarchy of needs provides a rational framework for motivation, and human nature determines that motivation is intrinsically linked to rewards.

CONTRIBUTION

The hierarchy of needs. There is an ascending scale of needs, which must be understood if people are to be motivated. First are the fundamental physiological needs of warmth, shelter, and food. It is quite true that man lives by bread alone—when there is no bread.

But what happens when there is plenty of bread?

> While the hierarchy of needs provides a rational framework for motivation, its flaw lies in the nature of humanity.

Emerging needs. Once basic physiological needs are met, others emerge to dominate. These can be categorised roughly as the safety needs. If man's state is sufficiently extreme and chronic, he may be characterised as living almost for safety alone.

Next on the hierarchy are social or love needs, and ego or self-esteem needs.

Self-actualisation. As each need is satisfied, eventually comes self-actualisation—the individual achieves his or her own potential.

From motivation to reward. While the hierarchy of needs provides a rational framework for motivation, its flaw lies in the nature of humanity. Man always wants more. When asked what salary they would be comfortable with, people routinely—no matter what their income—name a figure that is around twice their current income.

Instead of being driven by punishment and deprivation, motivation became intrinsically linked to reward.

CONTEXT

Abraham Maslow was a member of the Human Relations School of the late 1950s, which also included McGregor and Herzberg.

Motivation and Personality is best known for its hierarchy of needs—a concept that was first published by Maslow in 1943. He argues that there is an ascending scale of needs, which must be understood if people are to be motivated. While the hierarchy of needs provides a rational framework for motivation, its flaw lies in the nature of humanity.

Maslow's hierarchy of needs contributed to the emergence of human relations as a discipline, and to a sea-change in the perception of motivation.

Gary Hamel commented: 'However subtle and variegated the original theory, time tends to reduce it to its most communicable essence: hence Maslow's hierarchy of needs, Pascale's seven Ss, Michael Porter's five forces, and the Boston Consulting Group's growth/share matrix. Yet there is no framework that has so broadly infiltrated organisational life as Maslow's hierarchy of needs. Perhaps this is because it speaks so directly to the aspirations each of us holds for ourself.'

THE BEST SOURCES OF HELP

Maslow, Abraham. *Motivation and Personality.* 3rd ed. New York: Harper & Row, 1987.

The Motivation to Work
by Frederick Herzberg, Bernard Mausner, and
Barbara Bloch Snyderman

Herzberg's work has had a lasting influence on human resource management. Concepts such as job enrichment, self-development, and job satisfaction have evolved from his insight that motivation comes from within the individual, rather than from a policy imposed by the company. It has also influenced organisations' rewards and remuneration packages.

GETTING STARTED

Employee motivation can be improved through greater emphasis on human relations.

Research indicates that motivation at work takes two forms—hygiene factors and motivation factors. Hygiene factors, which cover basic needs at work, include working conditions, benefits, and job security. Motivation factors, which meet uniquely human needs, include achievement, personal development, job satisfaction, and recognition. Improvements in hygiene factors remove the barriers to positive attitudes in the workplace, although hygiene factors alone are not sufficient to provide true motivation to work.

Employers should aim to motivate people through job satisfaction, rather than reward or pressure.

CONTRIBUTION

The importance of employee attitudes. 'People are our greatest assets' has become one of the most over-used clichés in business. However, before Herzberg, 'people issues' took a low priority in management literature. Management thinkers rarely sought the opinions of employees, or considered them worthy of study. Herzberg and his colleagues, Mausner and Snyderman, highlighted the importance of employee attitudes through a study of 203 Pittsburgh engineers and accountants. By asking what pleased and displeased people about their jobs, he raised the wider question: 'How do you motivate employees?'

Identifying factors that motivate employees. Herzberg made a critical distinction between factors that cause unhappiness at work and factors that contribute to job satisfaction. This distinction was based on his earlier work in public health, where he had concluded that mental health was not the opposite of mental illness. Transferring that concept to the workplace, he suggested that the reverse of the factors that make people happy did not make them unhappy. His research indicated that motivation at work takes two forms—hygiene factors and motivation factors.

Hygiene factors. Hygiene factors cover basic needs at work. They include working conditions, supervision levels, company policies, benefits, and job security. If these are poor or deteriorate, they lead to poor job attitudes and dissatisfaction with work. Conversely, improvements in hygiene factors remove the barriers to positive attitudes in the workplace. However, improvement in hygiene factors alone is not sufficient to provide true job satisfaction.

Motivation factors. Herzberg discovered that the factors that lead to dissatisfaction are completely different from those that provide satisfaction. He called the positive factors 'motivation factors'. These meet uniquely human needs and include achievement, personal development, job satisfaction, and recognition. Improving these factors can make people satisfied with work.

Challenging the reward process. Herzberg concluded that organisations should aim to motivate people through job satisfaction, rather than reward or pressure. This led to the concept of job enrichment, which would enable organisations to liberate people from the tyranny of numbers and expand the creative role of an individual within the organisation.

CONTEXT

Herzberg was one of the humanist school of management thinking, emphasising the human aspects of organisations, in contrast to the mechanistic views of scientific thinkers. The humanist tradition includes Mary Parker Follett, Elton Mayo, Douglas McGregor, Abraham Maslow, Charles Handy, and Tom Peters.

Maslow's hierarchy of needs, formulated in 1943, influenced industrial psychologists like Herzberg by showing that work can be made more satisfying by giving greater emphasis to affection, ego, and self-actualisation needs.

Herzberg's breakthrough was to identify hygiene and motivation factors. His work has had a lasting influence on human resource management: concepts such as job enrichment, self development, and job satisfaction have evolved from his insight that motivation comes from within the individual, rather than from a policy imposed by the company. It has also influenced organisations' rewards and remuneration packages.

The trend towards 'cafeteria benefits' reflects Herzberg's belief that people choose the form of motivation that is most important to them. Many organisations believe that money is the sole motivation for workers; Herzberg's work offers a more subtle approach. There has been much subsequent academic debate on the extent to which pay or other factors are the most important motivators.

Guru Gary Hamel commented: 'Too many organisations believe that the only motivation to work is an economic one. Treating knowledge assets like Skinnerian rats is hardly the way to get the best out of people. Herzberg offers a substantially more subtle approach—one that still has much to recommend it.'

Critics of Herzberg argue that pay plays an important part in the motivational equation, and can be used to reinforce other motivational levers. Others point out that people frequently describe good work experiences in terms that reflect credit on themselves—success, greater responsibility, or recognition. Conversely, they will blame bad work experiences on factors that are outside their control, such as poor working conditions or a difficult boss.

Recent commentators believe that the main application of Herzberg's theories has been to non-manual workers, where the hygiene factors are normally well satisfied. They believe that employees who were reasonably well rewarded would tend to emphasise motivational factors as more important.

THE BEST SOURCES OF HELP

Herzberg, Frederick, Bernard Mausner, and Barbara Bloch Snyderman. *The Motivation to Work*. New York: John Wiley, 1959.

My Life and Work
by Henry Ford

My Life and Work is an account of Henry Ford's life and business philosophy. It provides unique insights into the man who took mass production to new levels and opened up mass markets through consistently low pricing and standardisation. It also highlights the risk of a single-product strategy and the problems of autocratic control.

GETTING STARTED

Ford's policy was to reduce the price, extend the operations, and improve the article. He did not bother about the costs. Price forces the costs down. Ford reduced prices by 58% at a time when demand was such that he could easily have raised them. Mass production was the result, not the cause, of his low prices.

Management and managers were dismissed by Ford as largely unnecessary—but his lack of faith in management, along with its total reliance on the Model T, later proved the undoing of the company.

CONTRIBUTION

Pricing and costs. Ford stated his policy as being, 'to reduce the price, extend the operations, and improve the article. The reduction of price comes first. We have never considered any costs as fixed. Therefore we first reduce the price to the point where we believe more sales will result. Then we go ahead and try to make the prices. We do not bother about the costs. The new price forces the costs down. The more usual way is to take the costs and then determine the price, and although that method may be scientific in the narrow sense, it is not scientific in the broad sense. What use is it to know the cost, if it tells you that you cannot manufacture at a price at which the article can be sold?'

> In a sense Ford was both the most brilliant and the most senseless marketer in American history.

Ford's commitment to lowering prices cannot be doubted. Between 1908 and 1916 he reduced prices by 58% at a time when demand was such that he could easily have raised them.
Marketing. In a sense Ford was both the most brilliant and the most senseless marketer in American history. He was senseless because he refused to give the customer anything but a black car. He was brilliant because he fashioned a production system designed to fit market needs.

We habitually celebrate him for the wrong reason, his production genius. His real genius was marketing.
Standardisation. Ford realised that the mass car market existed—it just remained for him to provide the products the market wanted.

Model Ts were black, straightforward, and affordable. At the centre of Ford's thinking was the aim of standardisation—something continually emphasised by the car makers of today.
Problems of a single product. The problem was that when other manufacturers added extras, Ford kept it simple and dramatically lost ground.

Henry Ford is reputed to have kicked a slightly-modified Model T to pieces, such was his commitment to the unadulterated version. But the company's reliance on the Model T nearly drove it to self-destruction. The man with a genius for marketing lost touch with the aspirations of customers.

Mass production. Ford is celebrated for his transformation of the production line into a means of previously unimagined mass production.

He calculated that the production of a Model T required 7,882 different operations. Production was based around strict functional divides or demarcations. Ford believed in people getting on with their jobs and not raising their heads above functional parapets. He didn't want engineers talking to salespeople, or people making decisions without his say so.

Authoritarian control. Management and managers were dismissed by Ford as largely unnecessary, and he made a systematic, deliberate, and conscious attempt to run the billion-dollar business without managers.

Ford's lack of faith in management proved the undoing of the huge corporate empire he assembled. Without his autocratic belligerence to drive the company forward, it quickly ground to a halt.

Innovation in business. In some respects Ford remains a good role model. He was an improviser and innovator who borrowed ideas and then adapted and synthesised them. He developed flow lines that involved people; now, we have flow lines without people, but no-one questions their relevance or importance.

Though he is seen as having de-humanised work, Ford provided a level of wealth for workers and products for consumers which weren't previously available. He introduced the $5 wage for his workers which, at that time, was around twice the average for the industry.

He had an international perspective that was ahead of his time. His plant at Highland Park, Detroit, produced. But the world, not just the United States, bought.

Ford was acutely aware that time was an important competitive weapon. 'Time waste differs from material waste in that there can be no salvage', he wrote.

CONTEXT

My Life and Work is a robust account of Ford's life and business philosophy, although it is notable for the dominance of the former and the lack of the latter. Ford's business achievements and contribution to the development of industrialisation are likely to be remembered long after his theories on politics, history, motivation, or humanity.

Leading author Gary Hamel said, 'Henry Ford may have been autocratic and paranoid, but he brought to men and women everywhere a stunningly precious gift—mobility. Whatever his faults, Henry Ford was driven by the dream of every great entrepreneur—to make a real difference in people's lives—and to do it globally.'

THE BEST SOURCES OF HELP

Ford, Henry. *My Life and Work*. New York: Doubleday, Page & Co, 1923.

My Years with General Motors
by Alfred Sloan

Alfred Sloan is one of the very few figures who undoubtedly changed the world of management. He was also one of the first managers to write an important theoretical book. *My Years with General Motors* is an account of his remarkable career and the creation of a new organisational form, the multi-divisional form, that spawned a host of imitators.

GETTING STARTED

Alfred Sloan, a leading figure at General Motors from 1917, became its chief executive in 1946 and honorary chairman from 1956 until his death in 1966.

When he joined, the automobile market was dominated by Ford, and GM's market share was a mere 12%. GM was then an unwieldy combination of companies with eight models that competed against each other as well as against Ford. Sloan cut the eight models down to five and targeted each at a particular segment of the market. The five ranges were updated regularly and came in more than one colour—unlike Ford's Model T. He also reshaped the organisation so that it was better suited to deliver his aspirations.

He created eight divisions—five car and three component divisions. In the jargon of 50 years later, these were strategic business units. Each had responsibility for its own commercial operations and its own engineering, production, and sales department. The divisions were supervised by a central staff responsible for overall policy and finance.

The main interest of *My Years with General Motors* for modern management thinkers lies in how Sloan managed to co-ordinate the semi-autonomous divisions with the centre and balance flexibility with control.

CONTRIBUTION

Balancing flexibility with control. The policy that Sloan labelled 'federal decentralization' marked the invention of the decentralised, divisionalised organisation.

The multi-divisional form enabled Sloan to utilise the company's size without making it cumbersome. Executives had more time to concentrate on strategic issues and operational decisions were made by people in the front line rather than at a distant headquarters.

> The book reveals that Sloan was committed to what at the time would have been regarded as progressive human resource management.

By 1925, with its new organisation and commitment to annual changes in its models, GM had overtaken Ford. More than that, however, Sloan's segmentation of the company changed the structure of the car industry and provided a model for how firms could do the same in other industries.

Commitment to employees. The book reveals that Sloan was committed to what at the time would have been regarded as progressive human resource management. In 1947 he established GM's employee-research section to look at employee attitudes, and he invested a large amount of his own time in selecting the right people for the job.

Problems in decentralisation. The decentralised structure built up by Sloan revolved around a reporting and committee infrastructure that eventually became unwieldy.

As time went by, more and more committees were set up. Stringent targets and narrow measures of success stultified initiative. The organisation proved quite incapable of creating and developing new businesses internally. This inability to manage organic expansion into new areas was caused by many factors:

- operating responsibilities and measurement systems focused on profit and market share in existing markets
- business unit managers were not expected to look for new opportunities
- the boxes in the organisation chart defined their product or geographic scope
- small new ventures could not absorb the large central overheads and return the profits needed to justify the financial and human investments

As Sloan himself put it: 'In practically all our activities we seem to suffer from the inertia resulting from our great size. There are so many people involved and it requires such a tremendous effort to put something new into effect that a new idea is likely to be considered insignificant in comparison with the effort that it takes to put it across.'

CONTEXT

Sloan established GM as a benchmark of corporate might, a symbol of American strength and success. 'What's good for GM is good for America', ran the popular mythology. Peter Drucker and Alfred Chandler celebrated his approach, but the deficiencies of the model were apparent to Sloan himself, have become more so since the publication of his book, and are most obviously manifested in the decline of GM.

By the end of the 1960s the delicate balance, which he had brilliantly maintained between centralisation and decentralisation, was lost. Finance emerged as the dominant function, and GM became paralysed by what had once made it great.

Gary Hamel commented: 'Can you be big and nimble? The question is as timely today as it was when Sloan took over General Motors. Despite divisionalisation and decentralisation, Sloan's organisational inventions, GM still fell victim to its size . . . [T]he corporate superstructure that emerged to manage GM's independent divisions was more successful in creating bureaucracy than in exploiting cross-divisional synergies. The challenge of achieving divisional autonomy and flexibility on one hand, while reaping the benefits of scale and co-ordination on the other, is one that has eluded not only GM, but many other large companies as well.'

One thing that should not be forgotten is that Sloan believed in managers and management in a way that his great rival Henry Ford did not. Nevertheless, as *The Economist* said: 'Alfred Sloan did for the upper layers of management what Henry Ford did for the shopfloor: he turned it into a reliable, efficient, machine-like process'.

Of the book as a whole, Peter Drucker remarked: 'It is perhaps the most impersonal book of memoirs ever written. And this was clearly intentional. Sloan's book knows only one dimension: that of managing a business so that it can produce effectively, provide jobs, create markets and sales, and generate profits.'

THE BEST SOURCES OF HELP

Sloan, Alfred. *My Years with General Motors*. New York: Doubleday, 1963.

Natural Capitalism
by Paul Hawken, Amory Lovins, and Hunter Lovins

The book offers an environmental perspective on economic activities. It includes practical advice on ways to transform business so that the Earth's resources are protected.

GETTING STARTED

Natural Capitalism recognises the critical relationship between the traditional creation of financial capital and the maintenance of the natural resources that are fundamental to any form of economic activity. The book suggests an approach for reconciling ecological and economic priorities, one that not only protects the Earth's environment, but also improves profits and competitiveness. The authors point out that environmental and economic priorities are normally considered contradictory, so that any state of balance requires trade-offs. However, they believe that the best solutions may be based on design integration at all levels of economic activity, an approach they call 'natural capitalism'.

CONTRIBUTION

The concept of natural capital. 'Natural capital', according to the authors, comprises the world's resources, living systems, and ecosystem services. These, they feel, are being depleted at a dangerous rate. They explain how increased resource productivity would enable business and consumers to obtain the same amount of utility from a product or process while using less material or energy. These natural efficiencies, they argue, go way beyond industry's current marginal performance gains. They believe that, if natural capitalism became widely accepted, resource productivity could grow at least fourfold, allowing people to live twice as well, yet use half as much.

The stages of natural capitalism. The authors divide natural capitalism into four key strategies:
- radical resource productivity
- biologically-inspired production models
- a solutions-based business model
- reinvesting in natural capital

These strategies, they say, offer benefits and opportunities in markets, finance, materials, distribution, and employment.

Radical resource productivity. According to the authors, radical resource productivity is the cornerstone of natural capitalism. It means obtaining the same amount of utility or work from a product, while using fewer materials and less energy. In simple terms, this means doing more with less. The authors believe that fundamental changes in production design and technology offer the opportunity to develop ways to make natural resources such as energy, minerals, water, and forests stretch 5, 10, even 100 times further than they do today.

In manufacturing, transportation, forestry, construction, energy, and other industrial sectors, their evidence suggests that radical improvements in resource productivity are both practical and cost-effective. Designers, they believe, are already developing ways to make natural resources work much harder. These efficiencies transcend the marginal gains in performance that industry constantly seeks as part of its evolution. According to the authors, these revolutionary leaps in design and technology will alter industry itself.

Biologically-inspired production models. Taking examples from the natural world, the authors show how living organisms can produce complex 'products' from recycled materials using minimal amounts of sustainable resources. Some of these products, such as the spider's silk or the cellulose produced by trees, have qualities that outperform their man-made equivalents. They argue that industry should learn from these natural techniques, a process they call 'bio-mimicry'. This approach seeks not only to reduce waste, but to eliminate the very concept of waste.

They demonstrate how every output, in closed-loop production systems modelled on nature's designs, is returned harmlessly to the ecosystem as a nutrient, like compost, or becomes an input for manufacturing another product. They point out how this compares with the inefficiency of many production processes where as little as 6% of the materials consumed actually end up in the product.

A solutions-based business model. The business model of traditional manufacturing rests on the sale of goods: a consumer uses the product for a limited period and disposes of it at the end of its useful life. This process, the authors argue, is extremely wasteful. They offer an alternative model, where a physical product owned by a consumer is replaced by a flow of services.

A simple example might be a washing machine that is owned, maintained, and upgraded by the manufacturer. When its useful life is finished, the manufacturer is responsible for recycling the product. Another example would be providing access to the entire catalogues of music companies by subscription rather than purchasing individual CDs. This shift of responsibility, they claim, would reduce consumption, but improve consumer choice.

Reinvesting in natural capital. According to the authors, sustaining, restoring, and expanding natural stocks of capital would work towards reversing worldwide planetary destruction, and governments are already recognising the importance of using resource productivity to achieve this. They use terms such as 'Factor Four', which means that resource productivity can and should grow fourfold, in other words, the amount of wealth extracted from one unit of natural resources can quadruple. On that basis, people could live twice as well yet use half as much.

CONTEXT

Natural Capitalism is one of the increasing number of books that argue for a more ecologically sound approach to business. Unlike many more confrontational books that attack industry and offer no solution, *Natural Capitalism* shows how industry can adapt by learning from the natural world. While most commentators believe that environmental and economic priorities are contradictory, this book attempts to reconcile them. Above all, it indicates opportunities that could lead to nothing less than a transformation of commerce and all societal institutions.

THE BEST SOURCES OF HELP

Hawken, Paul, Amory B. Lovins, and L. Hunter Lovins. *Natural Capitalism: The Next Industrial Revolution*. London: Earthscan Publications Ltd, 1999.

The Nature of Managerial Work
by Henry Mintzberg

Mintzberg is regarded by many as a leading contemporary management thinker, and this book was the first to explore what managers actually do at work. It goes behind the myths and the self-perceptions to describe the day-to-day work of a manager.

GETTING STARTED

What managers actually do, how they do it, and why, are fundamental questions.

What managers actually do, how they do it, and why, are fundamental questions. Managers believe they deal with big strategic issues—in reality they move from task to task dogged by diversions. Managerial work is marked by variety, brevity, and fragmentation.

Managers have three key roles and the prominence of each role varies in different managerial jobs.

CONTRIBUTION

What managers do—the myth. What managers actually do, how they do it, and why they do it, are fundamental questions. There are a number of generally accepted answers.

Managers believe:

- that they sit in solitude contemplating the great strategic issues of the day
- that they make time to reach the best decisions
- that their meetings are high-powered, concentrating on the meta-narrative rather than the nitty-gritty

The reality largely went unexplored until Henry Mintzberg's book.

What managers do—the reality. Mintzberg went in search of the reality. He simply observed what a number of managers actually did. The resulting book blew away the managerial mystique.

Managers did not spend time contemplating the long term. They were slaves to the moment, moving from task to task with every move dogged by another diversion, another call. The median time spent by a manager on any one issue was a mere nine minutes.

The characteristics of the manager at work. Mintzberg observed that the typical manager:

- performs a great quantity of work at an unrelenting pace
- undertakes activities marked by variety, brevity, and fragmentation
- has a preference for issues that are current, specific, and non-routine
- prefers verbal rather than written means of communication
- acts within a web of internal and external contacts
- is subject to heavy constraints but can exert some control over the work

Managers' key roles. From these observations, Mintzberg identified the manager's work roles as:

- interpersonal
- informational
- decisional

Interpersonal roles.

- Figurehead: representing the organisation/unit to outsiders.
- Leader: motivating subordinates, unifying effort.
- Liaiser: maintaining lateral contacts.

Informational roles.

- Monitor: overseeing information flows.
- Disseminator: providing information to subordinates.
- Spokesman: transmitting information to outsiders.

Decisional roles.

- Entrepreneur: initiating and designing change.
- Disturbance handler: handling non-routine events.
- Resource allocator: deciding who gets what and who will do what.
- Negotiator: negotiating.

All managerial work encompasses these roles, but the prominence of each role varies in different managerial jobs.

CONTEXT

Henry Mintzberg is perhaps the world's premier management thinker, according to Tom Peters. His reputation has been made not by popularising new techniques, but by rethinking the fundamentals of strategy and structure, management, and planning.

His work on strategy—in particular his ideas of emergent strategy and grass-roots strategy making—has been highly influential.

Influential author Gary Hamel commented: 'Five reasons I like Henry Mintzberg: he is a world class iconoclast. He loves the messy world of real companies. He is a master story-teller. He is conceptual and pragmatic. He doesn't believe in easy answers.'

The Nature of Managerial Work has produced few worthwhile imitators, but Mintzberg's rigour and originality have given his ideas staying power.

THE BEST SOURCES OF HELP

Mintzberg, Henry. *The Nature of Managerial Work*. New York: Harper & Row, 1973.

The New Corporate Cultures
by Terrence Deal and Allan Kennedy

Deal and Kennedy wrote the first significant book on corporate culture, *Corporate Cultures: Rites and Rituals of Corporate Life*, in 1982. Their later book, *The New Corporate Cultures*, re-examines its role in the light of accelerating changes in the business environment. They set out to demonstrate how organisations with a strong culture have survived and succeeded, despite the impact of globalisation, information technology, mergers, and downsizing, and how an understanding of corporate cultures, coupled with strong leadership, can prove an effective model for business.

GETTING STARTED

The authors argue that corporate culture is a unifying factor that enables people to co-operate to achieve a common goal. However, a number of factors have militated against the development and maintenance of an effective culture—the demand for short-term results, the impact of downsizing and mergers, the introduction of outsourcing, and the effect of computers on business relationships. Organisations wishing to regain lost ground must now rebuild their cultures from the bottom up through strong leadership and high performance.

CONTRIBUTION

Culture breeds financial success. The authors demonstrate the value of corporate culture by analysing financial performance. The companies they identified as top performers in 1982 outperformed average stock market growth by nearly 50%.

The impact of short-term needs. They also explain, however, how the rise of shareholder value played a key role in reducing the importance of corporate culture. The emphasis on short-term results, coupled with a growth in institutional ownership, meant that long-term actions proved unattractive to many organisations.

> Mergers create a climate of uncertainty for employees, because there are always winners and losers.

Short-termism, they believe, had a significant impact on employee loyalty and productivity, initiating a vicious circle that produced more and more short-term responses. Cutting costs to achieve short-term results led to a wave of downsizing and re-engineering. This, in turn, ended the concept of lifetime employment and destroyed trust within organisations.

Outsourcing, downsizing, mergers, and IT. Downsizing, say the authors, damages a corporate culture by destroying trust and breaking the link between leaders and employees.

Outsourcing, they claim, has a similarly damaging effect, since when organisations focus on their core activities and outsource everything else, employees may be transferred to other organisations, losing benefits and severing their links with the original employer.

The rapid increase in mergers has likewise tested corporate cultures. Mergers create a climate of uncertainty for employees, because there are always winners and losers.

Information technology too has, in their view, had a significant adverse effect. Although personal computers empower the people who use them, they can also isolate people from each other and break the informal links that are an important part of corporate culture.

The effect of globalisation. Globalisation, according to Deal and Kennedy, has accelerated the outsourcing and downsizing trends by enabling companies to source from around the world. Management is also affected by globalisation, as multinational managers struggle to operate in different cultures.

The need for cultural leadership. The authors believe that cultural leadership is key to overcoming the problems that have emerged. Managers must find out what employees really believe about the company and translate that into a statement that represents the company's position. Finding the common ground and turning it into set of shared beliefs helps to shape the overall corporate vision.

Challenge people. It is important, the authors suggest, to measure the progress of cultural revitalisation in financial terms. Celebrating victories can bring people together. However, as they explain, performance standards should not necessarily be based on financial targets. Setting people other challenges can help to create a strong culture.

Companies must rebuild trust by emphasising the importance of employees to the business. Transparency is an important part of that process. To ensure a high standard of performance, the authors recommend hiring and rewarding the right people. However, they point out that the organisational structure must be right to get the most from people. A rigid divisional structure tends to isolate people, so transferring them can help to redress the balance.

Building teamwork. The authors recommend the introduction of cultural revitalisation teams with access to senior management. The team should try to identify subcultures, small informal groups who work together and can form the basis of strong teams. Encouraging formal and informal meetings also helps to rebuild the connections inside a company.

Rebuilding the social context of work helps give people a sense of belonging. The authors explain how factors such as job security, job satisfaction, and a socially rewarding environment create a more attractive culture.

CONTEXT

When Deal and Kennedy introduced the term 'corporate cultures' in 1982, it received a mixed reaction. Supporters believed it gave a valuable insight into the inner workings of an organisation. Critics felt that it was a superficial application of the discipline of anthropology to management.

The term has now become an accepted part of business language and often forms a key element of corporate strategy. For example, Edgar Schein, writing in *Organization, Culture, and Leadership*, believes that the only important thing leaders do is create and manage corporate culture. John Kotter and James Hesketh, in *Corporate Culture and Performance*, analyse the performance of companies with a strong culture, and in *Built to Last* James Collins and Jerry Porras look at companies with a long history of success and compares their performance with companies lacking a strong corporate culture.

In 1995, *Fortune* magazine published a survey on corporate reputation and introduced the feature with a comment that robust culture appeared to be the factor that set the top-ranking companies apart.

THE BEST SOURCES OF HELP

Deal, Terrence, and Allan Kennedy. *The New Corporate Cultures*. London: Texere Publishing, 2000.

The New New Thing
by Michael Lewis

This is a biography of Jim Clark, a highly-successful technology entrepreneur. It provides a useful insight into the personal characteristics needed for success and into the nature of a technology start-up.

GETTING STARTED

The book portrays serial entrepreneur and billionaire Jim Clark. Clark changed the pattern of investment by taking Netscape public, with no profits and no revenue. The flotation, with stock value doubling in 24 hours, showed that massive growth potential was more critical than profits.

Clark's strategy for dealing with venture capitalists was to sell the dream, not the business plan. He believed that the moment of conception was the critical moment of any new enterprise, and that it was essential to employ people bent on changing the world, not just changing jobs.

Clark's original ambition was to have more money than Larry Ellison. Then he said he would be satisfied with a billion dollars after taxes.

CONTRIBUTION

Serial entrepreneurs. The book is a portrayal of billionaire Jim Clark, one of the Silicon Valley super-rich. Clark founded Netscape and Silicon Graphics, and was aiming to turn the trillion-dollar US healthcare industry on its head with his new project, Healtheon.

> The moment of conception is the critical moment of any new enterprise.

Changing the pattern of investment. Jim Clark decided to take Netscape public just 18 months after forming the company in 1994, despite it having no profits and no revenue to speak of. He rewrote the laws of capitalism by showing that massive growth was more critical than the need to show profits.

The Netscape flotation in 1995 remains perhaps the most famous share offering in the American stock market's history. The company's stock doubled in value within less than 24 hours and set the scene for a series of high-profile flotations.

Dealing with venture capitalists. Clark's strategy for dealing with venture capitalists was to sell the dream, not the business plan.

Perhaps the aura and mystique of a larger-than-life character like Clark plays a bigger part in selling a business idea than a convincing business plan. Silicon Valley, the engine-room of the new economy, may have a surreal sense of business logic.

Employing staff for a new venture. The moment of conception is the critical moment of any new enterprise. At that moment, it is important not merely to employ the people bent on changing the world but to avoid employing the people bent only on changing jobs.

Job changers were told, 'We're all confused here. We don't know what we're going to do yet'. Promising people were told, 'Here's exactly what we're going to do. It is going to be huge and you are going to get very, very rich'.

The real meaning of wealth. Clark's original ambition was to have more money than Larry Ellison (CEO of Oracle, worth about nine billion dollars). Once he had passed Ellison, Clark didn't feel he could overtake Bill Gates. He indicated that he just wanted to have a billion dollars, after taxes. Then he would be satisfied.

CONTEXT

The book gives occasional glimpses into the inner workings of Silicon Valley, but is light on business insights.

Although Clark's success as an entrepreneurial businessman goes without saying, the book does not teach the budding high-tech entrepreneur any lessons about how he managed to make his fortune.

Of the three enterprises Clark is most closely associated with, Silicon Graphics is struggling to survive, Netscape has been sold to online giant AOL, and Healtheon is still making a loss.

THE BEST SOURCES OF HELP

Lewis, Michael. *The New New Thing: How Silicon Valley Defines the Ways We Think and Live As We Enter a New Century.* London: Hodder & Stoughton, 1999.

New Patterns of Management
by Rensis Likert

The author was a pioneer of attitude surveys and introduced an attitude scale that is now widely used in business research. The book explains how he used his research tools to identify patterns of participative management and organisation that would bring success in an increasingly competitive environment.

GETTING STARTED

Rensis Likert was a pioneer of attitude surveys and poll design, as well as social research as a whole. According to Likert, there are four types of management style:

- exploitative and authoritarian
- benevolent autocracy
- consultative
- participative

Participative management is the best option, as increased participation and individualism is essential to meet increased competition. Participative groups can improve management and performance. The greater the loyalty of a group, the greater the motivation to achieve its goals.

An organisation's style can be linked directly to its performance. The route to understanding managerial performance is improved measurement.

CONTRIBUTION

Measuring attitudes. In his doctoral thesis, written in 1932 while Likert was at Columbia University, and entitled *A Technique for the Measurement of Attitudes*, he introduced a straightforward five-point scale by which attitudes could be measured. The now well-known scale ranges from 'strongly agree' to 'strongly disagree' and is known as the Likert Scale.

> Likert identified four types of management style, each of which tends to mould people in its own image.

The contribution of participative groups. Likert's business research focused on the ways in which participative groups could improve management and performance. It also examined the human systems that exist in organisations.

The greater the loyalty of a group, the greater is the motivation among members to achieve the goals of the group, and the greater the probability that the group will achieve its goals.

Management styles. Likert identified four types of management style, each of which tends to mould people in its own image. Authoritarian organisations tend to develop dependent people and few leaders. Participative management was seen by Likert as the best option, both in a business and a personal sense. Participative organisations tend to develop emotionally and socially mature people capable of effective interaction, initiative, and leadership.

Organisation style and performance. 'Managers with the best records of performance in American business and government are in the process of pointing the way to an appreciably more effective system of management than now exists', Likert wrote in the book's opening. With the assistance of social science research, it is now possible to state a generalised theory of organisation based on the management practices of these highest producers.

The importance of participation. Increased participation in the workplace and individualism are necessary consequences of increased competition and fast-accelerating technological improvement. There is much greater need for co-operation and participation in managing the enterprise than when technologies were simple and the chief possessed all the technical knowledge needed.

The importance of measurement. Management can make a difference, and the route to understanding managerial performance is improved measurement. An organisation should be outstanding in its performance:

- if it has competent personnel
- if it has leadership which develops highly-effective groups and uses the overlapping group form of structure
- if it achieves effective communication and influence, decentralised and co-ordinated decision-making, and high-performance goals coupled with high motivation

CONTEXT

Likert's research highlights the importance of participative styles of management. This book bids farewell to the world of blind obedience and corporate man. Likert picks up the mood of individualism, which was to sweep the world later in the 1960s. The book provides a blueprint for the ideal organisation, which has largely stood the test of time.

THE BEST SOURCES OF HELP

Likert, Rensis. *New Patterns of Management.* New York: McGraw-Hill, 1961.

The New Pioneers
by Tom Petzinger

The book is based on a series of interviews with entrepreneurs, and argues that the entrepreneur is more likely to succeed in the new economy than in large corporations. It provides a valuable insight into the way entrepreneurs have turned conventional business thinking upside-down and shows the huge opportunities that are available to people with the right attitude.

GETTING STARTED

In the new economy, everyone is an entrepreneur. Many small business owners are succeeding, despite turning traditional business thinking on its head. They are pioneers who have embarked on a new frontier of technologies, ideas, and values. They use technology to distribute, rather than consolidate, authority and creativity.

The entrepreneurial pioneers are part of a quiet revolution reshaping American business. This revolution is represented by the spectacular success enjoyed by small and medium firms, which are becoming the engine room of the new economy.

Such businesses have an entrepreneurial outlook that is team-centred. The people are individually passionate about what they do and use all of their resources to benefit the wider company. Entrepreneurial people have a genuine desire to belong and to contribute.

Information technology can support entrepreneurial middlemen by wiping out inefficiency. It has created a category of firms called 'infomediaries'.

CONTRIBUTION

Turning business thinking on its head. Many small business owners are succeeding, despite turning traditional business thinking on its head. They aren't just ignoring what the business books say they ought to do; more often than not, they are doing the complete opposite. This supports the view that, in the new economy, everyone is an entrepreneur.

The new pioneers. Today's pioneers have embarked on a new frontier, some in search of riches, others in search of freedom. This is a frontier of technologies, ideas and values.

The new pioneers celebrate individuality over conformity among their employees and customers alike. They deploy technology to distribute, rather than consolidate, authority and creativity. They compete through resilience instead of resistance, through adaptation instead of control.

In a time of complexity and change, they realise that tightly-drawn strategies are less important than shared purpose.

A quiet revolution in business. A revolution is quietly reshaping the face of American business and creating an opportunity-rich economy. This revolution is not to be found in the mega-mergers, takeovers, downsizing, fiscal crises, or bust-ups that dominate the financial press. The changes are visible in the spectacular success enjoyed by a growing number of small and medium-sized firms.

A revolution driven by entrepreneurs. Small and medium-sized businesses are the engine room of the new economy. This is normally described as populated by mega-corporations at one end of the scale or tiny start-ups at the other.

At the heart of these firms' success is an entrepreneurial outlook that is team- rather than self-centred.

The qualities of entrepreneurial firms. An open, selfless organisation is not only good for business, but also good for everyone involved, both inside and outside. An organisation like this needs people who are individually passionate about what they do and use all of their resources for the good of the team and the wider company.

There should be a fundamental shift in our collective thinking about the nature of organisations. In entrepreneurial companies, people have a genuine desire to belong and to contribute. Individual capability harnessed to a collective potential can create astonishing results.

Entrepreneurs and middlemen. Many commentators believe that information technology is wiping out the middleman by putting producers directly in contact with their customers. This process, known as 'disintermediation', collapses the distribution chain, wiping out all those who have made their living by taking orders or breaking big lots into smaller lots.

Information technology can support the middleman by wiping out inefficiency. It also makes possible the integration of services on the smallest of scales. It has created a category of firms called 'infomediaries'.

Technology explains how a single entrepreneur can create Amazon.com, the world's largest bookstore, on little more than a great idea.

CONTEXT

In *The New Pioneers*, Thomas Petzinger describes how many small business owners he interviewed had succeeded by turning traditional business thinking on its head.

These businesses didn't just ignore the advice of business books; more often than not, they were doing the complete opposite. Yet they were achieving astonishing success. This led to the conclusion that, in the new economy, everyone is an entrepreneur.

In 1962, Abraham Maslow also commented, 'The most valuable one hundred people to bring into a deteriorating society would not be one hundred chemists, or politicians, or professors, or engineers, but rather one hundred entrepreneurs'.

Thomas Petzinger takes issue with commentators who believe that technology is eliminating the middleman.

Don Tapscott wrote in the influential best-seller, *The Digital Economy*, 'Middleman functions between consumers and producers are being eliminated'. Patrick McGovern, chairman of International Data Group, the world's largest high-tech publisher, wrote: 'The intermediary is doomed. Technology strips him of effectiveness'.

Petzinger's view is different. 'I think the doomsayers are flat wrong. Information technology is the friend of the middleman. Technology wipes out inefficiency, it's true and thank goodness,' he wrote.

THE BEST SOURCES OF HELP

Petzinger, Thomas. *The New Pioneers: Men and Women who Are Transforming the Workplace and Marketplace*. New York: Simon & Schuster, 1999.

On Becoming a Leader
by Warren Bennis

Warren Bennis is widely respected as one of the foremost thinkers on leadership, and this book is regarded as a classic. It explains how people become leaders, how they lead, and how organisations respond to leadership. It is not based on academic theory, but offers practical advice based on interviews with a mix of leaders from many different fields.

GETTING STARTED

Bennis believes that there is no exact science of leadership. Leaders vary in background, education, and experience. However, he identifies certain characteristics as essential for success. According to Bennis, leaders should know what they want and should be able to communicate what they want to others in order to gain their support. Leaders should also understand their own strengths and weaknesses and use them to achieve their goals. Bennis explains the phenomenon of leadership by defining its distinctive qualities—especially those that set a leader apart from a boss or manager, by highlighting the experiences that were vital to the development of leaders, by identifying the turning points, and by examining the role of failure.

CONTRIBUTION

The importance of leadership. Bennis explains that leaders are important for three reasons:
- they are responsible for the effectiveness of organisations
- they provide a focal point
- they provide a recognisable constant in the midst of rapid change

Leading and managing. According to Bennis, the ingredients of leadership are wide-ranging and they include guiding vision, passion, integrity, self-knowledge, trust, and daring. Leaders, he argues, can be highly competent, but fail to win the hearts and minds of the people they are leading.

> **Leaders, according to Bennis, are their own best teachers.**

Bennis believes that there is a significant difference between a leader and a boss, especially a boss who comes up from a results-driven management role. The drive for short-term results can run counter to the effectiveness of a visionary leader.

There are also many important differences between managers and leaders, he argues. The former have short-term rather than long-term perspectives, focus on systems rather than people, accept the status quo rather than challenging it, and exercise control instead of inspiring trust.

Leaders and learning. Leaders, according to Bennis, are their own best teachers. They accept responsibility and gain from their own experience and that of others.

He distinguishes between maintenance learning and shock learning, both of which are familiar to managers, and what he calls innovative learning, which involves listening to others. This type of learning, he explains, means that people are free to express themselves, rather than just explain themselves. True intellect, he believes, is being able to see how things can be different.

The value of failure. Bennis suggests that leaders also learn from adversity. Making mistakes should not be punished. Leaders must operate on instinct, a process based on the use of the left- and right-hand sides of the brain. Managers, in contrast, rely on tried and tested processes.

According to Bennis, leaders should try everything, even in the face of failure. Few people venture into uncharted waters because of the risk of failure.

Achieving goals. Leaders should be able to shift perspective so that they can see what is most important.

Bennis argues that leadership, unlike any other skill, cannot be broken down into a series of repeatable manoeuvres. The creative process involved in reaching a goal is infinitely complex. As he explains, leaders have to be able to move through chaos and synthesise all the elements needed for success.

Gaining support. Bennis argues that leaders must get people on their side to effect change. Empathy is therefore an important characteristic of leadership. This, he explains, is in contrast to theories of leadership by force.

Leadership, he believes, requires persuasion, not giving orders. This requires an understanding of the needs of other people and the ability to communicate a vision.

CONTEXT

Leadership is now one of the most popular topics in management literature and training, and Warren Bennis has made an important contribution. Leadership did not attract serious academic interest until the 1985 publication of *Leaders: Strategies for Taking Change* written in conjunction with Burt Nanus.

Bennis's work is based on extensive research with leaders in every field. One project involved interviews with 90 of America's leaders, including astronaut Neil Armstrong, the coach of the LA Rams, orchestral conductors, and businessmen such as Ray Kroc of McDonald's.

Bennis argues that leadership is not a rare skill. Leaders are made rather than born; leaders are usually ordinary, or apparently ordinary, people rather than obviously charismatic figures. Leadership, moreover, is not solely the preserve of those at the top of the organisation—it is relevant at all levels.

THE BEST SOURCES OF HELP

Bennis, Warren. *On Becoming a Leader.* London: Arrow Books, 1998.

On the Economy of Machinery and Manufactures
by Charles Babbage

Charles Babbage was one of the great minds of the first industrial revolution. He is credited with pioneering the computer, and wrote extensively about the importance of data and manufacturing. The book offers fascinating insights into the early development of manufacturing techniques.

GETTING STARTED

In an age of economic theory, Babbage argued for a highly scientific approach. His emphasis on fact-finding influences not only the practical elements of factory management in the early industrial era, but the formation of interpretive theory. Mechanical principles govern manufacturing, and merchants and manufacturers are the best people to supply the data on which all the reasoning of political economists is founded. People should not fear bad deductions from good facts.

Good factory organisation is important, and factories require an entire system of operation. The most important principle of manufacture is the division of labour.

It is vital to calculate the life expectancy of capital equipment. In five years capital equipment ought to have paid for itself, and in ten it should be superseded by a better version.

CONTRIBUTION

Mechanical principles govern manufacturing. Babbage's fundamental approach was highly scientific. He held that mechanical principles regulate the application of machinery to arts and manufacture.

First, he said, it's essential to gather the evidence. Babbage did so through touring factories exhaustively in the United Kingdom and Europe. The book provides helpful hints and a checklist of questions on how to find the best information when touring a factory.

Make use of facts. Political economists have been reproached with too small a use of facts, and too large an employment of theory. 'If facts are wanting, the closet-philosopher is unfortunately too little acquainted with the admirable arrangements of the factory', Babbage wrote. 'The merchant and manufacturer are the best people to supply readily, and with so little sacrifice of time, the data on which all the reasoning of political economists are founded.'

Collecting data is essential. People should not fear that erroneous deductions may be made from recorded facts. The errors which arise from the absence of facts are far more numerous and more durable than those which result from unsound reasoning based on true data.

Babbage encourages managers to follow his example and gather their own data. Collecting data is essential for the manufacturer who wants to know how many additional customers he will acquire by a given reduction in the price of the article he makes.

Good factory organisation is important. The arrangements that should regulate the interior economy of a factory are founded on deeply-rooted principles. Babbage recognised that the factory requires an entire system of operation. It needs to be organised in a vastly different way to the conventional means of production.

Babbage provides insights in two central areas. First, economies of scale and second, the division of labour.

Calculating the right division of labour. Perhaps the most important principle on which the economy of manufacture depends is the division of labour among the people who perform the work.'The number of operations performed in a given time may frequently be counted when the workman is quite unconscious that any person is observing him', Babbage said. 'For example, the sound made by the motion of a loom may enable the observer to count the number of strokes per minute, even though he is outside the building in which it is contained.'

> Perhaps the most important principle on which the economy of manufacture depends is the division of labour among the people who perform the work.

Life expectancy of capital equipment. Machinery for producing any commodity in great demand seldom actually wears out. New improvements, by which the same operations can be executed either more quickly or better, generally supersede it long before that time arrives. To make such an improved machine profitable, it is usually reckoned that in five years it ought to have paid for itself, and in ten to be superseded by a better one.

CONTEXT

The book was a bestseller of its times. It is one of the first to recognise the importance of factories, economically and socially. In that sense, it is like the first book on the potential of the Internet.

Babbage was a pioneer of modern management. His approach bears more than a passing resemblance to that later adopted by the American champion of scientific management, Frederick Taylor. He beckoned in the industrial era and, in doing so, laid the intellectual groundwork for Marx, Engels, and John Stuart Mill. Contrasts can be made with Adam Smith whose economic viewpoint remained stuck in the agricultural era.

Joseph Schumpeter called the book 'a remarkable performance of a remarkable man'.

THE BEST SOURCES OF HELP

Babbage, Charles. *On the Economy of Machinery and Manufactures*. London: Frank Cass & Co, 1963.

The One Minute Manager
by Kenneth Blanchard and Spencer Johnson

Blanchard and Johnson start from the idea that the profession of management is not as compli-cated as it is sometimes made out to be. Following a few simple rules can guarantee increased productivity, profits, and job satisfaction for the employees. First published in 1982, this book has become a popular management classic. It is short, to the point, and the ideas that it advocates can be put into practice straight away.

GETTING STARTED

The 'carrot-and-stick' method of motivating employees does not work, say Blanchard and Spencer. It causes confusion and frustration, for two reasons: firstly it is inconsistent, and, secondly, it is unpredictable. And consistency and predictability are what count in human management. This 'allegory', as the authors describe it, recounts the story of a young beginner who sets out to find a really effective manager to model himself on. He finds what he is looking for in the One Minute Manager, who has three simple secrets: one minute goal-setting, one minute praising, and one minute reprimanding.

CONTRIBUTION

The search for the One Minute Manager. Really efficient managers deploy themselves and their employees so that both the business and its staff profit from what they do. Effective management, the authors say, is team-orientated. Managers should by and large keep out of decision-making by employees. They should be equally interested in results and people, because results are only achieved by people. A good manager, they suggest, acts on the principle that only people who feel good about themselves work well.

One minute goal-setting. In setting goals the One Minute Manager asks the following questions:

- What goals do I want to achieve?
- What kind of behaviour will best help me achieve these goals?

and goes through the following steps:

- writing each individual goal down on a separate sheet of paper in not more than 30 lines
- reading through the piece of paper, setting out the goal again periodically
- scrutinising his or her own working methods several times a day
- deciding, on the basis of self-observation, whether his or her own behaviour is helping to achieve the goal or not

One minute praising. Praising is effective, say the authors, if it is done like this.

- Always tell your employees what you think of their work.
- If you can praise someone, do it straight away.
- Tell your people what they have done well. Be concrete and go into detail.
- Let them know how pleased you feel about their good performance.
- Stop for a moment so that the person you are praising can share that feeling.

- Tell your employees to 'keep up the good work', as a way of letting them know that you actively support their professional success.

One minute reprimanding. A one minute reprimand works well, Blanchard and Spencer suggest, if this procedure is followed.

- Before the reprimand: tell staff from the outset that you will make absolutely clear to them what you think of their work.
- First part of reprimand: if you have to reprimand someone, do it straight away. Tell the person involved in detail what he or she has done wrong. Stop talking and wait long enough for the silence to become painful, that way the person you are criticising will share some of the feeling behind the reprimand.
- Second part of reprimand: offer your hand or show by some other gesture that, despite the fault, you are still on the person's side. It is important to make it clear to people that you value them as employees and think highly of them—apart from what they have done in this particular instance.
- After the reprimand: do not hark back. Once the reprimand is over, it is over.

Why one minute goal-setting works. Many managers, say the authors, act like this. They know what they want from staff, but do not take the trouble to tell them. They assume the employees will know. This is wrong. A manager should never take anything for granted, where goal-setting is concerned. Goals must be fixed in writing, so that employees can always look at them again to check their own performance.

Why one minute praising works. Most managers hold back praise until the employees have done something 'exactly right'. Consequently, the authors assert, many people never reach their full potential, because their superiors concentrate on catching them out making mistakes. That is wrong. When employees are introduced to a new task, the vital thing is to 'catch' them doing something 'nearly right', so that they go on to learn how to do it exactly right.

Why one minute reprimands work. In many businesses a 'blacklist' system operates. Managers collect up instances of unsatisfactory work they have spotted, and then one day—when giving a performance review or if they happen to be in a bad mood—they let the employee have it all at once. That, say Blanchard and Spencer, is wrong. Proper criticism is basically nothing but prompt feedback. Confront the person involved as soon as you have spotted a fault. Reprimands are fairer and clearer if they apply to someone's current behaviour. Criticism should also be directed only at the employee's behaviour, never at him or her as a person.

CONTEXT

The behavioural perspective in *The One Minute Manager* comes from Blanchard, a behavioural scientist and one of the creators of the situation-determined method of management. The psychological aspects of leadership are dealt with by Johnson, a specialist in social medicine and communications. Reviews praise the book's compact treatment of insights that are often presented at great length.

THE BEST SOURCES OF HELP

Blanchard, Kenneth, and Spencer Johnson. *The One Minute Manager.* London: HarperCollins Business, 2000.

On War
by Carl von Clausewitz

Business is a form of human competition resembling war. Military theory and practice frequently mirror management thinking in such areas as strategy, leadership, logistics, and human resources. Von Clausewitz provides a valuable insight into issues such as motivation, setting objectives, and achieving results with the most efficient use of resources.

GETTING STARTED

According to von Clausewitz, war is an important and continuing element of overall strategy. Decisions about war should be rational and based on estimated gains and losses. Any war, he argues, should have a clear objective, and all tactics should be focused on the single aim of winning. There is no such thing as a limited victory. Although theory plays an important part in developing strategy, plans should take account of practicalities such as the enemy's strengths and weaknesses. They should also be flexible enough to meet changing circumstances. The most effective leaders achieve their results by the most efficient use of their resources. Creative leaders who can motivate their people effectively can win, even with fewer resources.

CONTRIBUTION

War is a constant element in strategy. No-one, according to von Clausewitz, should wage a war simply for its own sake. War, which he defines as an act of force or violence designed to compel opponents to fulfil the other party's will, should be part of an overall strategy to achieve certain goals. It is a continuation of that strategy using other means. It should only be used when politics has failed.

War is used to achieve rational goals. He also suggests that we see war as a rational instrument of policy: in other words, it must have a clear goal based on an assessment of potential costs and benefits. The only true test of a war is victory, so all strategy and tactics must be directed towards winning.

Strategy and tactics are different. Strategy, according to von Clausewitz, is the overall plan for winning the war. Tactics are just part of that overall plan. Strategy does not change throughout the war. Tactics, on the other hand, can be changed on a day-to-day basis to deal with changing conditions and challenges. In changing the tactics, a leader should never lose sight of the overall strategy. He also points out that decisions about strategy appear, at first sight, to be simple but that that does not necessarily make them easy to achieve. Decisions about tactics, on the other hand, are made in the heat of the moment in response to an event.

> Strategy, according to von Clausewitz, is the overall plan for winning the war.

Information is important. Von Clausewitz believes that a leader should have a good understanding of all elements that could influence the outcome of a war. Part of that understanding is based on theoretical knowledge, part on knowledge of the terrain and the enemy. However, von Clausewitz also believes that the qualities of leadership supersede theoretical and local knowledge, and those qualities cannot be taught.

Concentrate on one objective at a time. He points out that it is essential to concentrate on one battle at a time. However, a leader should understand how each battle contributes to the achievement of the overall objective.

Leaders must be flexible. Plans must take into account the strengths and weaknesses of the enemy. A leader must be alert to those and be willing to adopt different tactics if circumstances change.

Achieve results with the least effort. Von Clausewitz argues that a leader should use the equivalent of cost-benefit analysis in planning for war. The most effective result uses the least possible resources to achieve the objective.

CONTEXT

Colonel F.N. Maude, in his editor's introduction to the 1908 edition of *On War*, pointed out that business is a form of human competition greatly resembling war. Von Clausewitz himself felt that comparisons between war and commerce were useful and valid. Commerce, he believed, was a conflict of interests and activities.

He was also one of the first to note the difference between strategy and tactics, although the debate on the difference still continues in management literature. The thinking behind the theory of 'management by objectives' can be seen in von Clausewitz's view that leaders should concentrate on one battle at a time, but consider each battle as part of a series that leads to the final goal of victory.

The military thinking of historical figures such as Sun Tzu, Hadrian, the Duke of Wellington, and Napoleon continues to play an important role in the development of management thinking. Sun Tzu, for example, is considered to be the first person to develop the concept of strategy. Hadrian believed a leader should stay close to the troops and share their conditions. Wellington demonstrated the importance of flexibility in resolving crises during the Napoleonic Wars. He too kept close to his troops and the action during a campaign. With that degree of involvement, he was able to deal with any crisis as it occurred and adjust his tactics to suit the circumstances.

More contemporary figures such as Basil Liddell Hart, Colin Powell, and Norman Schwarzkopf have also influenced both thinking and practice. Business guru Richard Pascale has also considered the views of military leaders and thinkers on current issues such as leadership, training, motivation, and strategy. In the November/December 1996 issue of *Human Resources*, he examines the role of training on motivation in the US Army.

THE BEST SOURCES OF HELP

von Clausewitz, Carl. *On War*. Ed. Anatol Rapoport. London: Penguin Books, 1968.

Onward Industry
by James Mooney and Alan Reiley

The book provides insights into early thinking about the nature of organisations and their impact on the performance of industry. The authors argue that organisation is a universal phenomenon and has a benefit on the overall standard of living.

GETTING STARTED

Organisation is a universal phenomenon that has occurred throughout history. The organisation of businesses is crucial to prosperity and living standards.

Production without distribution is worthless; the emphasis must be on finding and exploiting markets. Industry should encourage participation in business so that purchasing capacity can be created and extended. Organisational size is less important than knowing what to do with the organisation.

CONTRIBUTION

Organisation is a universal phenomenon. People love to organise, and organisation is as old as human society itself. Consider the scalar organisation of the Catholic Church, governmental organisation, and the evolution of different forms of organisation from Roman times to medieval times, through to the company of the early 20th century.

> The organisation of businesses is crucial to overall standards of living.

Organisation is crucial to standards of living. The organisation of businesses is crucial to overall standards of living. There is a direct link between industrial prosperity, built on modern management techniques, and the affluence of society as a whole.

'The highest development of the techniques both of production and distribution will be futile to supply the material wants of those who, because of poverty, are unable to acquire through purchase', the authors write. The final task of industry, therefore, is to organise participation in these activities, even in the poorest communities and countries, through which purchasing capacity can be created and extended.

Production without distribution is worthless. Before the 1930s, production was the overarching driving force. Later the emphasis shifted to finding new markets and enhancing and expanding distribution to make inroads into these markets.

The value of size. Size isn't everything. Modern business leadership has been generally characterised by the capacity to create large organisations, but by failure in knowing exactly what to do with them.

Key organisational principles. Mooney and Reiley's theory of organisations identified three central organisational principles:

- the co-ordinative principle, leading to effective co-ordination
- the scalar process, resulting in functional definition
- the functional effect, leading to interpretative functionalism

CONTEXT

The book provides an organisation model that is firmly of its time. It applies the reasoned science of Frederick W. Taylor to the broader organisational canvas.

The argument that production without distribution is worthless marks something of a watershed. Before the 1930s, production was the overarching driving force. From the second world war, the emphasis shifted to finding new markets and enhancing and expanding distribution to make inroads into these markets.

THE BEST SOURCES OF HELP

Mooney, James, and Alan Reiley. *Onward Industry*. New York: Harper & Bros, 1931.

The Organization Man
by William Whyte

From the point of view of the age of uncertainty, the age of downsizing, re-engineering, and 'discontinuous change', the 1950s and 1960s can easily seem like a golden age. The careers enjoyed by corporate executives were built on solid foundations, workers had jobs for life, suburbia was heaven, and everything seemed set to go on and on and on. William Whyte showed the downside to this corporate utopia. Read his brilliant, witty, and often poignant analysis to get both the post-war past and the present in perspective.

GETTING STARTED

William Whyte joined the staff of *Fortune* magazine in 1946 after graduating from Princeton and serving in the US Marines during the second world war. *The Organization Man* is based on articles he wrote for the magazine. He subsequently left *Fortune* and, in his later years, wrote mainly on the subject of urban sprawl, urban planning, and human behaviour in urban spaces.

1950s America still publicly and privately subscribed to the idea that rugged individualism was the hallmark of the American character and the foundation stone of American success. According to Whyte, this was a delusion. Average Americans in fact subscribed to a collectivist social ethic that was turning them into organisation people—and they needed to realise the fact and do something about it.

CONTRIBUTION

The social ethic. Whyte believed that the condition he was analysing did not affect America alone: he referred to 'a bureaucratization that has affected every country'.

The bureaucratic or collectivist ethic rested on three major principles:
- a belief in the group as the source of creativity
- a belief in 'belongingness' as the ultimate need of every individual
- a belief in the application of science to achieve belongingness

And above all he believed that, 'the fundamental principle of the new model executive is . . . that the goals of the individual and the goals of the organization will work out to be one and the same'.

The importance of loyalty. Grey-suited and obedient, corporate man was unstintingly loyal to his employer. He spent his life with a single company and rose slowly, but quietly, up the hierarchy.

Loyalty and solid performance brought job security. This was mutually beneficial.

The executive gained a respectable income and a high degree of security. The company gained loyal, hard-working executives.

But while loyalty is a positive quality, it can easily become blind. What if the corporate strategy is wrong or the company is engaged in unlawful or immoral acts? The corporation becomes a self-contained and self-perpetuating world supported by a complex array of checks, systems, and hierarchies. The company is right.

In a remark reminiscent of George Orwell's *1984*, Whyte suggested that the organisation man 'must not only accept control, he must accept it as if he liked it'.

Low-risk environment. Customers, who exist outside the organisation, are often regarded as peripheral.

In the 1950s, 1960s, and 1970s, it sometimes seems, no executive ever lost his job by delivering poor-quality or indifferent service. In some organisations, executives only lost their jobs by defrauding their employer or insulting their boss. Jobs for life was the refrain and, to a large extent for executives, the reality.

> Customers, who exist outside the organisation, are often regarded as peripheral.

Clearly, such an environment was hardly conducive to the fostering of dynamic risk-takers. It rewarded the steady foot soldier, the safe pair of hands, the organisation man living with his organisation wife.

CONTEXT

Reviewing the book in the *New York Times*, C. Wright Mills wrote: 'Whyte understands that the work-and-thrift ethic of success has grievously declined, except in the rhetoric of top executives; that the entrepreneurial scramble to success has been largely replaced by the organizational crawl.'

Chester Barnard noted in *The Functions of the Executive*: 'The most important single contribution required of an executive, certainly the most universal qualification, is loyalty [allowing] domination by the organization personality.'

Twenty years after the publication of Whyte's book, things had not changed very much. When she came to examine corporate life for the first time in her 1977 book, *Men and Women of the Corporation*, Rosabeth Moss Kanter found that the central characteristic expected of a manager was dependability.

Fortune founder Henry Luce commented: 'It was *Fortune's* William H. Whyte, Jr who made the "organization man" a household word, and the organization wife too. His was a fine achievement in sociological reporting. In it he related the phenomenon of the business organization to questions of human personality and values. The kind of people who are eager to hear the worst about American society assumed that Mr Whyte was predicting the destruction of individualism by the organization.'

Whyte was uneasy about corporate life, which seemed to stifle creativity and individualism. He was uneasy about the subtle pressures in the office and at home that called for smooth performance rather than daring creativity. However, he did not urge the organisation men to leave their secure environment. Rather he urged them to fight the organisation when necessary, and he was optimistic that the battle could be successful.

THE BEST SOURCES OF HELP

Whyte, William. *The Organization Man*. New York: Simon & Schuster, 1956.

Organizational Culture and Leadership
by Edgar Schein

Organizational Culture and Leadership clarified the entire area of corporate culture in a way no previous book had. It brought culture into the management debate and paved the way for a plethora of further studies. Even today, its perspectives on culture as a constantly changing force in corporate life remain as disconcerting as they are valuable.

GETTING STARTED

Schein is sometimes seen as the inventor of the term 'corporate culture'; he is, at the very least, one of its originators. After a long and distinguished academic career, he is currently the Sloan Fellows' Professor of Management Emeritus at the MIT Sloan School of Management.

In this book, he not only provides a sophisticated definition of culture, but he turns the abstract concept into a tool to assist managers in understanding the dynamics of organisations. In addition, he tackles the vital question of how an existing culture can be changed—one of the toughest challenges for leadership.

CONTRIBUTION

The basis of corporate culture. Culture is a pattern of basic assumptions invented, discovered, or developed by a given group as it learns to cope with its problems of external adaptation and internal integration. These assumptions have worked well enough to be considered valid and, therefore, to be taught to new members as the correct way to perceive, think, and feel in relation to those problems.

They can be categorised into five dimensions.

- humanity's relationship to nature—while some companies regard themselves as masters of their own destiny, others are submissive, willing to accept the domination of their external environment.
- the nature of reality and truth—organisations and managers adopt a wide variety of methods to reach what becomes accepted as the organisational truth.
- the nature of human nature—organisations differ in their views of human nature. Some follow McGregor's Theory X and work on the principle that people will not do the job if they can avoid it. Others regard people in a more positive light and attempt to enable them to fulfil their potential for the benefit of both sides.
- the nature of human activity—the West has traditionally emphasised tasks and their completion rather than the more philosophical side of work. Achievement is all. Schein suggests an alternative approach—'being-in-becoming'—emphasising self fulfilment and development.
- the nature of human relationships—organisations make a variety of assumptions about how people interact with each other. Some facilitate social interaction, while others regard it as an unnecessary distraction.

These five categories are not mutually exclusive, but are in a constant state of development and flux. Culture does not stand still.

Shaping organisational values. Key to the creation and development of corporate culture are the values embraced by the organisation. A single person can shape these values and, as a result, an entire corporate culture. The heroic creators of corporate cultures include such people as Henry Ford and IBM's Thomas Watson Sr.

Development of corporate culture. There are three stages in the development of a corporate culture.

- birth and early growth—the culture may be dominated by the business founder. It is regarded as a source of the company's identity, a bonding agent protecting it against outside forces.
- organisational mid-life—the original culture is likely to be diluted and undermined as new cultures emerge and there is a loss of the original sense of identity. At this stage, there is an opportunity for the fundamental culture to be realigned and changed.
- organisational maturity—culture, at this stage, is regarded sentimentally. People are hopelessly addicted to how things used to be done and unwilling to contemplate change. Here the organisation is at its weakest, as the culture has been transformed from a source of competitive advantage and distinctiveness to a hindrance in the marketplace. Only through aggressive measures will it survive.

Changing corporate culture. Each stage of the culture's growth requires a different method of change.

If culture is to work in support of a company's strategy, there has to be a level of consensus covering five areas:

- the core mission or primary task
- goals
- the means to accomplish the goals
- the means to measure progress
- remedial or repair strategies

Achieving cultural change is a formidable challenge, one that well-established executives in strong cultures often find beyond them. The exceptional executives who achieve cultural change from within a culture they are closely identified with (such as GE's Jack Welch) are rarities, and are known as cultural hybrids.

CONTEXT

Schein's findings gave rise to a host of other studies of the subject. His basic assumptions are rephrased and reinterpreted elsewhere in a variety of ways. Perhaps Chris Argyris comes closest to him when discussing 'theories-in-use'.

Gary Hamel says: 'It is impossible to change a large organisation without first understanding that organisation's culture. Ed Schein gave us an ability to look deeply into what makes an organisation what it is, thus providing the foundation of any successful effort at transformation or change. *Organizational Culture and Leadership* remains essential reading for all aspiring change agents.'

THE BEST SOURCES OF HELP

Schein, Edgar H. *Organizational Culture and Leadership*. 2nd ed. San Francisco, California: Jossey-Bass, 1997.

Organizational Learning
by Chris Argyris and Donald Schön

This book shows why organisational learning is the ultimate competitive advantage. It also explains two of the central paradoxes of business life—how individual initiative and creativity can work in an organisational environment, where rules will always exist, and how teamworking and individual working can co-exist fruitfully.

GETTING STARTED

Learning is a key business activity. Many organisational models only achieve single-loop learning, which—while this permits a company to carry on its present policies and achieve its current objectives—is limited to detection and correction of organisational error.

Double-loop learning, however, enables organisations to detect and correct errors in ways that involve the modification of underlying norms, policies, and objectives. With double-loop learning, managers can act on information and learn from others. Most organisations do quite well in single-loop learning, but have great difficulties with double-loop learning.

Deutero-learning is the process of inquiring into the learning system by which an organisation detects and corrects its errors. It underpins the concept of the learning organisation.

Increasingly, the art of management is managing knowledge—and effective leadership means creating the conditions that enable people to produce valid knowledge. Success in the marketplace increasingly depends on learning, yet most people don't know how to learn.

CONTRIBUTION

The weakness of single-loop learning. The authors investigate two basic organisational models.

Model 1 is based on the premise that we seek to manipulate and form the world in accordance with our individual aspirations and wishes. In Model 1, managers concentrate on establishing individual goals. They keep to themselves and don't voice concerns or disagreements. The onus is on creating a conspiracy of silence in which everyone dutifully keeps their head down. Defence is the prime activity in a Model 1 organisation, though occasionally the best means of defence is attack. Model 1 managers are prepared to inflict change on others, but resist any attempt to change their own thinking and working practices.

Model 1 organisations are characterised by single-loop learning—the detection and correction of organisational error that permits the organisation to carry on its present policies and achieve its current objectives.

The importance of double-loop learning. Model 2 organisations emphasise double-loop learning—where organisational error is detected and corrected in ways that involve the modification of underlying norms, policies, and objectives.

In Model 2 organisations, managers act on information. They debate issues and respond to change—as well as being prepared to change themselves. They learn from others. A virtuous circle emerges of learning and understanding.

Most organisations do quite well in single-loop learning, but have great difficulties with double-loop learning.

The challenge of deutero-learning. Deutero-learning offers even greater challenges. This is the process of inquiring into the learning system by which an organisation detects and corrects its errors. The examination of learning systems is central to the contemporary concept of the learning organisation.

The importance of managing knowledge. Learning is powerfully practical and increasingly, the art of management is managing knowledge. Organisations should not manage people per se, but rather the knowledge that they carry.

Leadership means creating the conditions that enable people to produce valid knowledge, and to do so in ways that encourage personal responsibility. Knowledge must relate to action, rather than knowledge for the purpose of understanding and exploring.

The learning imperative. There is a natural temptation for organisations and individuals to limit themselves to single-loop learning rather than its more demanding alternatives. However, the need better to understand learning in all its dimensions is now imperative. Any company that aspires to success in the tougher business environment of the 1990s and beyond must embrace learning—yet most people don't know how to learn. Those members of an organisation who are assumed by many to be the best at learning are, in fact, not very good at it.

CONTEXT

If you wished to trace the roots of the learning organisation, you would invariably find yourself reading *Organizational Learning*.

Organizational Learning grew out of Argyris and Schön's 1974 book, *Theory in Practice*.

Chris Argyris was part of the human relations school of the late 1950s and involved in the work of the National Training Laboratories. He was drawn to the riddles of human nature—in particular, why do people fail to live up to their own professed ideals? Why is so much human behaviour so self-frustrating, particularly within organisations?

In the last decade, Argyris's ideas have become fashionable. This is most apparent in the upsurge of interest in the concept of the learning organisation.

Organizational Learning appeared in 1978, but it took the 1990 bestseller from Peter Senge of MIT (Massachusetts Institute of Technology), *The Fifth Discipline*, to propel the learning organisation from an academic concept to mainstream acceptance.

Charles Hampden-Turner of the University of Cambridge's Judge Institute of Management says, 'There is an urgent need for alternative visions of science and Schön's work, along with that of Argyris, provides some of the best ideas and answers. Few have gone so far in reconciling the vigour of relevance and in building a bridge between the isolated academic fortresses of the sciences and the humanities.'

Gary Hamel concurs. 'If your organisation has not yet mastered double-loop learning, it is already a dinosaur. No one can doubt that organisational learning is the ultimate competitive advantage. We owe much to Argyris and Schön for helping us learn about learning.'

THE BEST SOURCES OF HELP

Argyris, Chris, and Donald Schön. *Organizational Learning*. New York: Addison-Wesley, 1978.

Out of the Crisis
by W. Edwards Deming

This book is regarded as a classic of literature on quality management. It reflects Deming's experience in introducing quality to Japan, and its aim was to transform the style of American management. Deming is regarded as the leading figure on quality and this book sets out the methods that taught industry the power of quality.

GETTING STARTED

Deming argues that profit comes from repeat customers—and they respond to good quality.

Statistical quality control produces spectacular results, so senior managers must take charge of quality, and quality training should begin at the top of the organisation.

Quality is a way of living, Deming says: it is not the preserve of the few but the responsibility of all. Deming argued that factory workers already understood the importance of quality but were stymied by managers focused on increasing productivity regardless of quality.

CONTRIBUTION

The importance of quality. Profit in business comes from repeat customers, customers who boast about your product and service, and who bring friends with them.

Quality is more than statistical control, though this is important. Statistical quality control produces spectacular results by using tools to improve processes in ways that minimise defects and eliminate rejects, rework, and recalls. Deming's work bridges the gap between science-based application and humanistic philosophy.

The quality gospel. The book's quality gospel revolves around a number of basic precepts.

- if consistent quality is to be achieved senior managers must take charge of it.
- implementation requires a cascade, with training beginning at the top of the organisation before moving downwards through the hierarchy.
- the use of statistical methods of quality control is necessary so that, finally, business plans can be expanded to include clear quality goals.
- quality is a way of living, the meaning of industrial life and, in particular, of management.

Deming's Fourteen Points.

- Create constancy of purpose for improvement of product and service.
- Adopt the new philosophy.
- Cease dependence on inspection to achieve quality.
- End the practice of awarding business on the basis of price tag alone. Instead, minimise total cost by working with a single supplier.
- Improve constantly and forever every process for planning, production, and service.
- Institute training on the job.
- Adopt and institute leadership.
- Drive out fear.
- Break down barriers between staff areas.
- Eliminate slogans, exhortations, and targets for the workforce.

- Eliminate numerical quotas for the workforce and numerical goals for management.
- Remove barriers that rob people of pride of workmanship. Eliminate the annual rating or merit system.
- Institute a vigorous programme of education and self-improvement for everyone.
- Put everybody in the company to work to accomplish the transformation.

The importance of empowerment. The simplicity of the Fourteen Points disguises the immensity of the challenge: quality is not the preserve of the few but the responsibility of all. In arguing this case Deming was anticipating the fashion for empowerment.

People all over the world think that it is the factory worker that causes problems. He or she is not your problem. 'Ever since there has been anything such as industry, the factory worker has known that quality is what will protect his job. He knows that poor quality in the hands of the customer will lose the market and cost him his job. He knows it and lives with that fear every day. Yet he cannot do a good job. He is not allowed to do it because the management wants figures, more products, and never mind the quality.'

The problem of management. Management is 90% of the problem, a problem caused in part by the Western enthusiasm for annual performance appraisals. Japanese managers receive feedback every day of their working lives.

The basic cause of sickness in American industry and resulting unemployment is failure of top management to manage. He that sells not can buy not.

The Japanese culture was uniquely receptive to Deming's message for a number of reasons. Its emphasis on group rather than individual achievement enables the Japanese to share ideas and responsibility. It also promotes collective ownership in a way that the West often finds difficult to contemplate, let alone understand.

CONTEXT

W. Edwards Deming has a unique place among management theorists. He had an impact on industrial history that others only dream of. Deming visited Japan after the second world war on the invitation of General MacArthur, and played a key role in the rebuilding of Japanese industry. During the 1950s, Deming and the other American standard bearer of quality, Joseph Juran, conducted seminars and courses throughout Japan.

Deming, and Japanese management, was eventually discovered by the West in the 1980s.

British management journalist Robert Heller says, 'Deming didn't invent quality but his sermons had a uniquely powerful effect because of this first pulpit and congregation: Japan and Japanese managers. Had his fellow Americans responded with the same intense application, post-war industrial history would have differed enormously.'

Management guru Gary Hamel adds, 'Of all the management gurus . . . there is only one who should be regarded as a hero by every consumer in the world—Dr Deming. He may have taken the gospel of quality to the Japanese first, but thank God his message finally penetrated the smug complacency of American and European companies. No senior executive ever sat through one of Dr Deming's harangues without coming away just a little bit more humble and contrite—a good beginning on the road to total quality.'

THE BEST SOURCES OF HELP

Deming, W. Edwards. *Out of the Crisis*. Cambridge, Massachusetts: MIT Center for Advanced Engineering Study, 1982.

Parkinson's Law
by C. Northcote Parkinson

Parkinson's Law, like *The Dilbert Principle*, takes a cynical look at business. The book treats the growth of bureaucracy in a humorous way, but the findings reflect real life situations, particularly in government organisations.

GETTING STARTED

Companies grow without thinking of how much they are producing and without making any more money. The time to complete a task depends on the person doing the job and their unique situation. Work expands to fill the time available for its completion and officials make work for each other.

CONTRIBUTION

How organisations grow. Parkinson's Law is simply that work expands to fill the time available for its completion. As a result, companies grow without thinking of how much they are producing.

> **Parkinson's Law is simply that work expands to fill the time available for its completion.**

Even if growth in numbers doesn't make them more money, companies grow and people become busier and busier.

The author contends that an official wants to multiply subordinates, not rivals, and that officials make work for each other.

Work expands to fill the time. The notion of a particular task having an optimum time for completion is wrong. There are no rules—it depends on the person doing the job and their unique situation. For example, an elderly lady of leisure can spend an entire day in writing and dispatching a postcard to her niece at Bognor Regis. The total effort which would occupy a busy man for three minutes may, in this fashion, leave another person prostrate after a day of doubt, anxiety, and toil.

Administration expands. Faced with the decreasing energy of age and a feeling of being overworked, administrators face three options:

- resign
- halve the work with a colleague
- ask for two more subordinates

There is probably no instance in civil service history of choosing any but the third alternative.

The number of admiralty officials in the British Navy increased by 78% between 1914 and 1928, while the number of ships fell by 67% and the number of officers and men by 31%.

As the author points out in this example, the expansion of administrators tends to take on a life of its own. The conclusion drawn is that officials would have multiplied at the same rate had there been no actual seamen at all.

CONTEXT

Parkinson's Law is an amusing interlude in management literature.

It is a kind of *Catch-22* of the business world, by turns irreverent and humorous, but with a darker underside of acute observation.

The book was written in the late 1950s when the Human Relations School in the United States was beginning to flower and thinkers were actively questioning the bureaucracy that had grown up alongside mass production.

Max Weber's model of a paper-producing bureaucratic machine appeared to have been brought to fruition as the arteries of major organisations became clogged with layer upon layer of managerial administrators.

Gary Hamel had this to say. 'Yes, I know that bureaucracy is dead. We're not managers any more, we're leaders. We're not slaves to our work, we've been liberated. And all those layers of paper-shuffling administrators between the CEO and the order takers—they're all gone, right? Well then, why does a re-reading of *Parkinson's Law*, written in 1958, at the apex of corporate bureaucracy, still ring true? *Parkinson's Law* was to the 50s what *The Dilbert Principle* is to the 1990s.'

THE BEST SOURCES OF HELP

Parkinson, C. Northcote. *Parkinson's Law*. London: John Murray, 1958.

The Peter Principle
by Laurence Peter

This book is one of the most enduring books to take a cynical view of management. It is a humorous book that sets the tone for later works like *The Dilbert Principle*.

GETTING STARTED

According to the author, in a hierarchy, every employee tends to rise to his or her level of incompetence. There are no exceptions to the Peter Principle. In time, every post tends to be occupied by an employee who is incompetent to carry out his duties. If at first you don't succeed, you may be at your level of incompetence. There are two kinds of failures: those who thought and never did, and those who did and never thought. There are two sorts of losers—the good loser, and the other one who can't act.

CONTRIBUTION

Finding a level of incompetence. Peter asserts that in a hierarchy every employee tends to rise to his level of incompetence.

A position of incompetence is the apotheosis of a corporate career—or, indeed, of any career in any profession in which there is a hierarchy.

> A position of incompetence is the apotheosis of a corporate career—or, indeed, of any career in any profession in which there is a hierarchy.

No-one is exempt from the Peter Principle.

The author contends that for each individual, the final promotion is from a level of competence to a level of incompetence. So, given enough time—and assuming the existence of enough ranks in the hierarchy—each employee rises to, and remains at, his or her level of incompetence.

In time, every post tends to be occupied by an employee who is incompetent to carry out his or her duties.

Dealing with failure. Peter asserts the following:

- If at first you don't succeed, you may have arrived at your level of incompetence.
- If you don't know where you are going, you will probably end up somewhere else.
- An economist is an expert who will know tomorrow why the things he predicted yesterday didn't happen.
- Human inadequacy is universal, as is the human capacity to build vacuous power structures. In our supposedly leaner and fitter times, there are still hierarchies aplenty. The difference is, perhaps, that we have simply become more adept at disguising them.
- There are two kinds of failures: those who thought and never did, and those who did and never thought.
- There are two sorts of losers—the good loser, and the other one who can't act.
- Fortune knocks once, but misfortune has much more patience.

Computerised incompetence. Computerised incompetence is the incompetent application of computer techniques or the inherent incompetence of a computer.

CONTEXT

Cynicism about the way businesses and managers operate is nothing new. For example, *The Dilbert Principle* is simply an accurate and amusing portrayal of corporate cynicism, updated for the 1990s.

From *Murphy's Law* to *Parkinson's Law*, from Pudd'nhead Wilson to Stanley Bing, a steady infusion of comic scepticism has been injected into the corporate canon.

The Peter Principle is perhaps the most enduring, cynical classic and along with *Parkinson's Law* carries many echoes of that other humorous classic of the 1960s, *Catch-22*.

The Peter Principle remains a poignant antidote to the blind optimism and sugary reality of most business books. It is a reminder that corporate reality is not usually about grand designs and great decisions. It is more mundane and frustrating. Too mundane and too frustrating to be taken seriously.

> *The Peter Principle* remains a poignant antidote to the blind optimism and sugary reality of most business books.

Dilbert creator Scott Adams commented, 'Now, apparently, the incompetent workers are promoted directly to management without ever passing through the temporary competence stage. When I entered the workforce in 1979, *The Peter Principle* described management pretty well. Now I think we'd all like to return to those Golden Years when you had a boss who was once good at something.'

The book remains relevant today. When Peter refers to codophilia (defined as speaking in letters and numbers instead of words), he could be talking of today's consultants.

Microsoft's Bill Gates echoes Peter saying, 'The art of management is to promote people without making them managers'.

THE BEST SOURCES OF HELP

Peter, Laurence. *The Peter Principle*. New York: William Morrow & Co, 1969.

Planning for Quality
by Joseph M. Juran

Juran, like W. Edwards Deming, was one of the key figures in the quality revolution. In this book he stresses that the human aspect of quality management is as important as statistical control. The book underscores the contribution that quality teams and empowerment give to the quality process.

GETTING STARTED

Unlike the West, the Japanese have made quality a priority at the top of the organisation.

The key elements in a quality philosophy are:
- quality planning
- quality management
- quality implementation

Juran contends that quality is nothing new, but it has become ignored in the West where it is treated as an operational issue. There is more to quality than specification and rigorous testing: it cannot be delegated and has to be the goal of each employee, individually and in teams. Quality can be seen as an invariable sequence of steps. Planning consists of developing processes to meet customers' needs; the human side is just as important.

CONTRIBUTION

National attitudes to quality matter. Talking to Japanese audiences in the 1950s, Joseph Juran's message was enthusiastically absorbed by groups of senior managers—the Japanese have made quality a priority at the top of the organisation. In the West, Juran's audiences were made up of engineers and quality inspectors. Quality was delegated downwards—an operational rather than a managerial issue.

In the post-war years, US businesses were caught unawares for two reasons:
- they assumed their Asian adversaries were copycats rather than innovators
- chief executives were too obsessed with financial indicators to notice any danger signs

Juran insisted that quality cannot be delegated, and he was an early exponent of what has become known as empowerment.

The quality trilogy. Juran's quality philosophy is built around a 'quality trilogy' based on 'Company-Wide Quality Management' (CWQM), which aims to create a means of disseminating quality to all. Juran insisted that quality cannot be delegated, and he was an early exponent of what has become known as empowerment.

Quality has to be the goal of each employee, individually and in teams, through self-supervision.

The historical context of quality. Manufacturing products to design specifications and then inspecting them for defects to protect the buyer was something the Egyptians had mastered 5,000 years previously when building the pyramids. The ancient Chinese set up a separate department of the central government to establish quality standards and maintain them.

Juran's message is therefore that quality is nothing new. But if it is so elemental and elementary, why had it become ignored in the West?

The human side of quality. There is more to quality than specification and rigorous testing for defects; Juran regarded the human side of quality as critical. He developed all-embracing theories of what quality should entail.

The quality planning process. Quality planning consists of developing the products and processes required to meet customers' needs. Quality planning includes the following activities:

- identifying the customers and their needs
- developing a product that responds to those needs
- developing a process able to produce that product

Quality planning can be produced through an invariable sequence of steps:

- identify the customers
- determine their needs
- translate those needs into our language
- develop a product that can respond to those needs
- optimise the product features to meet our needs as well as customers' needs
- develop a process which is able to produce the product
- optimise the process
- prove that the process can produce the product under operating conditions
- transfer the process to the operating forces

CONTEXT

Juran is critical of Deming (*Out of the Crisis*) as being over-reliant on statistics. Juran's approach is less mechanistic than Deming's and places greater stress on human relations. It is based on Company-Wide Quality Management (CWQM), a means of disseminating quality to all. Juran was an early exponent of what has become known as empowerment and believed that quality should be the goal of each employee.

Gary Hamel commented: 'The impact of Juran, and of Deming as well, went far beyond quality. By drawing the attention of Western managers to the successes of Japan, they forced Western managers to challenge some of their most basic beliefs about the capabilities of their employees and the expectations of their customers.'

THE BEST SOURCES OF HELP

Juran, Joseph M. *Planning for Quality*. New York: Free Press, 1988.

The Practice of Management
by Peter Drucker

Peter Drucker is regarded as the major management and business thinker of the century. *The Practice of Management* is a book of huge range, encyclopaedic in its scope and historical perspectives. It laid the groundwork for many of today's accepted management practices and is an excellent primer in management thinking.

GETTING STARTED

Drucker asserts that management will remain a basic and dominant institution, with managers being at the epicentre of economic activity.

A business's purpose is to create a customer, and the two essential functions of business are marketing and innovation. Organisation is a means to achieving business performance and results.

There are five basics of the managerial role—to set objectives; organise; motivate and communicate; measure; and develop people. Management has a moral responsibility, and must be driven by objectives.

CONTRIBUTION

The importance of management. Management will remain a basic and dominant institution perhaps as long as Western civilization itself survives. Drucker places management and managers at the epicentre of economic activity.

Rarely has a new basic institution emerged as fast as has management since 1900, and never before has a new institution proved indispensable so quickly.

A marketing attitude is critical. There is only one valid definition of business purpose: to create a customer.

Markets are created by businessmen. The want they satisfy may have been felt previously by the customer, but it was theoretical. Only when the action of businessmen provides a means to satisfy that want is there a customer, a market.

Since the role of business is to create customers, its only two essential functions are marketing and innovation. Marketing is not an isolated function, it is the whole business seen from the customer's point of view.

The nature of organisations. Though indispensable, organisation is not an end in itself, but a means to achieving performance and results. The wrong structure will seriously impair performance and may even destroy the business.

The first question in discussing structure must be: what is our business and what should it be? Organisation structure must be designed in such a way that it's possible to achieve business objectives for 5, 10, 15 years hence.

The managerial role. There are five basics of the managerial role. These are to: set objectives; organise; motivate and communicate; measure, and develop people.

The function that distinguishes the manager above all others is educational. The unique contribution he or she must make is to give others vision and ability to perform.

The importance of moral responsibility. It is vision and moral responsibility that, in the last analysis, define the manager. This morality is reflected in five areas.

- There must be high performance requirements; no condoning of poor or mediocre performance, and rewards must be based on performance.
- Each management job must be rewarding in itself, rather than just a step on the ladder.
- There must be a rational and just promotion system.
- Management needs clear rules on who has the power to make life-and-death decisions affecting a manager, and there should be some way to appeal to a higher court.
- In its appointments, management must realise that integrity is the one quality that a manager has to bring to the job and cannot be expected to acquire later on.

Management by objectives. A manager's job should be based on tasks, the performance of which will help attain the company's objectives. The manager should be directed and controlled by the objectives of performance, rather than by his or her boss.

The manager must know and understand what the business goals demand of him or her in terms of performance, and his or her superior must judge the manager accordingly.

Tasks for the manager of the future. Drucker identified seven new tasks for the manager of the future. Given that these were laid down over 40 years ago, their prescience is astounding. Tomorrow's managers must:

- manage by objectives
- take more risks and for a longer period ahead
- be able to make strategic decisions
- be able to build an integrated team, each member of which is capable of managing his or her own performance in relation to the common objectives
- be able to communicate information fast and clearly
- be able to see the business as a whole and to integrate his or her function with it

CONTEXT

The Practice of Management laid the groundwork for many of the developments in management thinking during the 1960s, and is notable for its ideas concerning the tools and techniques of management. The book is also important for the central role it argues management has in 20th-century society.

Drucker coined phrases such as 'privatisation' and 'knowledge worker', and championed concepts such as management by objectives. Many of his innovations have become accepted facts of managerial life. *The Economist* commented, 'In a field packed with egomaniacs and snake-oil merchants, he remains a genuinely original thinker.'

Influential author Gary Hamel says, 'No other writer has contributed as much to the professionalisation of management as Peter Drucker. Drucker's commitment to the discipline of management grew out of his belief that industrial organisations would become . . . the world's most important social organisations—more influential, more encompassing, and often more intrusive than either church or state. Professor Drucker bridges the theoretical and the practical, the analytical and the emotive, the private and the social more perfectly than any other management writer.'

THE BEST SOURCES OF HELP

Drucker, Peter F. *The Practice of Management*. Oxford: Heinemann, 1955.

The Prince
by Niccolò Machiavelli

Although written over 400 years ago, Machiavelli's advice to leaders remains relevant to managers today, and covers many popular topics such as motivation, dealing with change, and leadership qualities.

GETTING STARTED

Change management, leadership style, motivation, and international management were just as relevant in the 16th century as they are today. Executives continue to see themselves as natural rulers of an organisation, and to the leader, presentation is as important as ability.

Introducing change is extremely difficult. It's essential to keep motivation high—success is not down to luck or genius, but happy shrewdness. Leaders who rise rapidly often fall just as quickly, and people ruling foreign countries should be on the spot to prevent trouble. Sometimes leaders have to practise evil when necessary.

CONTRIBUTION

Executives have not changed. Machiavelli covers topics as apparently contemporary as change management, leadership style, motivation, and international management. Like the leaders Machiavelli sought to defend, some executives tend to see themselves as the natural rulers in whose hands organisations can be safely entrusted.

Theories abound on their motivation: is it a defensive reaction against failure, or a need for predictability through complete control? The effect of the power-driven Machiavellian manager is usually plain to see.

> In the author's opinion, success is not down to luck or genius, but happy shrewdness.

Presenting the right image. According to Machiavelli, 'It is unnecessary for a prince to have all the good qualities [I have] enumerated, but it is very necessary to appear to have them. It is useful to be a great pretender and dissembler.'

Managing change and motivation. 'There is nothing more difficult to take in hand, more perilous to conduct, or more uncertain in its success, than to take the lead in the introduction of a new order of things. A leader ought above all things to keep his men well organised and drilled, to follow incessantly the chase.'

Managing internationally. 'When states are acquired in a country with a different language, customs, or laws, there are difficulties; good fortune and great energy are needed to hold them. It would be a great help if he who acquired them should go and live there. If one is on the spot, disorders are seen as they spring up, and one can quickly remedy them; but if one is not at hand, they are heard of only when they are great, and then one can no longer remedy them.'

The qualities of leadership. In the author's opinion, success is not down to luck or genius, but happy shrewdness. He felt that a prince 'ought to have no other aim or thought, nor select anything else for his study, than war and its rules and discipline; for this is the sole art that belongs to him who rules'.

'In addition, those who solely by good fortune become princes from being private citizens have little trouble in rising, but much in keeping atop,' says the author. 'They have no difficulties on the way up, because they fly, but they have many when they reach the summit.'

It is all very well being good, but the leader 'should know how to enter into evil when necessity commands'.

CONTEXT

The Prince is the 16th-century equivalent of Dale Carnegie's *How to Win Friends and Influence People*. Many of its insights are as appropriate to today's managers and organisations as they were half a millennium ago. Antony Jay's 1970 book, *Management and Machiavelli* developed the comparisons.

The book offers something for everyone. It covers topics as apparently contemporary as change management, leadership style, motivation and international management.

Gary Hamel has said: 'We occasionally need reminding that leadership and strategy are not 20th-century inventions. It's just that in previous centuries they are more often the concerns of princes than industrialists. Yet power is a constant in human affairs, and a central theme of Machiavelli's *The Prince*. It is currently out of fashion to talk about power. We are constantly reminded that in the knowledge economy, capital wears shoes and goes home every night. No place here for the blunt instrument of power politics? But would Sumner Redstone, Bill Gates, or Rupert Murdoch agree? What is interesting is that after 400 years, Machiavelli is still in print. What modern volume on leadership will be gracing bookstores in the year 2500? Does Machiavelli's longevity tell us anything about what are the deep, enduring truths of management?'

THE BEST SOURCES OF HELP

Machiavelli, Niccolò. *The Prince*. (Trans. Bull.) London: Penguin, 2003.

Principles of Political Economy
by John Stuart Mill

Can liberalisation and ethics be combined? Is there a just way of distributing wealth? These are still very relevant issues in the age of globalisation and neoliberalism. They also exercised the mind of John Stuart Mill in the middle of the 19th century. He gives lucid and humane expression to the view that the goal of economic policy must be to ensure an appropriate material livelihood for everyone. Rejecting the premises of 'homo economicus', the rational maximiser of profit and consumption, and the unrestricted belief in the progress of his age, he evolved a concept of the 'good' society that is ultimately a vision of co-operative socialism.

GETTING STARTED

Mill deals with the principles of production and distribution, embedding economic issues in a broader socio-political context. Free competition is necessary, Mill believed, in order to liberate useful social energies. However, the state is not thereby relieved of all its responsibilities, though the scope of its interventions should be strictly limited. Mill draws the balance of a whole period of scientific research and connects economic principles with their practical applications.

CONTRIBUTION

Production and distribution. The national economy, Mill argues, has to be redefined. Production and distribution must be separated. Whereas the laws of production may be natural laws, the only laws to be investigated in the case of distribution are man-made.

Progress. Belief in progress should not, he believes, be unqualified. A 'stationary' state in which economic production stagnates is not a crisis signal or catastrophe for industrialised countries, but an opportunity to develop a more just, leisured, and cultivated society. It is not an unhappy and discouraging prospect but a chance to create a harmonious social order. He confessed that he was 'not charmed with the ideal of life held out by those who think that the normal state of human being is that of struggling to get on; that the trampling, crushing, elbowing, and treading on each other's heels, which form the existing type of social life are the most desirable lot of human kind or anything but the disagreeable symptoms of one of the phases of industrial progress'.

Progressive economic development, Mill thought, is characterised by the continuing and unlimited growth of human control over nature and the constant increase in the security of persons and property.

Production and prosperity. Increase in production remained of significance only for underdeveloped countries, in Mill's view. Distribution was much more important for developed countries. The objective there is not mere increase in the result of aggregate production, but prosperity for all.

Where producers join together to form co-operatives, Mill suggests, the overall productivity of industry increases. A strong impetus is given to productive energy, inasmuch as the workers are placed in relation to their work as a single body. But the material benefit is nothing in comparison to the moral transformation of society that would accompany this. Co-operatives reduce the profits of capitalists.

Private property. The principle of private property is, according to Mill, important for three reasons. First, individuals have a right vis-à-vis society, a claim to the rewards of the labour or their frugality. Second, the criterion of economic efficiency is operative in that people are motivated to perform to the best of their abilities when they can appropriate the results of their efforts to their own use. Third, private property develops as a function of individuality itself.

State interference. In Mill's opinion, state interventions in the economy are to be rejected. For one thing, individuals know what benefits them and what harms them; for this reason state interventions are always inferior to private initiatives. For another, state interventions increase the power of the state and tend to lead to despotic and centralised rule.

The good society. A happy society is characterised by the following elements. In Mill's words:

- 'a well-paid and affluent body of labourers'
- 'no enormous fortunes, except what were earned and accumulated during a single lifetime'
- 'a larger body of people than at present not only exempt from coarser toils, but with sufficient leisure . . . to cultivate freely the graces of life, and afford examples of them to the classes less favourably circumstanced for their growth'

Modern states, he says, will need to learn the lesson that the welfare of a nation must rest on the justice and the judicious self-determination of its individual citizens. Progress in the future depends on the degree to which they are educated to be able to think for themselves.

CONTEXT

The English economist, philosopher, and logician, John Stuart Mill, is one of the chief exponents of empirically-orientated thought and of utilitarianism. He made his name as an advocate of radical reform in political and social life and of equality for women. He wished to unite the political economy of capital with the demands of the working class. His thorough-going investigation of the methodological questions relating to national economies made him the epistemologist of the liberal school. His inquiries at the interface of pure economics, social philosophy, and ethics gave liberalism a new social cast and are still relevant today. Mill's reflections have once again attracted attention in the course of the debate on 'the limits of growth'.

THE BEST SOURCES OF HELP

Mill, John Stuart. *Principles of Political Economy with Some of Their Applications to Social Philosophy.* Oxford: Oxford University Press, 1999.

Principles of Political Economy and Taxation
by David Ricardo

David Ricardo (1772–1823) is one of the most important theorists in the history of political economy. *The Principles of Political Economy and Taxation* is one of the cornerstones of the classical approach to the subject. His ideas, especially the theory of comparative cost advantage, formed the basis for the discussion of free trade and protective tariffs throughout the 19th century. His work forms a bridge between that of Adam Smith, who was Ricardo's immediate inspiration, and that of Karl Marx. He is also often said to be the inspirer of the Chicago 'monetarist' school that had such a profound influence on the economics and the politics of the late 20th century. The book is still acknowledged as a masterpiece today for its isolation and abstraction of basic principles, its synthesis, and its logic.

GETTING STARTED

In this book, first published in 1817, Ricardo gets to grips with the concept of exchange value and expounds the theory of comparative cost advantage. His central argument runs as follows: the exchange of goods between two countries is worthwhile for both, even if one country can produce all the goods more cheaply than the other. He uses two trading nations, Britain and Portugal, and two types of good, cloth and wine, as examples. In addition, he sets out criteria for the objective valuation of goods. According to his doctrine, the value of any good is determined solely by how much labour is necessary for its production. He also deals with prosperity and poverty in the social classes, and the connections between the factors of production, labour, land, and capital, and develops general principles of taxation.

CONTRIBUTION

On value. Ricardo states that the value of a good depends on the relative quantity of labour required for its production. By this he means not merely the labour expended in actually creating it, but also that expended on the machines, tools, and buildings that support the immediate work of production.

On foreign trade. Expansion of foreign trade will not, according to Ricardo, immediately increase the sum of value in a country. As the value of all foreign goods is measured by the quantity of the products of the country's soil and labour expended in exchange for them, it will not possess greater value if, through the discovery of new markets, it receives double the quantity of foreign goods for a specific quantity of its own.

On taxes. Taxes, says Ricardo, are a part of the product of the land and labour of a country that is put at the disposal of the government. They are always paid out of the country's capital or revenue.

Taxes on luxury goods only affect those who use luxuries. Taxes on necessities, however, are a burden on consumers not only in proportion to the quantity they consume, but often in far greater measure. This is because, argues Ricardo, anything that increases wages reduces the profit from capital; any taxes on goods consumed by workers tend to bring down rates of profit.

Income taxes likewise increase wages and reduce the rate of profit on capital. Consequently, in Ricardo's view, only those who employ workers contribute to income tax, not money capitalists, nor landowners, nor any other social class.

He also argues, however, that a tax on essential consumer goods does not entail any particular disadvantage insofar as it raises wages and lowers profits. Profits are indeed reduced, but only to the extent of the worker's contribution to the tax, which in any event must be borne either by the worker's employer or the consumers of the products of his or her labour.

On currencies and banks. The exchangeability of paper money for metal is not essential to ensure its value, Ricardo says. It is only necessary that its quantity should be regulated in accordance with the value of the metal that has been declared as the standard. If gold of a specific weight and fineness is the standard, then the amount of paper money in circulation can be increased whenever gold declines in value or, which is the same thing in its effect, whenever the price of goods rises.

On the influence of supply and demand on prices. Production costs, Ricardo argues, determine the prices of goods, not the relationship between supply and demand. This relationship may influence the market price of a good for a time, until it is delivered in greater or lesser quantities depending on whether demand has risen or fallen. But this will only be a temporary effect.

CONTEXT

In his thoughts on foreign trade, Ricardo went against the spirit of his age. Whereas his homeland, Great Britain, protected its own economy with customs barriers, his theorem of comparative cost advantages argued in favour of free trade. His views on foreign trade are a guiding light in the liberalisation of world trade even today: his portrait adorns the website of the World Trade Organization (WTO).

Ricardo's arguments on the value of goods and his ideas on the division of income between workers, capitalists, and landowners influenced many later economists. In particular, his theory of added value was taken up by Karl Marx and became a weapon in the arsenal of socialism.

Before he began writing, Ricardo was one of the best-known speculators of his time. As a young man, he was a dealer in government securities and made a fortune through the stock exchange. In Ricardo's system of distribution, however, landowners come off best in the long run. He himself acted in accordance with his own principles: he sold his securities and bought an estate.

THE BEST SOURCES OF HELP

Ricardo, David. *The Principles of Political Economy and Taxation*. Loughton: Prometheus Books UK, 1996.

The Principles of Scientific Management
by Frederick Winslow Taylor

At the time *The Principles of Scientific Management* was published, 'business management as a discrete and identifiable activity had attracted little attention' as Lyndall Urwick, the British champion of scientific management, said. The book put management on the map, and its influence on working methods and managerial attitudes for most of the 20th century, especially in mass-production industries, was enormous. Taylor's principles have been alternately reviled, rejected, and rediscovered. They remain undeniably significant even today.

GETTING STARTED

Frederick Winslow Taylor was a US engineer and inventor, whose fame rests chiefly on this book. He shares with Henry Ford the dubious distinction of founding an '-ism'. Taylorism is the practice of the principles of scientific management, which emerged from Taylor's work at the Midvale Steel Works, where he was chief engineer. It involves rigorous measurement of work processes, total objectivity in the assessment of which methods work best, and the consequent mechanisation of work and elimination of the human element. The objective standards arrived at, however, are as binding on managers, who have to enforce them, as on the workers who have to meet them. Like the unstoppable assembly line, scientific management imposes its discipline on everyone. Not surprisingly, to most members of the humanistic school of management it is the enemy *par excellence*.

CONTRIBUTION

Measuring work. Taylor's science consisted in the minute examination of individual tasks. Having identified every single movement and action involved in doing something, he could determine the optimum time required to complete a task.

Armed with this information, the manager could determine whether a person was doing the job well.

Putting science before opinion. The most obvious consequence of scientific management is a dehumanising reliance on measurement.

The experts, who first analyse and then accurately time the various ways of doing each piece of work, will finally know from exact knowledge, and not from anyone's opinion, which method will accomplish the results with the least effort and in the quickest time.

The exact facts will have in this way been developed and they will constitute a series of laws, which are destined to control the vast multitude of our daily personal acts which, at present, are the subjects of individual opinion.

A system with no initiative. The Taylorist system envisages no room for individual initiative or imagination. People are labour, mechanically accomplishing a particular task and doing what they are told.

According to Robert McNamara, 'those who were so important in the early stages of American manufacturing, the foremen and plant managers, were disenfranchised. Instead of being creators and innovators, as in an earlier era, now they depended on meeting production quotas. They could not stop the line and fix problems as they occurred; they lost any stake in innovation or change' (quoted in *Promise and Power* by Debora Shapley).

Taylor's schemes for objectively determining best practices for every imaginable job could, on the other hand, be said to have freed front-line workers from the capricious discipline of unscientific, turn-of-the-century foremen.

CONTEXT

While Taylor's concepts are now usually regarded in a negative light, the originality of his insights and their importance are in little doubt. He himself announced that he was ushering in a revolution, 'a complete mental revolution on the part of the working man engaged in any particular establishment or industry, a complete mental revolution on the part of these men as to their duties toward their work, toward their fellow men, and toward their employees.'

Peter Drucker observed in *The Practice of Management*: 'Few people had ever looked at human work systematically until Frederick W. Taylor started to do so around 1885. Work was taken for granted and it is an axiom that one never sees what one takes for granted. *Scientific Management* was thus one of the great liberating, pioneering insights.'

Lyndall Urwick, adds: 'At the time Taylor began his work, business management . . . was usually regarded as incidental to, and flowing from knowledge of . . . a particular branch of manufacturing, the technical know-how of making sausages or steel or shirts. The idea that a man needed any training or formal instruction to become a competent manager had not occurred to anyone.'

The legacy of Taylor's work is most obvious in companies that tend to emphasise quantity over quality. His ideas were enthusiastically taken up by Henry Ford in the development of mass-production techniques.

Drucker goes on to identify two fundamental flaws in scientific management.

'The first of these blind spots is the belief that, because we must analyse work into its simplest constituent motions, we must also organise it as a series of individual motions, each if possible carried out by an individual worker; the second that it divorces planning from doing.'

Gary Hamel sums up the position thus: 'The development of modern management theory is the story of two quests: to make management more scientific, and to make it more humane. It is wrong to look at the latter quest as somehow much more enlightened than the former. Indeed, they are the yin and yang of business. The unprecedented capacity of 20th-century industry to create wealth rested squarely on the work of Frederick Winslow Taylor. While some may disavow Taylor, his rational, deterministic impulses live on. Indeed, re-engineering is simply late 20th-century Taylorism. Though the focus of re-engineering is on the process, rather than the individual task, the motivation is the same: to simplify, to remove unnecessary effort, and to do more with less.'

THE BEST SOURCES OF HELP

Taylor, Frederick Winslow. *The Principles of Scientific Management*. New York: Harper & Row, 1911.

Quest for Prosperity
by Konosuke Matsushita

This book describes how Konosuke Matsushita built a global business—Panasonic—from nothing. It contains lessons on customer service, business ethics, and marketing that would benefit any business.

GETTING STARTED

According to the author, customer service is critical to success—customers want goods that will benefit them. After-sales service is more important than assistance before sales.

Business with a conscience cements loyalty. We are using precious resources that could be better used elsewhere unless we make a good profit. Production efficiency and quality products are key. The mission of a manufacturer should be to overcome poverty, to relieve society as a whole from misery, and to bring it wealth.

CONTRIBUTION

Building a winning business. The Matsushita story is one of the most impressive industrial achievements of the 20th century.

The company's first break was an order to make insulator plates. The order was delivered on time and was high quality. Matsushita began to make money. He then developed an innovative bicycle light. Initially, retailers were unimpressed. Then Matsushita had his salesmen leave a switched-on light in each shop. This simple product demonstration impressed the retailers, and the business took off.

The importance of customer service. The company understood customer service before anyone in the West had even thought about it:

- don't sell customers goods that they are attracted to. Sell them goods that will benefit them.
- after-sales service is more important than assistance before sales. It is through such service that one gets permanent customers.

Efficiency and quality. Matsushita emphasised efficient production and quality products.

> To be out of stock is due to carelessness.

To be out of stock is due to carelessness. If this happens, apologise to the customers, ask for their address, and tell them that you will deliver the goods immediately.

Risk-taking pays. Matsushita took risks and backed his beliefs at every stage.

The classic example of this is the development of the videocassette. Matsushita developed VHS video and licensed the technology. Sony developed Betamax, which was immeasurably better, but failed to license the technology. The world standard is VHS and Betamax is consigned to history.

Business with a conscience. Matsushita advocated business with a conscience, reflected in his paternalistic employment practices. During a recession early in its life the company did not make any of its workers redundant. This cemented loyalty.

It is not enough to work conscientiously. No matter what kind of job, you should think of yourself as being completely in charge of and responsible for your own work.

The role of the leader. Big things and little things are the leader's job. Middle-level arrangements can be delegated.

Matsushita also explained the role of the leader in more cryptic style: 'The tail trails the head. If the head moves fast, the tail will keep up the same pace. If the head is sluggish, the tail will droop.'

The broader aims of business. Matsushita mapped out the broader spiritual aims he believed a business should have. Profit was not enough. The mission of a manufacturer should be to overcome poverty, to relieve society as a whole from misery, and bring it wealth.

He outlined his basic management objective as follows: 'Recognising our responsibilities as industrialists, we will devote ourselves to the progress and development of society and the well-being of people through our business activities, thereby enhancing the quality of life throughout the world.'

Failure to make a profit was regarded as a sort of crime against society: 'We take society's capital, we take their people, we take their materials, yet without a good profit, we are using precious resources that could be better used elsewhere.'

Business is demanding, serious, and crucial: 'Business, we know, is now so complex and difficult, the survival of firms so hazardous in an environment increasingly unpredictable, competitive, and fraught with danger, that their continued existence depends on the day-to-day mobilisation of every ounce of intelligence.'

CONTEXT

Matsushita created a $42 billion-revenue business from nothing. He also created Panasonic, one of the world's most successful brands, and amassed a personal fortune of $3 billion.

The book explains the principles that made his business a success.

THE BEST SOURCES OF HELP

Matsushita, Konosuke. *Quest for Prosperity*. Kyoto: PHP Institute, 1988.

Reengineering the Corporation
by James Champy and Michael Hammer

Reengineering the Corporation is seen as the key book in the re-engineering revolution. It encourages organisations to take a fresh look at inefficient and outdated processes, and to focus on dramatic improvements in cost, quality, service, and speed. Although the message has been misinterpreted, re-engineering remains a powerful tool for change.

GETTING STARTED

In the authors' view, re-engineering must focus on the fundamental rethinking and radical redesign of key business processes. Dramatic improvements in cost, quality, service, and speed are the objective, and organisations must make key processes as lean and profitable as possible, discarding peripheral processes and people if necessary.

Re-engineering should go far beyond altering and refining processes: the aim is 'to reverse the Industrial Revolution'. Organisations should start with a blank piece of paper and map out processes to identify how their business should operate. They should then attempt to translate the paper into concrete reality.

Re-engineering puts a premium on the skills and potential of the people at the centre of the organisation, and should also tackle three key areas of management—managerial roles, styles and systems.

CONTRIBUTION

Focus on improving core processes. In the context of a fiercely competitive environment and the ability of IT to transform business processes, the book encourages organisations to take a fresh look at inefficient and outdated processes. Re-engineering, according to the authors, is the fundamental rethinking and radical redesign of business processes.

> True re-engineering is a recipe for a corporate revolution, and should go far beyond altering and refining processes: the past is history; the future is there to be coerced into the optimum shape.

Create a lean organisation. The authors argue that organisations need to identify their key processes and make them as lean and profitable as possible. In some cases, peripheral processes and people need to be discarded.

Unfortunately, many organisations have taken this advice literally and downsized without re-engineering. CSC, the consultancy founded by Champy and Hammer, surveyed more than 600 companies involved in re-engineering projects in 1994. In the United States, an average 336 jobs were lost on each project. In Europe, the figure was 760 jobs per project.

Achieve a complete corporate revolution. Simple business process re-engineering is not enough, say the authors. True re-engineering is a recipe for a corporate revolution, and should go far beyond altering and refining processes: the past is history; the future is there to be coerced into the optimum shape.

The authors believe that re-engineering is concerned with rejecting conventional wisdom and received assumptions about the past. However, this can mean ignoring the experience of the past. Companies are discouraged from trying to understand why they have been successful and building on that.

Transform the future. The authors suggest that organisations should start with a blank piece of paper. They should map out their processes to identify how their business should operate, and then attempt to translate the paper into concrete reality.

In practice, this has proved difficult to achieve. The authors now believe that companies tend not to cast the re-engineering net widely; they find processes that can be re-engineered quickly and stop at that point. They lack a vision for the future and the revolutionary approach to take re-engineering forward.

Re-engineer management as well. Part of the problem, they now believe, is that managers fail to impose change on themselves—they concentrate on tearing down processes, but they leave their own jobs and management styles intact. However, the old ways of management could eventually undermine the very structure of their rebuilt enterprise. The re-engineering process should therefore tackle three key areas of management—managerial roles, styles, and systems.

Re-engineering should be built on trust, respect, and people. The authors believe that re-engineering actually puts a premium on the people at the centre of the organisation. Once peripheral activities have been cut away, the new environment puts a premium on skills of the people who are left. Experience suggests that this has not happened so far: downsizing creates a difficult environment in which trust is frequently absent.

CONTEXT

Re-engineering is seen by some as an old concept with a new label. Frederick W. Taylor's *Scientific Management* advocated similar change, but at an individual rather than an organisational level. Gary Hamel pointed out that re-engineering followed a line from scientific management, industrial engineering, and business process improvement.

The mechanistic theme has been a key focal point for critics, who have made the point that re-engineering owes more to visions of the corporation as a machine, rather than a human system. Peter Cohan, a former colleague, said the authors ignored the importance of people, describing them as objects who handle processes. Christopher Lorenz of the *Financial Times* believed that the authors failed to state whether organisations should undertake behavioural and cultural changes in parallel with re-engineering.

It has also been easy to take the book's messages too literally. Re-engineering has been seen as a synonym for redundancy, and the book has been blamed for a wave of downsizing.

THE BEST SOURCES OF HELP

Champy, James, and Michael Hammer. *Reengineering the Corporation*. New York: Harper Business, 1993.

Relationship Marketing
by Regis McKenna

Relationship marketing has become one of the most important determinants of corporate success. Retaining customers and maximising lifetime customer value are critical to long-term revenue and profitability. Regis McKenna's book sets out the principles of building successful relationships, using technology to understand customers and communicate effectively with them.

GETTING STARTED

The author restates the view that marketing is not a separate corporate function. It has moved away from the practice of mass marketing to customisation and personalisation. Technology is the enabler in this change, allowing companies to deal with the growing power of the customer and the accelerating pace of change in the marketplace. Products are no longer sufficient. Customers demand solutions. Communication has also moved from monologue to dialogue, based on a deeper understanding of customers.

CONTRIBUTION

Integrating the customer with the company. McKenna believes that technology and the choices it offers are transforming the marketplace—as well as the nature of marketing. The aim now is to integrate the customer into the company.

Dominating markets. According to the author, a strong brand is the reflection of a successful relationship. Market dominance is vital to attracting customers, business partners and the best employees. The starting point is to define a narrow market and dominate it, before deepening and widening the relationships.

Dialogue with customers. One-way advertising is no longer valid. Companies need to have dialogue with customers using trials, user groups, and other feedback mechanisms. This is 'experience-based marketing', based on a deep understanding of the customer.

Merger of products and services. In industries like computing, around 75% of the business consists of services such as consultancy, systems integration, and customer support. These are all essential to customers and form part of a solution that builds relationships.

Faster time to market. According to McKenna, companies must reduce time to market as much as possible—delay leads to lost opportunities. The marketplace is also changing rapidly so it is important to stay close to customers.

Market creation replaces market sharing. Companies must differentiate their products to dominate a market, says McKenna. This may mean starting with small sectors and acting like entrepreneurs. Market creation also means educating customers and listening to them. However, he points out that quantitative information can distract companies from entering small sectors. Qualitative judgement, he believes, may be more important.

The importance of relationships. Relationships, according to McKenna, are more important with complex high-risk products. Customers need reassurance, education, support, and services to build and maintain their confidence in a company.

Dynamic positioning. The author explains how dynamic positioning differs from traditional positioning. There are three elements:

- product positioning determines how a product fits into a competitive market
- market positioning requires a company to understand the infrastructure, influences, and distribution channels in its market
- corporate positioning determines whether a company is perceived as a credible and trusted supplier.

Product success. McKenna cites ten characteristics of a successful product:

- appeals to a new market
- takes advantage of the best existing technologies
- depends on the market infrastructure for newly-developed technologies
- timing is right
- adapted to market requirements
- developed by small entrepreneurial teams
- customers involved in development
- adopted by early users
- generates a new language
- used in demonstrations, workshops and user groups

Developing relationships. Successful companies develop relationships with the whole market, not just customers. This is the 'market infrastructure', and it includes analysts, developers, retailers, journalists, suppliers, and other organisations who are mutually dependent. The leaders set the standard for their market and everyone else works with them. McKenna describes these as structural relationships. Strategic relationships with partners are important. For larger companies, the relationships reduce development costs and speed up time to market. For smaller companies, they provide credibility and access.

Selling to the right customers. McKenna breaks buyers into four categories: innovators, early adopters, majority, and laggards. It is important for companies to identify the type of customers they are aiming at.

CONTEXT

This book was one of the first to highlight the importance of relationships with customers, suppliers, distributors, and other players in the marketplace. Relationship marketing has now entered mainstream marketing practice and is an essential tool for every company.

Since the book's publication, the practice of relationship marketing has been further refined by the development of personalisation techniques and one-to-one marketing via the Internet. The principles, however, remain the same.

The book uses examples mainly from high-tech companies where McKenna had a great deal of hands-on experience. The technique is now widely used in every sector and the lessons from the book can be easily adapted for other markets.

One of the key points in the book is the dependent relationships that have grown within technology markets. Companies in hardware, software, and related services depend on each other for success and even competitors have been known to form strategic alliances to ensure market development. This theme is explored in *Co-opetition* by Nalebuff and Brandenburger (HarperCollins Business, 1996).

THE BEST SOURCES OF HELP

McKenna, Regis. *Relationship Marketing: Successful Strategies for the Age of the Customer.* Cambridge, Massachusetts: Perseus Books, 1991.

Riding the Waves of Culture
by Fons Trompenaars and Charles Hampden-Turner

Riding the Waves of Culture is an examination of the cultural imponderables faced by managers in the global village. Based on exhaustive research, it systematically 'dimensionalises' cultural differences, identifying seven areas, such as attitude to rules and awareness of time, in which different nations have fundamentally different conceptions. Anyone whose work involves dealing with people from other cultures would benefit from reading it.

GETTING STARTED

Fons Trompenaars studied at a top American business school where he started thinking about cultural differences. 'I started wondering if any of the American management techniques I was brainwashed with in eight years of the best business education money could buy would apply in the Netherlands, where I came from, or indeed in the rest of the world.'

Charles Hampden-Turner is an international authority on cross-cultural communication who taught for many years in the United States and, like his co-author, worked for Shell.

The book is based on meticulous quantitative research (over 15 years 15,000 people from 50 countries were surveyed) and more than 900 seminars presented in 18 countries. Its main contentions are that basic to understanding other cultures is the awareness of cultural difference; that cultural difference can be systematically analysed; that flexibility, a certain amount of humility, and a sense of humour are needed in dealing with cultures other than our own; and that the reconciliation of difference is the supreme managerial art.

CONTRIBUTION

Culture. In the authors' view, culture is a series of rules and methods that a society has evolved to deal with the recurring problems it faces. They have become so basic that, like breathing, we no longer think about how we approach or resolve them.

People should be aware, first, that they belong to a culture and have a specific way of doing things, and they should be prepared, second, for a different response from the one they are accustomed to receiving when they do business with someone whose culture differs from theirs.

Seven dimensions of culture. In analysing cultural differences, the authors identify seven dimensions in which different or contrasting attitudes are particularly crucial. These are:

- universalism vs particularism
- individualism vs collectivism
- neutral vs emotional
- specific vs diffuse
- achievement vs ascription
- attitude towards time
- attitude towards the environment

Universalism and particularism. There are two fundamentally distinct ways of dealing with situations that the book labels 'universalism' and 'particularism'. Universalists (including

Americans, Canadians, Australians, and the Swiss) advocate one best way, 'what is good and right can be defined and always applies'. They focus on rules and procedure. Particularists (South Koreans, Chinese, and Malaysians) feel that circumstances dictate how ideas and practices should be applied. They focus on the peculiar nature of any given situation and on particular relationships.

Universalists doing business with particularists should be prepared for meandering or irrelevancies that do not seem to be going anywhere.

Particularists doing business with universalists should be prepared for rational and professional arguments and presentations, and little else.

Collectivist and individualist. The book also contrasts the collectivist mindset with the individualist one.

The United States again comes at one extreme of the spectrum, emphasising the individual before the group. Countries such as Egypt and France are at the other end.

Individualists working with collectivists must tolerate time taken to consult, and negotiators who can only agree tentatively and may withdraw an offer after consulting with superiors.

The role of the international manager. Given the wide range of basic differences in how different cultures perceive life, it is evident that the international manager is moving in a world riddled with potential pitfalls. There are also profound differences between those who show their feelings (such as Italians) and those who hide them (such as the Japanese); and those who accord status on the basis of achievement, and those who ascribe it on the basis of family and age.

The international manager needs to go beyond awareness of cultural differences, according to this book. He or she needs to respect these differences and take advantage of diversity through reconciling cross-cultural dilemmas. The international manager reconciles cultural dilemmas. In the end, the only positive route forward is through reconciliation. Those societies that can reconcile better are better at creating wealth.

CONTEXT

Tom Peters called *Riding the Waves of Culture* a masterpiece. 'What's not okay is cultural arrogance. If you come to another's turf with sensitivity and open ears . . . you're halfway home.'

Gary Hamel takes the authors to task for their criticisms of American cultural inflexibility: 'So Americans will never understand foreign cultures? Funny how American companies are out-competing their European competitors in Asia and Latin America. . . . Where I agree with Trompenaars is that the future belongs to the cosmopolitans.'

The cultural aspects of managing internationally are likely to gain in importance as the full force of globalisation affects industries and individuals. In this respect the value of the book's contribution is undeniable. It has been argued, however, that its stress on cultural relativism and adaptability might become outmoded if capital markets were to enforce 'global rules of the game', independent of different cultures.

THE BEST SOURCES OF HELP

Trompenaars, Fons, and Charles Hampden-Turner. *Riding the Waves of Culture*. 2nd ed. London: Nicholas Brealey, 1997.

The Rise and Fall of Strategic Planning
by Henry Mintzberg

Mintzberg shows how over-emphasising analysis and hard facts limits strategic planning. Planning should be something visionary and creative. The book has become an influential classic.

GETTING STARTED

Planning is concerned with analysis; strategy making is concerned with synthesis. Strategic planners tend to make false assumptions that discontinuities can be predicted; the future will resemble the past; and strategy making can be formalised. They tend to be detached from action and the reality of the organisation.

Planners typically gather hard data on their industry, markets, and competitors. Soft data—such as networks of contacts, talking with customers, suppliers, and employees—have been ignored. Strategy formulation has been dominated by logic and analysis. This narrows options. Intuition and creativity need to become part of the process.

CONTRIBUTION

Strategy and planning. Planning codifies, elaborates, and operationalises existing company strategy. In contrast, strategy is either an emergent pattern or a deliberate perspective, and cannot be planned. While planning is concerned with analysis, strategy making is concerned with synthesis.

The nature of planners. Planners do have value, but only as strategy finders, analysts, and catalysts. At their most effective, they unearth strategies in unexpected pockets of the organisation, whose potential can then be explored.

Problems with planning practices. The three main pitfalls are:

- the assumption that discontinuities can be predicted
- planners are detached from the reality of the organisation
- the assumption that strategy making can be formalised

The assumption that discontinuities can be predicted. Forecasting techniques often assume that the future will resemble the past. This gives artificial reassurance, and creates strategies that disintegrate as they are overtaken by events.

Detachment from the reality of the organisation. If the system does the thinking, strategy must be detached from operations, and thinkers from doers. This disassociation of thinking from acting lies at the root of strategic planning's problem.

Hard data and soft data. Planners typically gather hard data on their industry, markets, and competitors. Soft data—networks of contacts, talking with customers, suppliers, and employees, using intuition, and using the grapevine—have been all but ignored.

Hard data are often anything but. There is the fallacy of measuring what's measurable. There is a tendency to favour cost-leadership strategies (emphasising operating efficiencies, which are generally measurable) over product-leadership strategies (emphasising innovative design or high quality, which tends to be less measurable).

To gain useful understanding of an organisation's competitive situation, soft data need to be dynamically integrated into the planning process. They may be difficult to analyse, but they are indispensable for synthesis—the key to strategy making.

The assumption that strategy making can be formalised. The emphasis on logic and analysis creates a narrow range of options. Alternatives that do not fit into the predetermined structure are ignored.

The right side of the brain needs to become part of the process, with its emphasis on intuition and creativity. Planning defines and preserves categories. Creativity creates categories or rearranges established ones.

Thus strategic planning can neither provide creativity, nor deal with it when it emerges. Mould-breaking strategies grow initially like weeds—they are not cultivated and can take root anywhere.

The nature of strategy making. Mintzberg defines strategy making thus:

- It is derived from synthesis.
- It is informal and visionary, rather than programmed and formalised.
- It relies on divergent thinking, intuition, and using the subconscious. This leads to outbursts of creativity as new discoveries are made.
- It is irregular, unexpected, ad hoc, and instinctive. It upsets stable patterns.
- Managers are adaptive information manipulators—opportunists, rather than conductors who remain aloof.
- It is done in time of instability characterised by discontinuous change.
- It results from an approach that takes in broad perspectives and is, therefore, visionary, and involves a variety of actors capable of experimenting and then integrating.

CONTEXT

The book reflects a general dissatisfaction with strategic planning. Research by the US Planning Forum found that only 25% of companies considered their planning was effective.

The book attracted much attention and debate. It also brought a spirited response from the defenders of strategy. Andrew Campbell, co-author of *Corporate-level Strategy*, wrote: 'Strategic planning is not futile. Research has shown that some companies—both conglomerates and more focused groups—have strategic planning processes that add real value.' Campbell further argues that the corporate centre must develop a value-creating, corporate-level strategy and build the management processes needed to implement it.

Management guru Gary Hamel commented: 'Henry views strategic planning as a ritual, devoid of creativity and meaning. He is undoubtedly right when he argues that planning doesn't produce strategy. But rather than use the last chapter of the book to create a new charter for planners, Henry might have put his mind to the question of where strategies actually do come from!'

THE BEST SOURCES OF HELP

Mintzberg, Henry. *The Rise and Fall of Strategic Planning*. London: Prentice Hall International, 1994.

Six Sigma
by Mikel Harry and Richard Schroeder

Six Sigma is a management instrument that is designed to optimise processes so that they attain zero-fault quality. The authors use practice-based examples to show how the concept can be applied and what it can do for companies of various sizes and in various branches of industry. The book should therefore be of interest to anyone who is interested in improving quality and thereby market share, customer satisfaction, and, ultimately, profits.

GETTING STARTED

Under the Six Sigma system, say the authors, processes are organised in such a way that faults and errors cannot occur. It is intended to change fundamentally the ways in which businesses conduct their operations and to have a direct and improving effect on profit margins. Instead of planning projects years ahead in the future, Six Sigma concentrates on attaining financial goals in 12-month stages.

CONTRIBUTION

The path to change. There are six areas to which the Six Sigma programme applies:

- improving processes
- improving products and services
- looking after shareholders
- improving design
- improvements in suppliers
- training and appointing staff

Being better is cheaper. Since quality saves the company money, say the authors, it is sensible to produce a product or service in such a way that you get it right first time. Quality costs can be improved in the following key areas:

- basic organisational competence
- deviations in industrial processes
- deviations in the business process
- the technical design process and documentation
- the quality of technical data
- supplier competence

Benchmarking: discovering who really is the best. According to the authors, quantitative benchmarking enables a company to evaluate performance in every area. Standard indices are used for performance and ability. Performance can then be compared not only between different areas in-house, but against other companies as well.

Changing what companies measure. Statistics alone, however, do not bring about a breakthrough, though they are a very powerful instrument for changing the playing field on which the company operates. Measuring systems (metrics) create a common language and permit process measurements to be communicated openly and honestly.

Uncovering the hidden factory. Harry and Schroeder suggest that companies inadvertently create ad hoc systems and processes ('hidden factories') that are designed to correct faults that occur during production processes. These take up space, time, and resources unnecessarily. As the incidence of faults increases, 'hidden factories' expand and costs escalate.

The breakthrough strategy. The integration of Six Sigma takes place in four stages:

- Identification: in this phase managers begin to ask questions about processes instead of simply looking at the end product.
- Characterisation: quality criteria for the process are described and measured at this stage.
- Optimisation: this is a phase of improvement and control in which enhanced processing capability is first maximised then preserved.
- Institutionalisation: quality and the Six Sigma strategy are woven into corporate culture.

Measuring performance on the Sigma scale. Over a particular period the processing average may run according to plan, but as time goes on, for various reasons, it may deviate. Such distortions and fluctuations are catered for in the Six Sigma strategy, say the authors. The strategy allows for them when assessing process capability.

Implementation. The authors identify the following principles as requisite for carrying out a Six Sigma strategy successfully:

- highly visible top-down promotion of the initiatives by management
- a measuring system so that progress can be followed
- internal and external benchmarking of products, services, and processes
- 'stretch' goals to focus employees on changing processes
- further training for all levels
- 'champions' and 'black belts' to encourage the initiative

Six Sigma players. The most important internal actors in Six Sigma are these:

- *Champions* who ensure that all key company functions are linked to Six Sigma
- *Black Belt Masters* who work to co-ordinate project selection and project training
- *Black Belts* who apply the instrumentation and knowledge of the Six Sigma strategy to specific products
- *Green Belts* who are workers through the organisation who carry out Six Sigma as part of their normal work.

Guidelines for project selection. Six Sigma projects need to be tied in with the highest levels of company strategy and directly support specific business objectives. Where projects are designed to improve company productivity, both top-level management and the operational level in individual plants must be in accord, and people must be appointed to be responsible for the project and to carry it out.

CONTEXT

Mikel Harry and Richard Schroeder developed their comprehensive quality-management initiative, Six Sigma, at Motorola in the 1980s. It is compatible with quality norm ISO 9000. Its goal is the achievement of zero-fault quality both in production processes and in the service sector. The main criticism that has been levelled at Six Sigma is that it neglects the employees' side of things and tolerates the loss of jobs that may result from radical process optimisation and achieving the greatest possible cost savings.

THE BEST SOURCES OF HELP

Harry, Mikel, and Richard Schroeder. *Six Sigma: The Breakthrough Management Strategy Revolutionizing the World's Top Corporations.* New York: Bantam Doubleday Dell Books, 2002.

Small Is Beautiful
by E.F. Schumacher

Schumacher's book has become one of the most influential works ever on environmental issues and business. It looks at traditional Western economics in a radical way, arguing that big is not always best. His work has struck a chord with politicians, environmentalists, and a growing number of business leaders.

GETTING STARTED

Schumacher argues that the relentless pursuit of profit and progress has resulted in economic inefficiency, environmental pollution, and inhumane working conditions. Instead, he proposes greater use of 'intermediate technology', based on smaller work units, communal ownership, and the use of local labour and resources.

CONTRIBUTION

The problem of production. Schumacher believes that business has not solved the problem of production. Businesses are using up the store of natural capital, and he cites the spiralling demands on fossil fuels and other finite natural resources. The proposal to replace fossil fuels with man-made energy sources such as nuclear fuels creates its own problems.

The author's view is that the concept of peace through universal prosperity is also unachievable. He argues that, if prosperity grew in line with population growth, the impact on fuel consumption and subsequent atmospheric pollution would be extremely damaging.

Changing the emphasis of economics. The solution, he claims, lies in a re-orientation of science and technology. The emphasis should not be on concentrating production in larger and larger units, it should be on making technology accessible and suitable for small-scale application. He also believes that technology should leave room for human creativity, rather than replacing it.

Traditional economic theories are driven by market forces. Schumacher believes that they ignore humanity's dependence on the natural world. Economics, he says, is also over-dependent on quantitative measures such as gross domestic product and consequently overlooks qualitative measures such as the impact of the economy on the environment.

> Traditional economic theories are driven by market forces.

According to Schumacher, economics looks upon human labour as a necessary 'input' to wealth. Business takes every opportunity to reduce the cost, making work meaningless. An alternative point of view says that work should enable people to utilise their faculties and join in a common cause. This is in contrast to the theory that consumption is the only real end.

Towards a smaller scale. Schumacher points out that scale is another important element of economic thinking. The traditional theory is that economic organisations, such as businesses, should be as large as possible. He counters that they only need to be big enough to meet real needs.

Schumacher also argues for the more effective use of land. It is not simply a factor of production. He cites the flight from the land as evidence of this misunderstanding.

The efficiency gap. The author is critical of modern industrial efficiency. The United States, for example, has around 5% of the world's population, yet requires almost 40% of the world's primary resources to sustain its economy.

Apart from the demand on resources, Schumacher argues that this situation also creates problems between producer and consumer countries. An economy that is so dependent on other resources must in the long term suffer.

A human face for technology. Schumacher believes that technology needs a human face. Technology should free people from the burdens of work. He describes how the Intermediate Technology Development Group aims to broaden the use of technology, supporting production by the masses, instead of mass production. This approach, he feels, would be an effective way to support regional economic development around the world.

Despite his emphasis on small-scale regional development, Schumacher accepts that large organisations will remain an important part of the economy. He believes that setting up smaller units within a larger organisation could help to overcome any inherent problems of size.

CONTEXT

Schumacher, like Hawken and Lovins in *Natural Capitalism*, highlights the conflict between business growth and the destruction of natural resources. He proposes a system of environmentally-friendly business that takes account of limited resources and offers everyone a stake in success.

He draws on a wide range of influences and sources to develop his themes, including Buddhist economics, Adam Smith, Ghandi, and economists such as Galbraith.

Although Schumacher's work could be regarded as utopian, he proposes practical working solutions, some of which have already been put into successful practice.

THE BEST SOURCES OF HELP

Schumacher, E.F. *Small Is Beautiful: A Study of Economics As If People Mattered.* London: Vintage, 1993.

Strategy and Structure
by Alfred Chandler

Chandler's book is regarded by many commentators as a masterpiece. It demonstrates the critical link between a company's strategy and its structure, and played an influential role in the profitable decentralisation of many leading corporations. The book's findings remain relevant to new forms of organisation such as the federated organisation, the multi-company coalition, and the virtual company.

GETTING STARTED

According to the author, structure should be driven by strategy—and if it isn't, inefficiency results. The structure of many corporations is driven by market forces: recognition that production had to be market-driven led large organisations to change to a looser divisional structure.

Increases in scale also led to business owners having to recruit a new breed of professional manager, as professional management co-ordinates the flow of product to customers more efficiently than market forces.

A planned economy is important to long-term organisational success.

CONTRIBUTION

Structure should be driven by strategy. Strategy is the determination of the long-term goals and objectives of an enterprise, and the adoption of courses of action and the allocation of resources necessary for reaching these goals.

A firm's structure is dictated by its chosen strategy—and unless structure follows strategy, inefficiency results.

> Organisations and their managements require a planned economy rather than a capitalist free-for-all dominated by the unpredictable whims of market forces.

A company should establish a strategy and then seek to create the structure appropriate to achieving it.

Structure driven by market forces. Organisational structures in companies such as Du Pont, Sears Roebuck, General Motors, and Standard Oil were driven by the changing demands and pressures of the marketplace.

The market-driven proliferation of product lines in Du Pont and General Motors led to a shift from a functional, monolithic organisational form to a more loosely-coupled divisional structure.

The rise of the multi-divisional organisation. The multi-divisional organisation removed the executives responsible for the destiny of the entire enterprise from the more routine operational responsibilities.

It gave them the time, information, and even psychological commitment for long-term planning and appraisal.

The professionalisation of management. The managerial revolution was fuelled by the rise of oil-based energy, the development of the steel, chemical, and engineering industries, and a dramatic rise in the scale of production and the size of companies.

Increases in scale led to business owners having to recruit a new breed of professional manager. The roles of the salaried manager and technician are vital, as the visible hand of management co-ordinates the flow of product to customers more efficiently than Adam Smith's 'invisible hand' of the market.

The importance of a planned economy. Organisations and their managements require a planned economy rather than a capitalist free-for-all dominated by the unpredictable whims of market forces.

CONTEXT

The book is based on Chandler's research into major US corporations between 1850 and 1920. Its subtitle is 'Chapters in the history of the American industrial enterprise', but its impact went far beyond that of a brilliantly-researched historical text. Alfred Chandler's *Strategy and Structure* is a theoretical masterpiece which has had profound influence on both practitioners and thinkers.

Chandler was highly influential in the trend among large organisations for decentralisation in the 1960s and 1970s. While in 1950 around 20% of Fortune 500 corporations were decentralised, this had increased to 80% by 1970. In the 1980s, Chandler's thinking was influential in the transformation of AT&T from what was in effect a production-based bureaucracy to a marketing organisation.

Until recent times, Chandler's conclusion that structure follows strategy has largely been accepted as a fact of corporate life. Now, the debate has been rekindled.

Tom Peters said, 'I think he got it exactly wrong. For it is the structure of the organisation that determines, over time, the choices that it makes about the markets it attacks.'

In *Managing on the Edge*, Richard Pascale said, 'The underlying assumption is that organisations act in a rational, sequential manner. Yet most executives will readily agree that it is often the other way around. The way a company is organised, whether functional focused or driven by independent divisions, often plays a major role in shaping its strategy. Indeed, this accounts for the tendency of organisations to do what they best know how to do—regardless of deteriorating success against the competitive realities.'

Gary Hamel, author of *Leading the Revolution*, said, 'Those who dispute Chandler's thesis that structure follows strategy miss the point. Of course strategy and structure are inextricably intertwined. Chandler's point was that new challenges give rise to new structures. The challenges of size and complexity, coupled with advances in communications and techniques of management control, produced divisionalisation and decentralisation. These same forces, several generations on, are now driving us towards new structural solutions—the federated organisation, the multi-company coalition, and the virtual company. Few historians are prescient. Chandler was.'

THE BEST SOURCES OF HELP

Chandler, Alfred. *Strategy and Structure*. New York: Doubleday, 1962.

Strategy Safari
by Henry Mintzberg, Bruce Ahlstrand, and Joseph Lampel

The landscape of strategic management, according to the authors, is a wilderness—confusion reigns, the most heterogeneous forms of thinking co-exist, and there is no recognisable order or structure. This book offers itself as a jargon-free guide to those who wish to explore the wilderness. Its aim is to clarify and critique a variety of approaches, which the authors have shaped into distinct schools of thought. It ends with a plea for synthesis.

GETTING STARTED
The authors present eight 'schools of strategy' and compare them to one another.

CONTRIBUTION
The Design School—strategy as a conceptual process.
- Premises: Strategy development should be a conscious process, with control remaining in the hands of the chief executive. The model of strategy development must be kept simple and informal. The best strategies are the result of an individualised formation process.
- Criticism: The Design School puts too great an emphasis on thinking divorced from action, because it does not view the strategy-developing process as a learning one.
- Contribution and context: In principle, an individual person is capable of dealing with all the information needed to develop a strategy.

The Planning School—strategy development as a formal process.
- Premises: Strategies result from planning; they are divided into separate steps, which are presented in the form of checklists, and conducted by means of concrete techniques. The strategies that emerge from this process are ready-formulated.
- Criticism: Plans provide a clear direction and give an organisation stability, but they undermine flexibility.
- Contribution and context: Planning strategists make good analysts; they feed the black box with data and scrutinise strategies to see if they are feasible.

The Positioning School—strategy development as an analytical process.
- Premises: Strategies deal with generic, general, and recognisable market positions. Strategy development, therefore, is a matter of choosing these generic positions on the basis of analytical calculations.
- Criticism: The Positioning School's perspective is narrow. It concentrates on the purely economic and quantifiable, and leaves other factors out of the account.
- Contribution and context: The role of positioning must be to support the process; it should not be the actual process.

The Entrepreneurial School—strategy formation as a visionary process.
- Premises: Strategy exists in the mind of the chief executive as a feeling for the long-term direction and a vision of the future of the organisation. Strategy development takes place, at best, only half consciously.

- Criticism: Strategy development is presented as a process that is, as it were, 'wrapped up in' the behaviour of a single individual.
- Contribution and context: Businesses profit from the firm sense of direction and the high degree of integration and definition provided by this approach.

The Cognitive School—strategy formation as a mental process.

- Premises: Strategies form in the head of the strategist as ways of seeing—concepts, maps, schemata, and frameworks—that shape the way in which people act on information from their environment.
- Criticism: Strategic management hobbles a long way behind cognitive psychology.
- Contribution and context: Good strategists are creative; they create a world in their heads collectively and then bring it into being.

The Learning School—strategy formation as a self-developing process.

- Premises: The complex nature of the organisational environment excludes conscious control. It is the collective system that learns. There are many potential strategists.
- Criticism: Learning is costly. It takes time, it produces endless meetings and floods of electronic mail, and it runs off in all directions.
- Contribution and context: The research of the Learning School rests on simple methods that are well suited to explaining complex systems.

The Environmental School—strategy development as a reactive process.

- Premises: The decisive factor in the strategy development process is the environment, which presents itself to the organisation as an array of forces to which it must react.
- Criticism: In reality no organisation has to do with an environment that is generous or complex or hostile or dynamic. The attempt to orientate strategies in accordance with such general conditions seems foolhardy.
- Contribution and context: Both practitioners and theoreticians have to come to grips with a multifarious world that prompts imaginative action.

The Configurational School—strategy development as a process of transformation.

- Premises: In a business, phases of stability are occasionally interrupted by processes of transformation—there is a quantum leap to another configuration. These consecutive states and phases over time become ordered into structured sequences.
- Criticism: It is doubtful whether businesses either are static or change by means of great leaps forward.
- Contribution and context: It brings order to the chaotic world of strategy development.

Integration. Every strategy-making process demands a combination of various elements from the individual schools. Shaping strategy has mental and social aspects, must take the demands of the environment into account, and is unthinkable without leadership and powers of organisation, or without balancing step-by-step and revolutionary development.

CONTEXT

Henry Mintzberg enjoys the reputation of being the scourge of orthodox thinking. In his opinion, businesses and even official bodies are only able to function because people break the rules—not because they act in accordance with them.

THE BEST SOURCES OF HELP

Mintzberg, Henry, Bruce Ahlstrand, and Joseph Lampel. *Strategy Safari: The Complete Guide Through the Wilds of Strategic Management.* Harlow: Financial Times Prentice Hall, 2001.

Du système industriel
by Henri de Saint-Simon

Henri de Saint-Simon (1760–1825) was a social reformer and a seminal figure in the history both of socialism as a political movement and sociology as an academic discipline. In this work, a collection of essays and open letters which first appeared in 1821, Saint-Simon describes and justifies the claims of 'les industriels' to play the decisive role in any society, an *industriel* being, in Saint-Simon's terms, anyone who is in the broadest sense productively active: a farmer or labourer, a craftsperson or manufacturer, a merchant or banker, a scholar or an artist.

GETTING STARTED

The king should reign, but the government should be in the hands of the producers, *les industriels*. They, according Saint-Simon, are the embodiment of 'all manner of useful work, both intellectual and manual, its theory as well as its practical application'. In the future state as Saint-Simon envisages it, this class of people is entrusted with two tasks: to take over the leadership role and to emancipate the working class. The nobility, clergy, and the bourgeoisie must be removed from their ruling positions within the monarchy. Knowledge is to be the guiding spirit of society, directing it so that it operates for the good of all and the removal of oppression.

CONTRIBUTION

Workers and idlers. As Saint-Simon saw it, the basic division in society was between those who were productively active and those who were idle. The active (*industriels*) were those whose income was dependent on their work. (Industrialists in the modern sense are termed *manufacturiers* or *fabricants* by Saint-Simon; his term for modern industry is *fabrication*.) He contrasted the position of the *industriels* with that of the *rentiers*, those who lived on unearned income, the landowners, the royal dignitaries, and the military. He classified all these as 'idlers' (*oisifs*) because they did not contribute to production in any way.

Saint-Simon's aim was to convince the *industriels* that they should rely on the king to be their support, represent their interests, and take care of state business. His parallel aim was to convince the king that the *industriels* were his natural allies and that he could rely on them to guarantee the stability of the monarchy.

Lawyers, he said, occupied all the important offices of state, and provided both the ideas and the leadership for political parties. But in everything relating to the economy, lawyers lacked the necessary technical knowledge. It was therefore incumbent on the *industriels* to form the grassroots of a party of those who work for a living, and to organise themselves as an interest group in order to make their views count.

Financial planning. The best kind of budget, Saint-Simon argued, was one that did justice to the interests of the earning classes. They were the best administrators, because, in contrast to officials, they had to administer (that is, to make productive use of) not only income but also capital assets. The drawing up of financial plans for the state ought therefore, in his view, to be left to the *industriels*. They, in turn, should internalise the power that they represented so that they would no longer hesitate to demand the prominent position to which they were entitled in the administration of public affairs.

Constitutional reform. Saint-Simon created a plan for constitutional reform that envisaged that the position of minister of finance could be held only by an ordinary citizen. The minister would preside over a council of *industriels*, which was to be called the *chambre de l'industrie* (chamber of industry) and would be made up of experienced members of the productive classes of society. This chamber would meet once a year to debate and decide upon the state budget. The budget would be the basic legislative measure that would determine the policy of the kingdom.

The working class. In all the states on earth, said Saint-Simon, the working class was the most numerous class, but its interests were those in which governments had least interest. The common people needed the basic essentials of life. They must be provided with as great a livelihood as possible, that is, they should be given as much work as possible. Saint-Simon wished to entrust entrepreneurs with the task of deciding on large-scale state projects that would be financed from the public purse.

Bankers. The plans of the entrepreneurs could only be implemented if they were approved by the bankers. Business enterprises, therefore, found themselves in a kind of hierarchy, with the banks at the top. According to Saint-Simon, the class of *industriels* dominated by the banks ought in consequence to draft the budget.

The state. The nobility being politically dead, the state would relinquish its traditional powers in favour of the members of the productive classes who led business enterprises. In the *système industriel*, the attributes of the state would be reduced to the minimum necessary. Long before Karl Marx, therefore, Saint-Simon announced the 'withering away of the state'.

CONTEXT

Saint-Simon was one of the most influential thinkers of the 19th century. He was an advocate of 'utopian socialism', striving for a just society in which rights would be grade in accordance with productivity. He was the founder of the first socialist school, his work prepared the way for the socialist movement and became on if its seminal texts. In contrast to Marx—whose forerunner he is often said to be—Saint-Simon focused on the intellectual superstructure of society rather than its economic substructure.

THE BEST SOURCES OF HELP

de Saint-Simon, Henri. *Selected Writings.* (Trans. F.M.H. Markham.) Westport, Connecticut: Hyperion Press, 1991.

Tableau Economique
by François Quesnay

Even before the French Revolution, François Quesnay (1694–1774) was setting up what reads like a modern catalogue of economic demands: a state guarantee of private property, the removal of high taxes and customs tariffs, the dismantling of state subsidies, free competition, and liberalised access to the market. Quesnay, though originally a barber surgeon by trade, is perhaps the first economist proper. His work influenced Adam Smith. The famous zigzag diagram in the *Tableau Economique* is the first macroeconomic model depicting economic activity as a balanced circular flow and demonstrating the interdependence of all economic sectors. His 'physiocratic' terminology also formed the basis of the technical language of economics as an academic discipline.

GETTING STARTED

Quesnay describes the national economy as a circulatory system. His overall view of a system in which goods, services, and money continually circulate is a groundbreaking one. The model shows the flows of money and goods between various sectors: agriculture (the productive sector), landowners (the distributive sector), and the 'sterile' sector (merchants, craftspeople, officials, and factory workers). The productive sector produces added value— 'net product'—which also allows net investment. The distributive sector receives a portion of the net product. The sterile sector produces only reproduction costs and therefore no added value. That is the peculiarity of Quesnay's system. Land is, for him, the only production factor that produces added value. It is through agriculture, therefore, that wealth creation processes become transparent and the significance of net investment and capital accumulation are recognised.

CONTRIBUTION

The tableau. Quesnay looks at three types of expenditure, their source, the 'advances' that they necessitate, their distribution, their effect, their 'reproduction', their relationship with each other, and their relationships with the population, with agriculture, with industry, with trade, and with the mass of wealth of a nation.

The tableau or table has three columns.

- Column one shows productive expenditure on agriculture (annual advances 600 in order to produce 600 units (U) of 'revenue').
- Column two shows how the revenues are spent (minus tax, they are distributed between productive and sterile tasks).
- Column three shows sterile expenditure on industry (annual advances for items manufactured with sterile expenditures).

Quesnay summarises the results of his calculations using the circulatory system as follows: Reproduced in total: 600 U of revenue; in addition the annual costs of the 600 U plus the interest on the original advance by the landowner, which the land pays back in the sum of 300 U. Thus reproduction runs to 1500 U, inclusive of the revenues of 600 U, which, not taking into account tax and the advances required for reproduction, represents the basis of calculation.

Explanatory notes. Expenditures, explains Quesnay, may preponderate on one side or the other. If they are balanced, then large revenues are renewed year by year through reproductive spending. But it is easy to see how the annual reproduction of revenues would change, depending on whether sterile or productive expenditures preponderated to a greater or lesser extent.

The 300 U in revenue, which in accordance with the regular operation of the table flow to productive expenditure, are a repayment of cash advances, which again produce 300 U net and thus a portion of the revenues of the landowner. This process of circulation and mutual redistribution continues in the same manner down to the last penny of the sums that flow alternately from one class of expenditure to another.

Extract from the rules for the royal budget. For such a distribution, according to Quesnay, it is assumed:

- that from the mass of revenues nothing is exported abroad without an equivalent return in money or goods
- that taxation is not destructive in its effects and does not stand in a false relation to the mass of national revenue; that it is increased only after revenues increase
- that foreign trade is not impeded by products from the domestic harvest, for as sales are, so is reproduction
- that the price of foodstuffs and other goods in the kingdom is not artificially depressed, because trade with foreign countries would then become disadvantageous. As the exchange value, so the revenues. From superfluity and devaluation comes no wealth. From scarcity and price rises comes want. From superfluity and high prices comes prosperity
- that the means to provide for extraordinary needs of the state are to be expected from the wealth of the nation, not from the credit of financiers. Riches in the form of money are hidden riches, recognised neither by the king nor the country

CONTEXT

The work was conceived under the absolutist monarchy in France. The king's extravagant lifestyle and expenditure on wars led to large state deficits, and the peasants were impoverished by high taxes.

Quesnay was one of the most important exponents of an Enlightenment school of thought known as 'physiocracy'. The physiocrats extended the idea of a 'natural order' to society and concluded that there must be positive laws governing social activities, and that scientific knowledge of those laws could be made to serve useful human purposes. They claimed to show how these laws operated in the economy and to reveal economic theory as an exact science. Physiocracy was also a countermovement to mercantilism, criticising mercantilist economic policies as being against nature. Its weakness, however, lay in its insistence that agriculture was the only productive sector and its dismissal of trade and industry as sterile. Despite his status as the founding father of economic theory, it is sometimes argued that the practical financial reforms that Quesnay persuaded Louis XV to introduce were more significant than his theoretical writings.

THE BEST SOURCES OF HELP

Quesnay, François. *Quesnay's Tableau Economique*. (Trans. Marguerite Steinfeld Kuczynski and Ronald L. Meek.) London: Macmillan, 1972.

The Theory of Economic Development
by Joseph Schumpeter

One of Schumpeter's claims to fame—many have rated him one of the greatest economists of the 20th century— is that he was among the first to set out a clear concept of entrepreneurship and its function within an economy. The key factor is innovation. Entrepreneurs innovate. Innovations create dynamism. Schumpeter's work was for a long time overshadowed by that of Keynes, but increased interest in innovation since the 1980s has led to a renaissance of Schumpeterian economics and a renewal of interest in this book in particular.

GETTING STARTED

The Theory of Economic Development sets out to uncover the forces within an economy that produce endogenous change. Schumpeter explains the processes of economic development by means of microtheory; he bases his study on innovative entrepreneurs and uses them to make large-scale factors, such as capital accumulation, interest, and company profits, understandable as dynamic processes.

CONTRIBUTION

Static and dynamic phenomena. According to Schumpeter, static general concepts of the workings of national economies are inadequate to explain the periodic changes in their stationary equilibrium, that is, the fluctuations of the economic cycle, and economic progress. This is because such concepts ascribe change solely to external influences. The central element in any overall concept ought, in his view, to be economic development, which alters the existing balance endogenously, that is, from within.

It is necessary then to distinguish between static phenomena, in which no changes take place, and dynamic ones, which constitute a disturbance of the static balance and lead to changes until counteracting forces bring the economy into a new state of balance. This development is apparent in alternating phases of boom and recession, which, consequently, represent necessary manifestations accompanying economic development.

The stationary economy. Schumpeter's starting point is a stationary economy, that is, a system in a state of balance that periodically repeats itself. These are some of its features.

- All economic plans are aimed at achieving an optimum and need only be updated from period to period.
- In all private households and businesses the income corresponds exactly to the outgoings.
- In each period only those goods are consumed that were produced in the foregoing period and then exchanged.
- The possibilities of production are fixed in advance, this means that the production function is invariable, with the result that there are no possibilities for improvement or further investment.
- Perfect competition reduces aggregate profit to zero and consequently removes any incentive to entrepreneurial action.

But the function of capitalism is not, says Schumpeter, to administer existing structures, but to change them:

- In the static concept, there is no endogenous mechanism that could lead out of the status quo. Consequently, changes can only be brought about exogenously, that is, by external factors, social, political, and cultural influences, such as population growth, capital growth, or altered preferences and technical or organisational improvements (organic growth).
- In the dynamic concept, on the other hand, economic development originates in innovations. Here too, progress in production methods and organisational improvements play a part, but as a result of entrepreneurial action.

Innovations. Innovations, according to Schumpeter, consist in the practical implementation of knowledge, ideas, or discoveries, and rely, therefore, not on inventiveness as such, but on entrepreneurial abilities. Technically speaking, technological and organisational improvements could be described as new possibilities for factor combination. The innovation could, therefore, lie in the introduction of new products or production methods, in the opening up of new markets or supplies of resources, or in organisational changes.

These innovations are put into practice by dynamic entrepreneurs; they represent the microfoundation of the macrophenomenon of social development. Schumpeter posits two conditions as necessary for innovative entrepreneurs to appear as economic actors:

- Development takes place by means of individual actions and of incentives and appears as the aggregate of the consequences of individual actions. Only when profits can be realised through innovations, will the latter happen.
- Companies must have the opportunity to react to these incentives by changing the way they act. In balanced conditions, all production capacity is fully exploited. Consequently banks must make capital available so that potentially profitable investment opportunities can be realised through a change in the input of resources.

The outcomes of innovation. Profits from innovation make it possible to meet interest payments. As a result the rate of interest will be determined by the demand for capital and this demand, in turn, by the extent of profitable investment opportunities. How high interest rates are is consequently an indicator of economic progress. Profit and interest can thus be explained as outcomes of economic dynamism.

CONTEXT

Joseph Schumpeter (1883–1950) was an Austrian professor of political economy who belonged to the Vienna School of National Economics. He later emigrated to the United States and held a professorship at Harvard. He is considered to be a precursor of econometrics.

Schumpeter's roots were in Karl Marx, but since Marx's doctrine of the value of labour was in disrepute, he chose the neoclassical theory of value as the foundation for his work. This makes it difficult to assign Schumpeter a place in economic history. He proclaimed the significance of the business organisation, but at the same time believed in the victory of socialism, famously answering 'no' when asked if capitalism would survive. He realised himself that his work was likely to be overshadowed by Keynes's, and for most of the latter part of the 20th century this proved indeed to be the case.

THE BEST SOURCES OF HELP

Schumpeter, Joseph A. *The Theory of Economic Development: An Inquiry into Profits, Capital, Credit, Interest, and the Business Cycle.* (Trans. Opies.) New Brunswick, New Jersey: Transaction Publishers, 1982.

The Theory of Social and Economic Organization by Max Weber

It is quite easy to make Weber's book sound as if it was intended to be a source text for Franz Kafka's novels and Charlie Chaplin's film *Modern Times*, not to mention George Orwell's *1984*. Weber is often incorrectly assumed to have been an advocate of bureaucracy and a mechanistic society, rather than someone who described bureaucracy—with at least some degree of correctness—as the most efficient and rational means of organisation. In fact, as R.J. Kilcullen puts it 'bureaucracy was for Weber what capitalism was for Marx, the admired enemy'. No understanding of the way modern organisations work would be complete without a study of this book.

GETTING STARTED

Max Weber was a versatile thinker who was a professor of political economy at the universities of Freiburg and Heidelberg in Germany. He is best known today as one of the founding fathers of modern sociology.

The Theory of Social and Economic Organization grew out of his philosophical inquiries into the nature of authority and how it is transmitted. Weber identified three types of authority: the 'charismatic', based on the individual qualities of a leader and reverence for them among his or her followers; the 'traditional', based on custom and usage; and the 'rational-legal' based on the rule of objective law. Bureaucracy is the most efficient way of implementing the rule of law.

CONTRIBUTION

How bureaucracy works. There are four main principles identified by Weber as characteristic of a rational-legal bureaucracy:

- the organisation is structured around official functions which are bound by rules, each area having its own specified competence.
- functions are structured into offices organised into a hierarchy that follows technical rules and norms for which training is provided.
- the administration is separated from the ownership of the means of production.
- the rules, decisions, and actions of the administration are recorded in writing.

The impersonality of bureaucracy. The most important feature of bureaucracy—its main strength as well as its main weakness—is its impersonality.

Impersonality is a strength, in that it minimises the abuse of power by leaders because:

- offices are ranked in hierarchical order
- operations are conducted in accordance with impersonal rules
- officials are allocated specific duties and areas of responsibility
- appointments are made on the basis of qualifications and suitability for the post

It is a weakness in that:

- their characteristic information processing and filtering to the top makes bureaucracies cumbersome and slow to react

- their machinery makes it difficult to handle individual cases, because rules and procedures require all individuals to be treated as if they were the same
- bureaucratisation leads to depersonalisation, because the roles of officials are circumscribed by written definitions of their authority, and there is a set of rules and procedures to cater for every contingency

Towards ultimate efficiency. The purely bureaucratic type of administrative organisation is, from a purely technical point of view, capable of attaining the highest degree of efficiency. It is, in this sense, the most rational known means of carrying out imperative control over human beings. It is superior to any other form of organisation in precision, in stability, in the stringency of its discipline, and in its reliability.

CONTEXT

Bureaucratic organisation as expounded by Max Weber became the model for the 20th-century organisation, and was encapsulated in Alfred Sloan's General Motors and Harold Geneen's ITT. Strictly implemented, and in combination with regimented mass-production as practised by Henry Ford, who echoed some of Weber's thoughts in his faith in strict demarcations and his fervently mechanistic approach to business, it could produce a nightmare scenario for the world of work in the 20th century.

Weber himself could see no realistic substitute for bureaucracy. He regarded its triumph with distaste, but as inevitable. Only in the latter part of the 20th century did new and more humane concepts of the organisation emerge and start to win adherents. The roots of some of the latest are in biology and the new sciences of chaos and complexity, areas unknown to Weber. Today's organisations are talked of in terms of fractal and amoebae—they are imagined as elusive and ever-changing, rather than efficient and static.

The regularity of the machine age has given way to the tumult, ambiguity, and complexity of the information age.

Even so, Max Weber remains important. In his book *Gods of Management*, Charles Handy chose as one of the gods Apollo, who is characterised by a Weber-like faith in rules and systems. Aspects of the bureaucratic model remain alive and well in a great many organisations where hierarchies, demarcations, and exhaustive rules dominate.

The influential author Gary Hamel notes: 'Every organisation wrestles with two conflicting needs: the need to optimise in the name of economic efficiency, and the need to experiment in the name of growth and renewal. Authoritarian bureaucracies, of the sort that rebuilt the Japanese economy after the war, serve well the goal of optimisation. While there is experimentation here, it is tightly constrained. Anarchical networks, of the sort that predominate in Italy's fashion industry, allow for unfettered experimentation, but are always vulnerable to more disciplined competitors. Weber staked out one side of the argument; Tom Peters the other. As always, what is required is a synthesis.'

THE BEST SOURCES OF HELP

Weber, Max. *The Theory of Social and Economic Organization*. New York: Free Press, 1947.

Theory Z
by William Ouchi

The book is subtitled *How American Business Can Meet the Japanese Challenge*, and the issue is still as important as it was when *Theory Z* was published in 1981. Ouchi believes that one of the major differences between Japanese and Western companies is their respective approach to managing people. He claims that Western companies who adopt the Japanese approach and adapt it to the Western business environment will be able to transform their business.

GETTING STARTED

Ouchi believes that Japanese success is derived from a very strong company philosophy, a distinct corporate culture, long-range staff development, and decision-making based on consensus. The result, he claims, is lower staff turnover, increased job commitment, and higher productivity—all important factors in determining competitiveness. He argues that Western companies should not simply adopt Japanese practices, but adapt them. These are the firms that he calls Type Z organisations and he gives detailed insights into US companies that have transformed themselves in this way.

CONTRIBUTION

The real forces behind productivity. Ouchi believes that productivity is not just working harder. Trust is an essential factor, enabling people to make a contribution that will be respected. Subtlety is also important, allowing teams to balance their skills in line with their skills, rather than seniority. According to the author, intimacy is a feature of all aspects of Japanese life, and this enables people to cooperate effectively at work.

Lifetime employment. The author reports that major firms hire people just once a year. Staff are guaranteed employment until their retirement at 55, and any promotion takes place from within. The employment system is mirrored in the satellite system of suppliers and sub-contractors that surround a major firm and its bank. The trading relationships are permanent and stable.

Job rotation. Ouchi points out that the Japanese employment system features non-specialist career paths so that staff gain a broader experience of the ways of the whole company. This is a form of life-long job rotation. The Western system, he claims, rewards specialists and there is less chance of interaction between staff.

Working to common objectives. According to the author, the basic mechanism of control in Japan is the corporate philosophy and objectives. All other company policy is derived from that. The company values and beliefs are also derived from the overall philosophy.

Decision-making by consensus. Ouchi explains that, in this method of decision making, everyone gets involved. This may not result in the best decision, but it means that everybody understands the reasons for the decision and shares a commitment and responsibility for its success.

Japanese and Western companies compared. According to Ouchi, these are the key differences between the two approaches:

- lifetime employment versus short-term employment
- slow promotion versus rapid promotion
- non-specialist career path versus specialist career path
- implicit control mechanisms versus explicit
- collective decision making versus individual decision making
- collective responsibility versus individual responsibility

Type Z companies. Ouchi uses the term to describe Western companies that have adapted Japanese practices. They encourage employees to stay longer, but have a faster promotion ladder. They substitute 'management by walking about' for the job rotation of Japanese firms. Type Z companies encourage collaboration, but still maintain individual responsibility for decision making.

Creating a Type Z company. The author outlines the key stages for leaders who want to transform their company:

- understand a Type Z company and your own role in it
- audit your company's philosophy to detect inconsistencies
- define a suitable company philosophy
- create structures and incentives to support the new philosophy
- develop staff interpersonal skills
- involve employees and unions in the transformation
- stabilise employment
- broaden career-path development
- encourage participation

CONTEXT

Comparing Japanese and Western business practice has a long tradition.

W. Edwards Deming, paradoxically, took Western ideas on quality to Japan after the second world war. He made an important contribution to Japanese economic recovery and the country's subsequent reputation for quality. It was only when Western observers realised the potential impact of Japan on Western economies that they took notice of Deming's writings.

William Ouchi offers a valuable insight into the human factors that make Japanese business so successful. However, Nonaka and Takeuchi in their 1994 book *The Knowledge-creating Company* caution readers about over-reliance on contributory factors such as lifetime employment. They focus on the management of innovation within Japanese companies as a key competitive weapon.

Richard Pascale's *The Art of Japanese Management*, published in 1981, argues that Japanese success is largely attributable to what he called 'soft factors'— style, shared values, skills, and staff. Western companies concentrated on 'hard factors' such as strategy, structure, and systems.

THE BEST SOURCES OF HELP

Ouchi, William. *Theory Z*. Reading, Massachusetts: Addison-Wesley, 1981.

The Third Wave
by Alvin Toffler

The obvious reason for reading a work of futurology more than 20 years after its publication is to see if the futurologist got it right. In many respects Toffler did. But there is a danger there also. Toffler predicted the electronic office and its effects. Now that most people work in electronic offices and live with their effects, perhaps it seems redundant to read a book simply in order to be able to congratulate the author on his foresight. What is startling about *The Third Wave* is that it was written so recently, and yet the technological leaps made since its publication have been so immense. The intriguing thing now is whether the author's broader analysis encompassed the developments that flowed from the developments he immediately foresaw. For many people Toffler's ideas are still intriguing.

GETTING STARTED

Alvin Toffler began his career as a journalist but shot to international fame as a futurologist with the publication of his first book *Future Shock* in 1970. *The Third Wave* appeared ten years later, and *Power Shift* ten years after that.

The 'Third Wave' referred to in the title is the super-industrial society that emerged towards the end of the 20th century and is still taking shape. It succeeded the 'Second Wave', the industrialised society produced by the Industrial Revolution, which itself succeeded the agricultural phase of human development, the 'First Wave'. Each new wave was ushered in by the development of new technology. Electronics brought in the third.

Though the various waves followed one another in time, they did not affect the whole of the human race simultaneously—many people are still living under First Wave conditions. Toffler's main concern is with the transition from the Second to the Third Wave in advanced societies, but he also deals with possible areas of friction between people co-existing at different stages of development.

CONTRIBUTION

Towards mass customisation. The Third Wave, according to Toffler, is characterised by mass customisation rather than mass production.

The essence of Second Wave manufacture was the long run of millions of identical standardised products. By contrast, the essence of Third Wave manufacture is the short run of partially or completely customised products.

The Second Wave strictly separated consumer and producer. The Third Wave will see the two become almost indistinguishable, as the consumer becomes involved in the actual process of production, expressing choices and preferences.

The growth of flexible working. Toffler predicted the demise of the nine-to-five working day.

Machine synchronisation shackled the human to the machine's capabilities and imprisoned all of social life in a common frame. It did so in capitalist and socialist countries alike. Now, as machine synchronisation grows more precise, humans, instead of being imprisoned, are progressively freed. They are freed into more flexible ways of working, whether it is flexitime or working at home.

Changes in working relationships. A partial shift towards the electronic office will be enough to trigger an eruption of social, psychological, and economic consequences. The coming word-quake means more than just new machines. It promises to restructure all the human relationships and roles in the office.

The Third Wave will produce anxiety and conflict as well as reorganisation, restructuring, and, for some, rebirth into new careers and opportunities. The new systems will challenge all the old executive turfs, the hierarchies, the sexual role divisions, the departmental barriers of the past.

The impact on the corporation. Instead of clinging to a sharply-specialised economic function, the corporation, prodded by criticism, legislation, and its own concerned executives, is becoming a multipurpose institution.

The organisation is being driven to redefinition through five forces.

- Changes in the physical environment. Companies must take greater responsibility for the effect of their operations on the environment.
- Changes in the line-up of social forces. The actions of companies now have greater impact on those of other organisations such as schools, universities, civil groups, and political lobbies.
- Changes in the role of information. As information becomes central to production, as information managers proliferate in industry, the corporation, by necessity, impacts on the informational environment exactly as it impacts on the physical and social environment.
- Changes in government organisation. The profusion of government bodies means that the business and political worlds interact to a far greater degree than ever before.
- Changes in morality. The ethics and values of organisations are becoming more closely linked to those of society. Behaviour once accepted as normal is suddenly reinterpreted as corrupt, immoral, or scandalous. The corporation is increasingly seen as a producer of moral effects.

The organisation of the future will be concerned with ecological, moral, political, racial, sexual, and social problems, as well as traditional commercial ones.

CONTEXT

Other studies of the future of working life tend to plunge head-first into celebrations of the miracles of technology with little attempt to understand the human implications. Toffler is aware of them.

Many of his ideas have since been developed further by others. Charles Handy, for instance, has done a lot of work on the rise of homeworking.

Gary Hamel, author of *Leading the Revolution*, commented: 'The post-industrial society is here! And Alvin Toffler saw it coming in 1980 . . . One of the challenges for anyone reading Toffler, or any other seer, is that there is no proprietary data about the future. Your competitors read Toffler, Naisbitt, and Negroponte too! The real challenge is to build proprietary foresight out of public data!'

THE BEST SOURCES OF HELP

Toffler, Alvin. *The Third Wave*. New York: Bantam, 1980.

Toyota Production System
by Taiichi Ohno

During the last 40 years, Western car-makers have lurched from one crisis to another. They have always been one step behind. The company they have been following is the Japanese giant Toyota, and the reasons for this are explained by Taiichi Ohno in his brief book *Toyota Production System: Beyond Large-scale Production*.

GETTING STARTED

The Toyota Production System was developed to help the company catch up with the United States. US car workers were producing nine times as much as their Japanese counterparts. The Toyota system differed from the Western approach, emphasising a reduction in costs rather than an increase in selling price.

According to the author, the company should be seen as a continuous and uniform whole, including suppliers as well as customers. Asking the question 'why?' five times at each stage helps identify and solve problems before moving on.

CONTRIBUTION

Catching up with the West. The roots of the Toyota Production System lie in the immediate post-war years. Toyoda Kiichiro, president of Toyoda Motor Company, demanded that the company should catch up with the United States. He gave his company three years to do so. Otherwise, he anticipated, the Japanese car industry would cease to exist.

At that time in the car industry, an average US worker produced around nine times as much as a Japanese worker.

A different approach to production. The Toyota Production System evolved by Ohno was strikingly different from approaches used in the West.

In the West, selling price was regarded as the combination of actual costs plus profit.

Toyota, believing that the consumer actually sets the price, concluded that profit resulted when costs were subtracted from the selling price. Its emphasis therefore was on reducing costs rather than increasing the selling price.

The principles of the Toyota system. Three simple principles underlie the Toyota system:

- just-in-time production
- wider responsibility for quality
- concept of value stream

Just-in-time production. In the author's view, there is no point in producing cars, or anything else, in blind anticipation of someone buying them; production has to be closely tied to the market's requirements.

Wider responsibility for quality. Responsibility for quality rests with everyone.

Any quality defects need to be rectified as soon as they are identified.

Concept of value stream. The company should not be seen as a series of unrelated products and processes. It should be seen as a continuous and uniform whole, a stream including suppliers as well as customers.

The five whys. Another central element in Ohno's system was the process of the five whys. This suggested that by asking 'why?' five times and discovering the answer at each stage, the root of any problem can be discovered and solved.

CONTEXT

These concepts were brought to mass Western audiences thanks to work carried out at the Massachusetts Institute of Technology as part of its International Motor Vehicle Programme. The MIT research took five years, covered 14 countries, and looked exclusively at the worldwide car industry.

The researchers concluded that US car-makers remained fixed in the mass-production techniques of the past. In contrast, Japanese management, workers, and suppliers worked to the same goals as each other—resulting in increased production, high quality, happy customers, and lower costs.

This research was the basis for the 1990 bestseller by James Womack, Daniel Jones, and Daniel Roos, *The Machine that Changed the World*. From lean production, Womack and Jones went on to propose the lean enterprise (based on research covering 25 US, Japanese, and German companies) and lean management. As with most management fads, it was wilfully misinterpreted. It became linked to re-engineering and, more worryingly, with downsizing.

The reality is that lean production as introduced by Ohno and Toyota is a highly-effective concept. It can provide the economies of scale of mass production, the sensitivity to market needs usually associated with smaller companies, and job enrichment for employees.

The West continues to see lean production as a means of squeezing more production from fewer people. This is a fundamental misunderstanding. Reducing the number of employees is the end rather than the means. Western companies have tended to reduce numbers and then declare themselves as lean organisations.

Womack argues that while lean production requires fewer people, the organisation should then accelerate product development to tap new markets to keep the people at work.

Inevitably, lean production has its downside. The most obvious one is that its natural home is the mass-manufacturing world of car making. It can be more difficult to apply in other industries.

The second obvious problem with lean production is that it fails to embrace innovation and product development. It is one thing being able to make a product efficiently, but how do you originate exciting and marketable products in the first place?

Womack and Jones would suggest that the critical starting point for lean thinking is value, but this is effectively one stage beyond the initial one of generating ideas. Even so, lean production has raised awareness, provided a new benchmark, and brought operational efficiency to a wider audience.

Harvard Business School's Michael Porter argues, 'Organisations did well to employ the most up-to-date equipment, information technology, and management techniques to eliminate waste, defects, and delays. They did well to operate as close as they could to the productivity frontier. But while improving operational effectiveness is necessary to achieving superior profitability, it is not sufficient.'

THE BEST SOURCES OF HELP

Ohno, Taiichi. *Toyota Production System*. Cambridge, Massachusetts: Productivity Press, 1988.

Up the Organization
by Robert Townsend

Like any good satire, *Up the Organization* is not only irreverent and wickedly humorous, it is based on shrewd insight and sound common sense. Its questioning of the ghastly, stifling orthodoxies of corporate thinking, corporate behaviour, and corporate society is, many commentators note regretfully, as relevant now as it was when the book was first published over 30 years ago.

GETTING STARTED

Townsend's first concern is for the people who are trapped in rigid organisational structures and unable to realise anything like their full potential. He has no time for the adornments of executive office, or indeed anything that separates a management elite off from the experiences of ordinary workers. Turning his attention to more general issues, he suggests that all major organisations are operating on the wrong assumptions.

CONTRIBUTION

The organisational trap. According to Townsend, in the average company, the boys in the mailroom, the president, the vice-presidents, and the girls in the typing pool have three things in common: they are docile, they are bored, and they are dull.

He claims that they are trapped in the pigeonholes of organisation charts and that they have been made slaves to the rules of private and public hierarchies that run mindlessly on and on because nobody can change them.

The problems of business schools. Townsend's advice to companies is not to hire Harvard Business School graduates.

> All the special perquisites of executive office are anathema to Townsend.

He believes that this so-called elite is lacking in some pretty fundamental requirements for success: humility; respect for people in the firing line; deep understanding of the nature of the business and the kind of people who can enjoy themselves making it prosper; respect from way down the line; a demonstrated record of guts, industry, loyalty, judgement, fairness, and honesty under pressure.

The end of executive office perks. All the special perquisites of executive office are anathema to Townsend.

His list of no-nos includes:
- reserved parking spaces
- special-quality stationery for the boss and his elite
- muzak
- bells and buzzers
- company shrinks
- outside directorships and trusteeships for the chief executive
- the company plane

The wrong kind of leaders. According to Townsend, those with power, or who think they have power, are dangerous beings.

He claims that there is nothing fundamentally wrong with the United States except that the leaders of all its major organisations are operating on the wrong assumptions.

Townsend believes that the country is in this mess because for the last 200 years it has been using the Catholic Church and Caesar's legions as the patterns for creating organisations.

He argues that until 40 or 50 years ago it made sense. The average churchgoer, soldier, and factory worker was uneducated and dependent on orders from above. And authority carried considerable weight because disobedience brought the death penalty or its equivalent.

CONTEXT

Townsend's genius lies in debunking the modern organisation for its excess, stupidity, and absurdity. He collected his material in the course of his successful career as a director of American Express and president of Avis Rent-a-Car, then transformed himself into a witty commentator on the excesses of corporate life.

His bestseller *Up the Organization* is subtitled *How to Stop the Corporation from Stifling People and Strangling Profits*. Robert Heller called the book 'the first pop bestseller on business management'. It is in the tradition of humorous bestsellers debunking managerial mythology and the high-minded seriousness of the theorists. In the 1950s there was *Parkinson's Law*, at the end of the 1960s came Townsend. More recently the Dilbert series has followed in their footsteps.

Townsend also belongs in the tradition of people-orientated business writing. His humour should not blind one to the underlying seriousness of his purpose.

Given that over 30 years have passed since its publication, the book still retains its freshness and originality, and its insights into the blind deficiencies of too many organisations remain sadly apt.

THE BEST SOURCES OF HELP

Townsend, Robert. *Up the Organization*. London: Michael Joseph, 1970.

Valuation
by Tom Copeland, Jack Murrin, and Tom Koller

Prompted by more intensive competition, the restructuring of industries, and ever more sophisticated shareholders, managers are checking over their company portfolios more critically than ever before in order to find out precisely where value is being created or destroyed. At a time when shareholder value is gaining ground and share options play an ever more important role in the remuneration of leading employees, value-orientated portfolio structuring and resource allocation are becoming central factors in strategic thinking.

GETTING STARTED

The authors provide management with the necessary equipment to help them identify the sources and extent of value appreciation and depreciation within the company. In a series of theoretical analyses based on capital market research, they present the discounted cash flow (DCF) method and supplement their explanatory material with numerous case studies drawn from business practice.

CONTRIBUTION

Company value and company strategy. Companies, say the authors, need competitive strategies not only for the familiar goods and services markets, but also for the market in the disposal rights of companies. This is where the success of efforts to increase company value, which derives from cash flows, will be felt. Managers must pursue active value-management policies.

There are two stages in the development of a value-orientated policy:
- a restructuring that frees up the values locked into the company
- establishing priorities for enhancing value

Managers should regularly create and make use of opportunities to increase value. In this way they can avoid having to react under pressure later.

Company value on a cash flow basis: a guide for practitioners. The procedure that combines best with the aim of long-term value enhancement, the authors suggest, is the discounted cash flow (DCF) method.

The DCF method has the following advantages:
- The bases for valuation are free cash flows, as only these are available for servicing invested capital.
- Future expectations are systematically taken into account.
- Capital structure, financing costs, and risk are fully covered, so that the whole debit side of the company balance sheet is taken into consideration.
- An objective yardstick for comparing strategic options is created.
- Almost all the information needed to calculate the value of the company can be derived from existing and projected figures given in the company accounts.

In accordance with the DCF 'component model', the value of a company's equity capital is equivalent to the value of various cash flows that lead ultimately to the cash flow to shareholders (dividends, share repurchases, share issues). This, say the authors, has four advantages.

1. Evaluating the relevant components of the company helps to identify and understand the individual sources of investment and finance that influence the value of the company.

2. It identifies operating drivers with the greatest prospects for enhancing value.

3. It can be applied at various levels and combined with investment accounting.

4. It is sufficiently differentiated to cope with the complex situations and can be conducted using simple data-processing technology.

Using the DCF component model to value a company. This process splits into five stages:

- **Stage one: analysis of historical performance**. First the relevant components of free cash flows are determined. Then a comprehensive profile of past performance is drawn up. It provides important clues to forecasting future performance.

- **Stage two: determining capital costs**. The first step is to establish the capital structure of the company. From this the weighting factors for the weighted average cost of capital (WACC) formula can be derived. Next, external capital costs are determined. Finally, equity capital costs are assessed, a process best conducted using the capital asset pricing model (CAPM) or the arbitrage pricing model (APM).

- **Stage three: prognosis of future performance**. Here the assumptions and scenarios relevant to a prognosis of the company's economic situation and competitive position in its industry are worked out. Forecasts also need to be made for the decisive drivers of value: growth and return on capital.

- **Stage four: estimating continuance value**. First the most suitable DCF method to apply must be decided on. The choice is between the long-term detailed prognosis, the continuing-value formula taking account of growing cash flows, and the value factor formula. The time frame for a detailed prognosis is established. The parameters are then assessed: these are the operating result after tax, free cash flow, the return on new investment, the growth rate, and the WACC. Finally, the continuing value is discounted to the present.

- **Stage five: calculation and interpretation of results**. The final phase comprises the calculation and checking of the value of the company, together with the interpretation of the results in the light of the circumstances surrounding the decision.

This method of calculation, the authors say, is also suitable for valuing companies under more complex framework conditions. It allows the options price theory to be applied to both their assets and their liabilities.

CONTEXT

Insufficient attention to value has meant that the value of companies worldwide has been reduced without this becoming apparent in their published accounts. This development prompted the consultancy firm McKinsey to conduct extensive research that ultimately resulted in the DCF method. This book, whose three authors are partners at McKinsey, supplements accounting disciplines with a comprehensive plan for company evaluation. It was hailed on its appearance by finance experts worldwide as a must-read for managers, security analysts, and investors alike. The new edition shows how the system can be applied in the valuation of companies from the new economy.

THE BEST SOURCES OF HELP

McKinsey & Co. Inc, Tom Copeland, Jack Murrin, and Tim Koller. *Valuation: Measuring and Managing the Value of Companies*. 3rd ed. New York: John Wiley and Sons, 2000.

The Visual Display of Quantitative Information by Edward Tufte

The book is widely regarded as one of the most authoritative guides to the graphical treatment of statistical information through charts, graphs, and other graphic devices. It draws on the work of experts in the field and includes hundreds of examples of good and bad design.

GETTING STARTED

Statistical graphics are used to communicate complex information clearly through words, numbers, and pictures. The author reports that, each year, somewhere between 900 billion and 2 trillion images of statistical graphics are produced, demonstrating the importance of the subject. Excellence, he believes, should lead the viewer to think about the content and explain complex ideas with clarity, precision, and efficiency.

CONTRIBUTION

Tufte illustrates how graphics should tell a story in a way that ordinary statistics could not do. He points out that good graphics must be based on sound data sources. However, graphics can sometimes be used to distort data. He distinguishes between perceived visual effects and attempts to deceive. Design variations, such as changing scale, can also distort information.

The author suggests two ways to avoid distortion:
- the representation of numbers should be directly proportional to the numbers themselves
- clear labelling should be used to remove ambiguity

> Tufte illustrates how graphics should tell a story in a way that ordinary statistics could not do.

Tufte argues that it is a mistake to think that graphics should be used because data is intrinsically dull. This, he claims, is responsible for over-elaborate graphics produced by designers who may not understand the significance of the numbers. The use of graphics should not be treated as decoration.

The author sets out principles for good design:
- above all else, show the data
- erase non-data information
- erase redundant data information

He also suggests that presentation can be inspired by combining words, numbers, and pictures.

CONTEXT

The author is regarded as an authority on the presentation of statistical information. The book was based on a series of seminars on the use of statistical graphics. This, he believes, is an under-developed field. Most books on graphics concentrate on design technique, rather than on the information the graphics are communicating.

Tufte's collaboration with statistician John Tukey set out to bridge the gap. The collaboration, he believes, made the subject intellectually respectable.

As well as giving the subject a more intellectual dimension, Tufte also uses the book to demonstrate the tradition of excellence in graphics since the 18th century.

THE BEST SOURCES OF HELP

Tufte, Edward R. *The Visual Display of Quantitative Information.* Godalming: Graphics Press UK, 2001.

The Wealth of Nations
by Adam Smith

Many books are claimed to be classics or seminal works: *The Wealth of Nations* is indisputably both. It is a broad-ranging exploration of commercial and economic first principles. In it Adam Smith laid the philosophical foundations for modern capitalism and the modern market economy. There are few economists over the last 200 years—and fewer politicians of a free-market persuasion—who have not been influenced by it. Smith has helped shape the economic policies of British prime ministers and chancellors of the exchequer from the days of Lord North (1770–82) to those of Margaret Thatcher—and even Tony Blair.

GETTING STARTED

Adam Smith was a Scottish philosopher. He was professor of logic and professor of moral philosophy at Glasgow University, but left his university posts in order to travel on the continent as tutor to a young nobleman. In France he was greatly influenced by a school of philosophical economists known as the 'physiocrats'. Returning to his native town of Kirkcaldy in Fife, he spent ten years preparing *An Inquiry into the Nature and Causes of the Wealth of Nations*, which was published—a significant coincidence perhaps—in the year of the signing of the American Declaration of Independence, 1776.

His central thesis is that capital can best be used for the creation of both individual and national wealth in conditions of minimal interference by government. The 'invisible hand' of free-market competition ensures, in his view, both the vitality of commercial activity and the ultimate good of all a nation's citizens.

CONTRIBUTION

The invisible hand. According to Smith, conscious and well-meaning attempts to better the lot of a nation and its population are generally doomed to failure. The unintended cumulative effects of self-interested striving are far more effective. As he puts it: 'Every individual is continually exerting to find out the most advantageous employment for whatever he can command . . . [and] necessarily labours to render the annual revenue of the society as great as he can. He generally neither intends to promote the public interest nor knows how much he is promoting it. He intends only his own gain, and he is in this, as in many other cases, led by an invisible hand to promote an end which was no part of his intention.'

Value and labour. The value of a particular good or service is determined by the costs of production. If something is expensive to produce, then its value is similarly high.

'The real price of everything, what everything really costs to the man who wants to acquire it, is the toil and trouble of acquiring it. What everything is really worth to the man who has acquired it, and who wants to dispose of it or exchange it for something else, is the toil and trouble of which it can save himself, and which it can impose on other people.'

'What is bought with money or with goods is purchased by labour, as much as what we acquire by the toil of our own body. They contain the value of a certain quantity of labour which we exchange for what is supposed at the time to contain the value of an equal quantity.'

The division of labour. Smith's legacy to scientific management was the concept of the division of labour.

'The division of labour occasions in every art a proportionable increase of the productive powers of labour. The separation of different trades and employments from one another seems to have taken place in consequence of this advantage.'

> Smith's legacy to scientific management was the concept of the division of labour

'Men are much more likely to discover easier and readier methods of attaining any object when the whole attention of their minds is directed towards that single object than when it is dissipated among a great variety of things.'

CONTEXT

For a book that is over 200 years old, there is a surprisingly modern-sounding ring to a great deal of what *The Wealth of Nations* has to say. This is mainly owing to the acuteness and lasting value of Smith's analysis—the book was the first comprehensive exploration of the foundations, workings, and machinations of a free market economy—but also to the familiarity of many of its basic concepts. *The Wealth of Nations* continues to have a role as a right-wing manifesto, a gloriously logical exposition of the beauty of market forces. And the appeal is not only to the right wing in politics.

Smith's system of demarcation and functional separation provided the basis for the management theorists of the early 20th century, such as Frederick Winslow Taylor, and practitioners such as Henry Ford. They translated the economic rigour of his thinking to practices in the workplace, though in ways and to a scale that Smith could never have imagined.

History has, however, put its own limitations on Smith's theorising.

- Physical labour is no longer so important.
- The 20th century saw the emergence of management as a profession. It is barely acknowledged by Smith.
- Smith wrote without knowledge of the power and scope of modern corporations, let alone the power of brand names and customer loyalty.
- He also wrote in harder times where self-interest was not a choice but a necessity.

Nevertheless, as Gary Hamel commented: 'Revisionists be damned. Citizens from Prague to Santiago to Guangzhou to Jakarta owe much of their new-found prosperity to the triumph of Adam Smith's economic ideals. [He] laid the philosophical foundations for the modern industrial economy. Enough said.'

THE BEST SOURCES OF HELP

Smith, Adam. *The Wealth of Nations*. London Penguin Books, 1982.

The Will to Manage
by Marvin Bower

Marvin Bower is the man who did more than anyone else to create the modern management consulting industry. The book gives a valuable insight into the management practices that made McKinsey & Company such a long-lasting success.

GETTING STARTED

Marvin Bower's success grew on his principle that building trust with clients is critical to consultancy success. The interests of the client should precede increasing the company's revenues: if you look after the client, the profits look after themselves.

He also believed that using values to help shape and guide an organisation is extremely important. One of those values is that regard for the individual is based not on title, but on competence, stature, and leadership. Instead of experienced consultants, McKinsey recruited graduate students who could learn how to be good problem solvers and consultants. The company also developed 'virtual' project teams, bringing in the best people in the organisation wherever they were based in the world. Clear, simple employment policies and change through empowerment helped to maintain high professional standards.

CONTRIBUTION

A new way of looking at consultancies. Bower did not change the name of his company, McKinsey, as he shrewdly decided that clients would demand his involvement in projects if his name was up in lights. His vision was to provide advice on managing to top executives and to do it with the professional standards of a leading law firm. Due to a belief that in all successful professional groups, regard for the individual is based not on title but on competence, stature, and leadership, McKinsey consultants were associates who had engagements, rather than mere jobs, and the firm was a practice rather than a business.

Building trust with clients. The entire ethos of McKinsey was to be very respectable, the kind of people CEOs naturally relate to. Bower's gospel was that the interests of the client should precede increasing the company's revenues: unless the client could trust McKinsey, the company could not work with them. If McKinsey looked after the client, the profits would look after themselves. High charges were not a means to greater profits, but a simple and effective means of ensuring that clients took McKinsey seriously.

Other central principles were that consultants should keep quiet about the affairs of clients, should tell the truth, and be prepared to challenge the client's opinion. They should only agree to do work which is both necessary and which they could do well. Using values to help shape and guide an organisation was extremely important.

New patterns of recruitment. Instead of hiring experienced executives with in-depth knowledge of a particular industry, Bower recruited graduate students who could learn how to be good problem solvers and consultants. This changed the emphasis of consulting from passing on a narrow range of experience to using a wide range of analytical and problem-solving techniques.

Developing virtual project teams. Another element of Bower's approach was the use of teams. He thought of McKinsey as a network of leaders. Teams were assembled for specific projects, and the best people in the organisation were brought to bear on a particular problem, no matter where they were based in the world. McKinsey's culture fostered rigorous debate over the right answer, without that debate resulting in personal criticism.

Clear, simple employment policies. The company's policy remains one of the most simple: seniority in McKinsey correlates directly with achievement. If a consultant ceases to progress with the organisation, or is ultimately unable to demonstrate the skills and qualities required of a principal, he or she is asked to leave McKinsey.

> The company's policy remains one of the most simple: seniority in McKinsey correlates directly with achievement.

Change through empowerment. 'There have been thousands of changes in methods, but not in command and control. Many companies say they want to change, but they need to empower people below. More cohesion is needed rather than hierarchy,' Bower said in 1995.

CONTEXT

Under Bower's astute direction, McKinsey became the world's premier consulting firm. Recent years have also seen the structure and managerial style of the company receiving plaudits. McKinsey is special because it has developed a self-perpetuating aura that it is unquestionably the best. Marvin Bower was the creator of this organisational magic.

American Express chief, Harvey Golub, says that Bower led McKinsey according to a set of values, and it was the principle of using values to help shape and guide an organisation that was probably the most important thing he took away.

THE BEST SOURCES OF HELP

Bower, Marvin. *The Will to Manage*. New York: McGraw-Hill, 1966.

Author Index

Credits

Ultimate Business Library © Stuart Crainer 2002

Writing the New Economy © John Middleton 2002